Greenhill Books

WHY THE
GERMANS LOSE AT WAR

GREENHILL MILITARY PAPERBACKS

WHY THE GERMANS LOSE AT WAR

The Myth of German Military Superiority

Kenneth Macksey

Greenhill Books, London
Stackpole Books, Pennsylvania

Greenhill Books

Why the Germans Lose at War was first published 1996 as *From Triumph to Disaster* by Greenhill Books, Lionel Leventhal Limited, Park House, 1 Russell Gardens, London NW11 9NN
and
Stackpole Books, 5067 Ritter Road, Mechanicsburg, PA 17055, USA

British Library Cataloguing in Publication Data
Macksey, Kenneth, 1923–
Why the Germans lose at war: the myth of German military superiority. –
(Greenhill military paperback) 1. Germany – Armed Forces – History 2. Germany – History, Military – 20th century
I. Title
943'.08

ISBN 1-85367-383-8

Library of Congress Cataloging-in-Publication Data
Macksey, Kenneth
[From triumph to disaster]
Why the Germans lose at war: the myth of German military superiority / by Kenneth Macksey.
p.   cm. – (Greenhill military paperbacks)
Originally published: From triumph to disaster. London: Greenhill Books, 1996.
Includes bibliographical references and index.
ISBN 1-85367-383-8
1. Leadership – History – 19th century. 2. Leadership – History – 20th century.
3. Generals – Germany – History – 19th century. 4. Generals – Germany – History –
20th century. 5. Military art and science – Germany – History – 19th century.
6. Military art and science – Germany – History – 20th century. 7. Germany – History,
Military – 19th century. 8. Germany – History, Military – 20th century.
I. Title II. Series.
UB210.M22 1999
355.3'31'0943–dc21   99-16559
CIP

Publishing History
Why the Germans Lose at War was first published as *From Triumph to Disaster* in 1996 by Greenhill Books. It is now reproduced with the new title and in paperback exactly as the first edition.

Printed and bound in Great Britain
by Biddles Limited, Guildford and King's Lynn.

Contents

List of Illustrations

Charts and Maps

Charts and Maps drawn by John Richards

The Principal German Leaders

ARNIM, JÜRGEN VON (1889–1962): A forceful panzer commander who was overwhelmed in Tunisia. Good with his soldiers.

BAYERLEIN, FRITZ (1899–1970): An outspoken and very able commander and staff officer. An admirer of Rommel.

BECK, GENERAL LUDWIG (1880–1944): The indecisive Chief of the General Staff who botched the Bomb Plot.

BISMARCK, OTTO VON (1815–1898): The great Prussian Chancellor who united Germany.

BLASKOWITZ, JOHANNES VON (1878–1948): A General Staff officer of the old school who deprecated SS behaviour but side-stepped the issue.

BLOMBERG, FIELD MARSHAL WERNER VON (1878–1943): The Minister of Defence who handed power to Hitler before resigning due to a personal scandal.

BLÜCHER, GEBHARD VON (1742–1819): Victorious commander of the Prussian Army against Napoleon.

BLUMENTRITT, GÜNTHER VON (1892–1967): A fine example of the well-trained, polished General Staff officer.

BOCK, FIELD MARSHAL FEDOR VON (1885–1945): An aggressive commander of great talent with no love for Hitler and his gang.

BRAUCHITSCH, FIELD MARSHAL WALTHER VON (1881–1948): The Nazi-dominated Army Commander-in-Chief who yielded to Hitler.

BRUCHMÜLLER, GEORG (1863–1939 (?)): The architect of Germany's improvements in artillery techniques in World War I.

BUSCH, FIELD MARSHAL ERNST (1885–1945): An able, keen supporter of Hitler who, in 1944, was sacked for failing to do the impossible on the Eastern Front.

CLAUSEWITZ, KARL VON (1780–1831): The author of *On War* who founded modern military philosophy.

DIETRICH, SS COLONEL GENERAL JOSEP (Sepp) (1892–1966): A

brutal Nazi supporter of Hitler from before the war with limited military talent.

DÖNITZ, GRAND ADMIRAL KARL (1891–1980): Creator of the U-boat fleet, last Commander-in-Chief of the Navy and Hitler's successor in April 1945.

FALKENHAYN, ERICH VON (1861–1922): A classic example of the pre-World War I General Staff officer who dominated German politics and military development.

FALKENHORST, NIKOLAUS VON (1885–1968): An orthodox officer whose conduct of the Norwegian campaign was exemplary.

FELLGIEBEL, ERICH FRITZ (1886–1944): Creator of the Wehrmacht Signal Service. Hater of Hitler and casualty of the Bomb Plot due to ineptitude.

FRITSCH, GENERAL WERNER VON (1880–1939): A most able Army Commander-in-Chief who was no match for Hitler.

FROMM, FRIEDRICH (1888–1945): A Hitler supporter with a keen sense of survival and ambition.

GEHLEN, REINHARD (1902–1972): One of the brightest and most prescient of Army Intelligence officers.

GNEISENAU, AUGUSTUS WILHELM VON (1760–1831): Co-founder with Scharnhorst of the restored Prussian Army after Jena.

GÖRING, REICHSMARSCHALL HERMANN (1893–1946): Hitler's right-hand man, ruthless, lazy and of only moderate military talent.

GRÖNER, WILHELM (1867–1939): The brilliant administrator who solved many logistic problems in World War I and had the courage to abandon his oath to the Kaiser for the good of Germany and the Army.

GUDERIAN, HEINZ (1888–1954): A most charismatic Prussian officer who put patriotism before self. Also a fine strategist, tactician and technologist.

HALDER, FRANZ (1884–1972): The dry, very able Chief of Staff whose distaste for Hitler was never translated into resistance.

HINDENBURG, FIELD MARSHAL PAUL VON (1847–1934): The dominant politico-military figurehead of 1916–1933 who failed in old age to curb Hitler.

HOEPNER, ERICH (1886–1944): A fine panzer commander who, having been unjustly sacked, took part in the Bomb Plot and paid with his life.

JESCHONNEK, HANS (1899–1943): The able Luftwaffe Chief of Staff who lacked the strength of character to withstand Göring and

Hitler. Committed suicide under extreme pressure from Hitler to do so.

JODL, GENERAL ALFRED JOSEF (1890–1946): The very able and extremely ambitious staff officer who sacrificed his integrity in the cause of Hitler whom he blindly followed in nearly all his excesses.

KEITEL, FIELD MARSHAL WILHELM (1882–1946): The third-rate General Staff officer, whose servility to Hitler contributed to his own and Germany's downfall.

KESSELRING, FIELD MARSHAL ALBERT (1885–1960): Arguably the most able, cultured and versatile General Staff officer of his generation.

KLEIST, FIELD MARSHAL EWALD VON (1881–1954): An aristocratic Prussian cavalryman of great insight and drive. After the war he was found guilty of war crimes and spent the rest of his life in prison.

KLUGE, FIELD MARSHAL GÜNTHER VON (1882–1944): One of the most talented Prussian gunner officers with numerous great achievements to his credit. Loyal, but not blindly so, to Hitler, he destroyed himself by becoming involved with the Bomb Plot without grasping its implications.

KÜCHLER, FIELD MARSHAL GEORG VON (1881–1968): A most able general who steered a narrow course between loyalty and resistance to Hitler.

LEEB, FIELD MARSHAL WILHELM VON (1872–1956): He was among the pre-war high flyers for whom the initial set-backs in Russian in 1941 proved too much.

LIST, FIELD MARSHAL WILHELM VON (1880–1971): A very calm and imperturbable officer for whom Hitler held no terrors. He was pleased to be relieved of command in September 1942.

LÖHR, ALEXANDER (1885–1947): Had the distinction of proposing the airborne invasion of Crete and was among the most competent of the Luftwaffe generals.

LUDENDORFF, ERICH (1865–1937): One of the most dynamic and efficient pre-World War I generals whose greatest distinction in a lost cause was the introduction in 1916 of Total War.

MANSTEIN, FIELD MARSHAL ERICH VON (1887–1973): Considered by many to be Germany's best strategist, in World War II he was ill at ease with Hitler and pleased in 1944 to be relieved of command.

MANTEUFFEL, HASSO VON (1897–1978): Among the most able practitioners of armoured warfare.

MILCH, FIELD MARSHAL ERHARD (1892–1972): A most able aviator to whose credit, along with Kesselring, goes the making of the Luftwaffe.

MODEL, FIELD MARSHAL WALTER (1891–1945): A brilliant panzer commander whose final defeats prior to committing suicide in 1945 were no fault of his.

MOLTKE, HELMUTH VON (1800–1891): The greatest German Chief of the General Staff.

MOLTKE, HELMUTH JOHANNES VON (1848–1916): The shadow of his uncle, he proved unequal to the strain of real war in 1914.

PAULUS, FRIEDRICH (1890–1957): A brilliant staff officer who proved unequal to the responsibilities of Army Commander at Stalingrad.

PRAUN, ALBERT (b. 1894): One of the elite signals branch officers who, along with Fellgiebel, created the excellent (though security-flawed) communications system.

RAEDER, GRAND ADMIRAL ERICH (1876–1960): Trod in the footsteps of Tirpitz in attempting to create a Navy without hope of victory.

REICHENAU, FIELD MARSHAL WALTHER VON (1884–1942): A leading proponent of what became OKW, he distinguished himself until 1942 when he died from heart failure in Russia.

REINHARDT, GEORG-HANS (1887–1963): Made his name in France in 1940 as panzer corps commander.

RICHTHOFEN, WOLFRAM VON (1895–1945): The brilliant exponent of close air support of land forces. Died of natural causes.

ROMMEL, FIELD MARSHAL ERWIN (1891–1944): The charismatic, very ambitious tactician who pinned his star to Hitler. Not regarded as General Staff calibre.

ROON, ALBRECHT VON (1803–1879): A bullying force behind the German Army in the 1860s.

RUNDSTEDT, FIELD MARSHAL GERD VON (1875–1953): Doyen of the German officer corps who toadied to Hitler throughout World War II.

SCHARNHORST, GERHARD JOHANN VON (1755–1813): Founder of the Prussian Army and General Staff after Jena.

SCHLEICHER, KURT VON (1882–1934): The very ambitious founder of the Freikorps whose subsequent involvement in high politics, linked with resistance to Hitler, led to his murder.

SCHLIEFFEN, ALFRED VON (1833–1913): Creator of the famous plan to win a major war quickly, which failed in 1914.

SCHMUNDT, RUDOLF (1896–1944): Hitler's loyal and sensible adjutant who became a vital king maker until killed by the bomb in the plot to assassinate Hitler.

SCHÖRNER, FIELD MARSHAL FERDINAND (1892–1973): The courageous and brutal mountain war expert whose excesses could not prevent collapse in the East in 1945.

SEECKT, HANS VON (1866–1936): Brilliant staff officer in victory and defeat, it was he who, in the 1920s, established the 'non political' Reichswehr which Hitler exploited as a striking force.

SPEERLE, FIELD MARSHAL HUGO (1885–1953): An 'old eagle' who transferred to the Luftwaffe in 1935 and, from 1940 onwards, commanded the air force in the West, causing destruction but suffering eventual defeat.

STUDENT, KURT (1890–1978): The airborne forces enthusiast whose initial successes in 1940 led to Crete and the subsequent eclipse of his forces.

THOMA, WILHELM VON (1891–1948): A gloomy early tank pioneer in Spain who fought in many campaigns until captured in November 1942.

TIRPITZ, GRAND ADMIRAL ALFRED VON (1849–1930): Founder of the modern German Navy which proved an albatross round his country's neck.

UDET, ERNST (1896–1941): Air ace and failed technical head of the Luftwaffe who committed suicide.

VIETINGHOFF, HEINRICH VON (1887–1952): Imaginative and tough commander who started the Army's surrender process on 30 April 1945.

WALDERSEE, FIELD MARSHAL ALFRED VON (1832–1904): One of the most ambitious but least impressive German Chiefs of the General Staff.

WARLIMONT, WALTER (1894–1976): Among those who proposed OKW, he worked without a break in that organisation, under Jodl, until 1945.

WEICHS, FIELD MARSHAL MAXMILLIAN VON (1881–1954): One of the less spectacular field marshals who consistently produced sound results even in desperate situations.

WESTPHAL, SIEGFRIED (b. 1902): A most competent staff officer who managed with great success to win the confidence of Kesselring and Rommel.

WITZLEBEN, FIELD MARSHAL ERWIN VON (1881–1944): A fine soldier who, after being sacked by Hitler, led the resistance against him and paid with his life.

ZEITZLER, KURT VON (1895–1963): An armoured chief of staff who attracted attention in 1940 and became the none-too-effective Chief of General Staff from September 1942 until July 1944.

GENERALSTAB
THE PRUSSIAN STAFF SYSTEM
(1816-78)

GREAT GENERAL STAFF
(BERLIN)

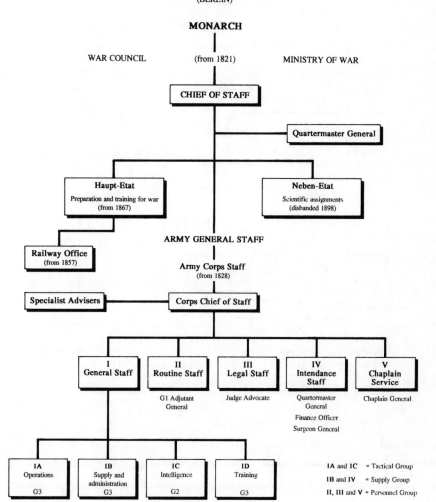

MONARCH

WAR COUNCIL   (from 1821)   MINISTRY OF WAR

CHIEF OF STAFF

Quartermaster General

Haupt-Etat
Preparation and training for war
(from 1867)

Neben-Etat
Scientific assignments
(disbanded 1898)

ARMY GENERAL STAFF

Railway Office
(from 1857)

Army Corps Staff
(from 1828)

Specialist Advisers   Corps Chief of Staff

I General Staff	II Routine Staff	III Legal Staff	IV Intendance Staff	V Chaplain Service
	G1 Adjutant General	Judge Advocate	Quartermaster General	Chaplain General
			Finance Officer	
			Surgeon General	

1A Operations G3	1B Supply and administration G3	1C Intelligence G2	1D Training G3

1A and 1C = Tactical Group

1B and IV = Supply Group

II, III and V = Personnel Group

ARMY HIGH COMMAND
(OKH)
1941 - 42

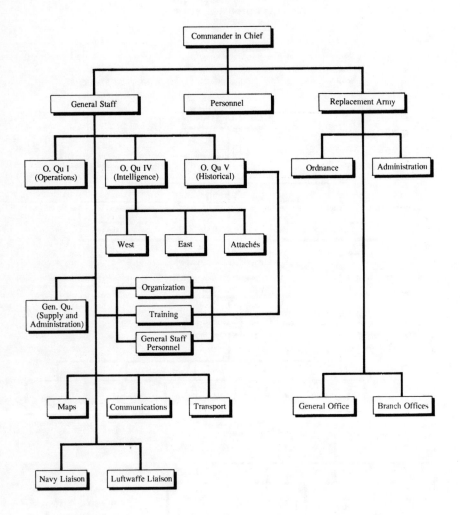

SUPREME HIGH COMMAND
(OKW)
1941-42

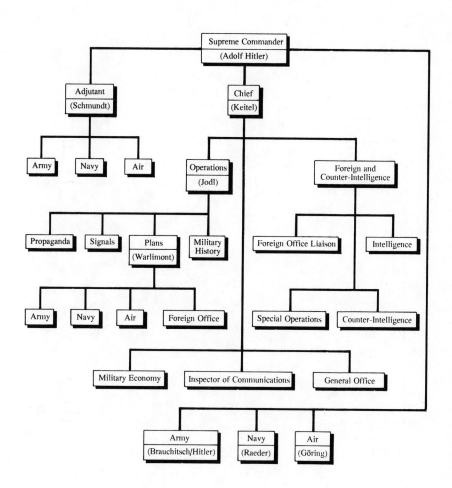

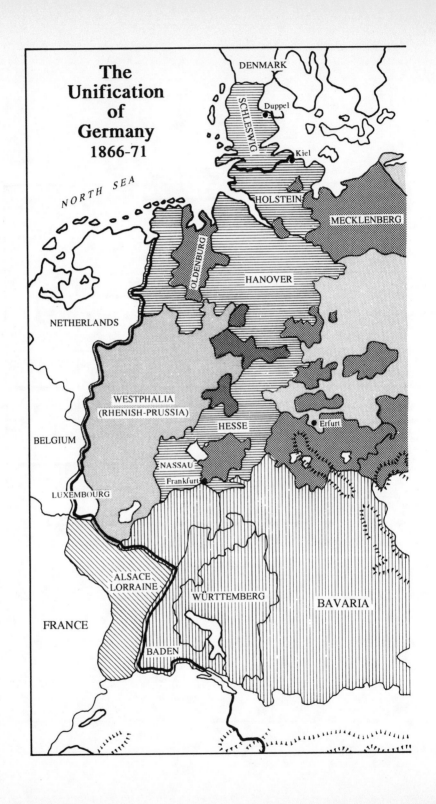

**The
Unification
of
Germany
1866-71**

DENMARK

SCHLESWIG

Duppel

Kiel

NORTH SEA

HOLSTEIN

MECKLENBERG

OLDENBURG

HANOVER

NETHERLANDS

WESTPHALIA
(RHENISH-PRUSSIA)

HESSE

Erfurt

BELGIUM

NASSAU

Frankfurt

LUXEMBOURG

ALSACE
LORRAINE

WÜRTTEMBERG

BAVARIA

FRANCE

BADEN

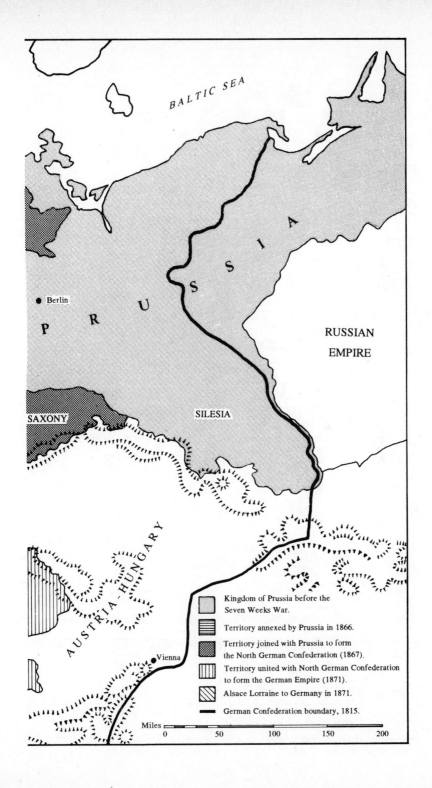

BALTIC SEA

● Berlin

P R U S S I A

RUSSIAN
EMPIRE

SAXONY

SILESIA

AUSTRIA-HUNGARY

● Vienna

Kingdom of Prussia before the
Seven Weeks War.

Territory annexed by Prussia in 1866.

Territory joined with Prussia to form
the North German Confederation (1867).

Territory united with North German Confederation
to form the German Empire (1871).

Alsace Lorraine to Germany in 1871.

German Confederation boundary, 1815.

Miles

0   50   100   150   200

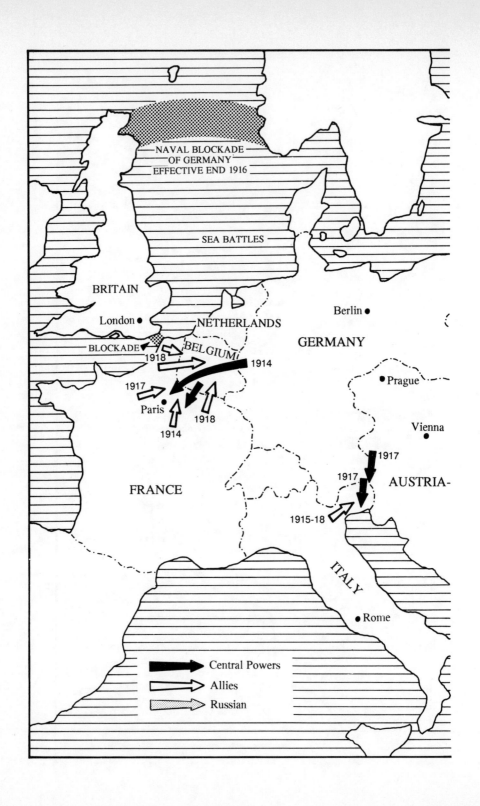

NAVAL BLOCKADE
OF GERMANY
EFFECTIVE END 1916

SEA BATTLES

BRITAIN

London

NETHERLANDS

Berlin

GERMANY

BLOCKADE
1918

BELGIUM

1914

1917

Paris

1918

1914

Prague

Vienna

FRANCE

1917

1917

AUSTRIA-

1915-18

ITALY

Rome

Central Powers

Allies

Russian

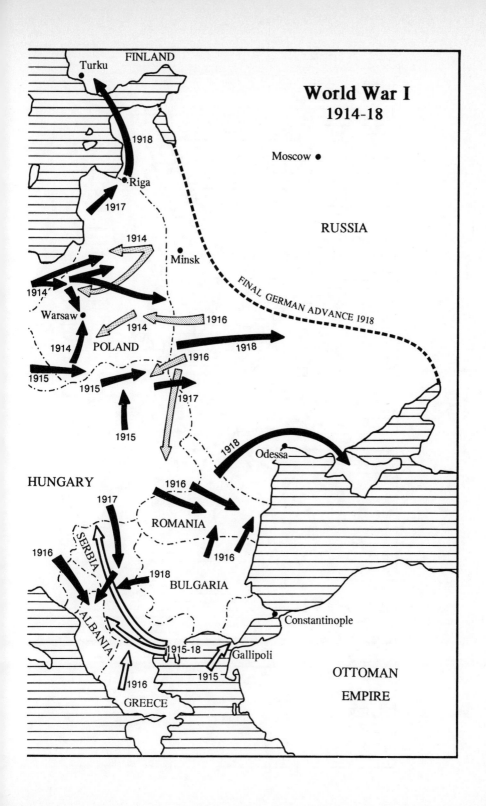

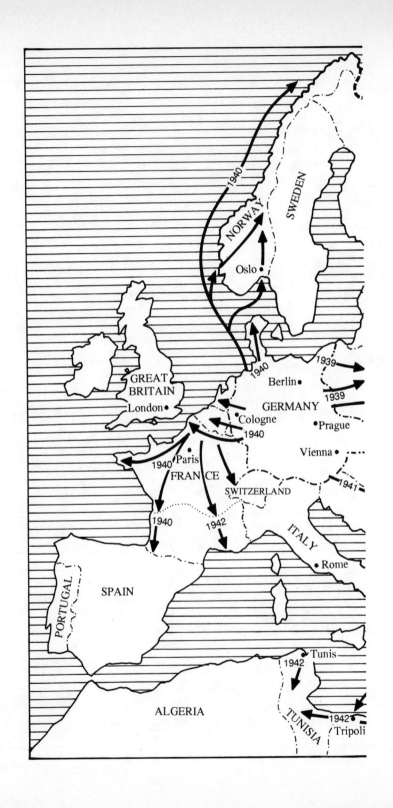

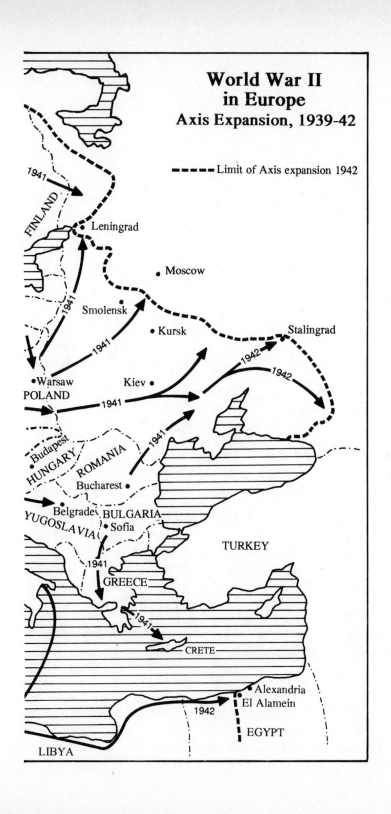

World War II in Europe
Axis Expansion, 1939-42

- - - - - Limit of Axis expansion 1942

FINLAND

1941

• Leningrad

• Moscow

Smolensk

• Kursk

Stalingrad

1941

1941

1941

•Warsaw
POLAND

Kiev •

1941

1942

1942

Budapest

HUNGARY

ROMANIA

1941

Bucharest •

Belgrade

BULGARIA

YUGOSLAVIA

• Sofia

TURKEY

1941

GREECE

1941

CRETE

• Alexandria
El Alamein

1942

EGYPT

LIBYA

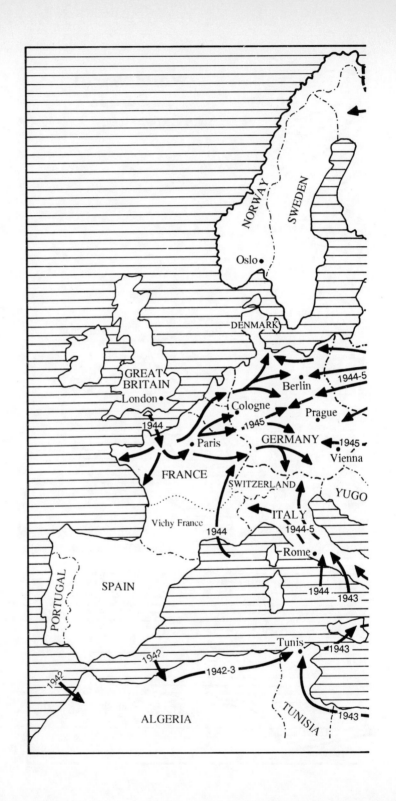

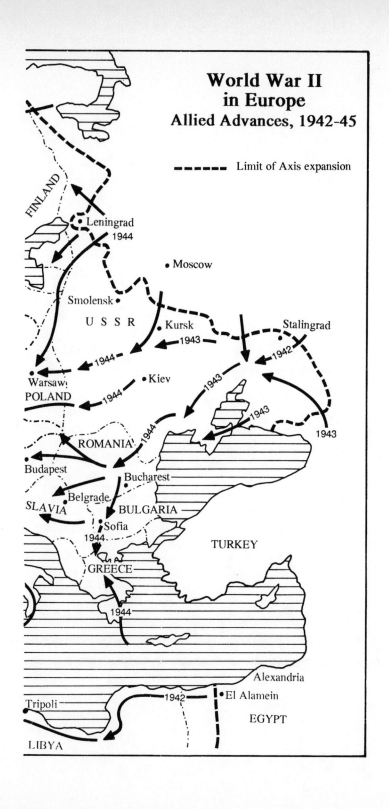

World War II
in Europe
Allied Advances, 1942-45

- - - - - - Limit of Axis expansion

FINLAND

Leningrad
1944

• Moscow

Smolensk •

U S S R

• Kursk
1943

Stalingrad

1944

1942

1943

• Kiev

1943

1944

Warsaw
POLAND

1944

1943

ROMANIA

1944

Budapest

Bucharest

Belgrade •

SLAVIA

BULGARIA

• Sofia

1944

TURKEY

GREECE

1943

1944

Alexandria

Tripoli

1942

• El Alamein

EGYPT

LIBYA

Götterdämmerung at Nürnberg

In 1946, at the end of a ten-month trial which had fascinated the world, the International Military Tribunal delivered its judgement at Nürnberg. In the court all eyes and the cine-cameras were focused upon the reaction of the twenty-two Germans accused of war crimes during World War II, and naturally it was the nineteen found guilty (of whom five were leaders of the Armed Forces and two members of the General Staff, which had also been accused of war crimes) who attracted most attention. For they were notorious as monsters, almost without parallel in history – criminals whom many people believed deserved maximum punishment to fit their crimes. Much less interest, therefore, was given to the trio who escaped the death penalty or a long prison sentence. And only meagre comment was afforded to the acquittal of the General Staff and High Command, even though it was difficult for members of the public to understand this verdict, given the damning opinion of the Tribunal – especially since Reichsmarschall Hermann Göring (Commander-in-Chief of the Luftwaffe), Field Marshal Wilhelm Keitel and General Alfred Jodl (the heads of Oberkommando der Wehrmacht (OKW)) and Grand Admirals Erich Raeder and Karl Dönitz (each at one time Commander-in-Chief of the Navy) individually had been found guilty.

There were those who thought the escape from punishment of the General Staff and High Command was fairly irrelevant. After all, it was personalities, not organisations, upon whom retribution was most desired. And in any case both military bodies had been effectively abolished the day the war with Germany ended in May 1945. As far as the General Staff was concerned, this was the second time it had experienced that ignominious fate at the hands of victors after a World War. For the Treaty of Versailles had imposed a similar condition in 1919, although that time nothing like the vilification at Nürnberg was expressed.

Yet these were but the latest episodes when the German peoples had been characteristically led by their own excesses from triumphs to disasters, and the Tribunal certainly did not pull its punches when it berated their military leaders: 'They have been responsible in large measure for the miseries and sufferings that have fallen upon millions of men, women and children. They have been a disgrace to the honourable profession of arms. Without their military guidance the aggressive ambitions of Hitler and his fellow Nazis would have been academic and sterile. Although they were not a group falling within the words of the Charter, they were a ruthless military caste. The contemporary German militarism flourished briefly with its recent ally, National Socialism, as well or better than it had in the generations of the past ...'

There, by inference, was the rub. The General Staff had escaped justice through a legal loophole in the Charter laid down by the London Agreement setting up the Tribunal on 8 August 1945. As a result, and for compelling political and security reasons, a future President of the USA, General Dwight Eisenhower, felt free to say in 1949 that he did not consider German military honour had been sullied. Clearly the British, French, Russian and American judges had felt otherwise when they reflected upon the record of the General Staff which in 1934 had been restored by the German Chancellor, Adolf Hitler.

They could reflect that, sixteen years after Germany's defeat in 1918, and a further forty-eight since Prussia had defeated France in 1870 (and Austria and Denmark in 1866 and 1864 respectively), thus creating the German Empire, the General Staff had raised German military might and prestige to a pinnacle of arrogance. They might also have recalled that after the routing of the Prussian Army in the battles of Jena and Auerstadt in 1806, a fledgling General Staff had gone on to help free Germany and Europe from French domination in 1815.

How was it that a sophisticated organisation which had contributed decisively to the unification of Germany in 1871, and whose members prided themselves upon honour and prowess, twice managed to stage and lose a World War and, as part of the last act of their follies, stand in the dock accused of unimaginably terrible crimes against humanity?

*   *   *

Central European nations are accustomed to being trampled over by neighbours, especially when like Germany they lack easily defended frontiers and terrain. Countries such as Switzerland and Austria which are shielded by mountains are extremely difficult to overrun. But the north German plain is wide open from east and west, protected mainly by rivers – barriers which are notoriously difficult to defend against determined and properly equipped enemies. So at various times over the centuries, when Scandinavians and Balts thrust southwards into Germany, when Mongols and Poles swept through from the east, Romans and Turks from the south and the French from the west, the Germans have been hard pressed to survive. Consequently their tribes, who gradually began to coalesce for security and trade, always had to do better than simply attempt to hold their frontiers intact. From bitter experience they learnt that the best defence was pre-emption, attacking their threatening neighbours, and that this sort of deterrent was dependent upon possession in peacetime of superior land forces.

This was one reason, for example, why the Knights of the Teutonic Order (emerging from western Germany) diverged in the thirteenth century from the pastime of Crusading in Palestine against the Muslims in order to stamp out paganism more profitably on the eastern fringes of the homeland. Like many autocratic orders of the Middle Ages, the celibate (supposedly) and mercenary Knights were a highly proficient and greedy combat organisation which, like most feudal cliques, waged war for profit on the lines of business ventures. When Hermann von Salza was Grand Master, the Hungarians invited them in 1205 for assistance against raiding, pagan Kumans. But twenty-five years later the deal was cancelled and the Knights were expelled for attempting to take over their hosts.

Meanwhile, however, the Knights had become involved in the curbing of pagan Prussians from the North who preferred raiding to adopting Christianity. Tentatively to begin with, but later much more vigorously, this led to the outward thrusting of German frontiers beyond the River Vistula, which the Knights fortified as they ruthlessly crushed the Prussians. But once again they arrogantly overstepped the mark, this time by threatening the Christianised Poles and Lithuanians, until, in 1410, a combined force of 46,000 Lithuanians, Poles, Russians and Bohemians under Wladyslaw II Jagiello, with only sixteen cannon, met and defeated an army of 32,000 over-confident, well-armoured Germans with 100 cannon at Grunwald (Tannenberg). Jagiello won the day by superior tactics and the encirclement of the elite Knights whom he provoked into a wild charge. Some 200 of the 250 knights, including the impulsive Grand Master, Ulrich von Junginnen, were killed. But the underlying reason for this crushing German defeat was overstretch, and the consequences a Wagnerian 'Twilight of the Gods' when the Knights' morale collapsed and they were ultimately forced to evacuate Poland.

It was nearly three hundred years before another predominant German state emerged in the midst of what could be regarded as a World War – that of the Spanish Succession. During this period, ferocious Religious Wars and the incursions of predatory foreign armies had inflicted immense damage and created lasting hatreds among the afflicted German tribes. Nevertheless, a new much more stable Prussia was born at the end of the War of the Spanish Succession in 1713, when the Brandenburger, Frederick Wilhelm I, became ruler of the combined provinces of Brandenburg and Prussia, separated as they were by Poland.

As inheritor of a power similar to that of a Grand Master of the Teutonic Order (which had expired in 1525), Frederick assumed the Knights' expansionist ambitions through power diplomacy and small wars. Central to determining his policy was the perennial need to maintain employment for an impoverished aristocracy through a militarism geared to a centralised bureaucracy run by the General Directorate. Under this strong monarch, who assumed a Divine Right, conscription expanded the Army to four per cent of the population: an Army which became notorious for its harsh disciplinary code and control by an elitist officer corps, drawn from a class of society working self-interestedly within the General Directorate. At the same time, however, Frederick I ensured that the General Directorate kept expenditure within bounds while accumulating a strong credit balance.

In effect, the new Prussian Army burgeoned as 'A prosperous State within the State' controlled by a prudent ruler whose son, in 1740, inherited the splendidly trained military machine he was only too eager to lead in battle. For Frederick II, known as the Great, was a monarch whose ambitions matched those of Salza and whose tendency to take risks those of Junginnen. Eager for military adventures, he managed within seven months of mounting the throne to launch a pre-emptive invasion of Silesia. This precipitated a successful war with Austria which eventually so frightened Russia, France and Sweden that they allied with Austria and Saxony against the Prussians, thus starting in 1756 the Seven Years' War, in which Britain was Frederick's only ally.

This confrontation, for all the prowess of the Prussian Army and Frederick's skilful generalship, would have ended in victory for the Alliance had not Tsar Peter III of Russia suddenly withdrawn from it in 1762 when Prussia was down to her last 60,000 soldiers and on the verge of capitulation. Frederick the Great, indeed, was luckier than many of his predecessors and also his successors. The collapse of the Alliance in 1763, linked to a few British and Prussian victories, not only rescued him but also so strengthened Prussia that, in 1772, it was possible for her, without war, to acquire northern Poland along with a position of growing world-wide influence. Furthermore it established Prussian military doctrine and training as models of excellence. German officers were in demand as instructors and leaders by other armies (including the American Continental one when at war with Britain in the 1770s). Some went as far as to copy Prussian dress and extremely harsh disciplinary measures, such as running the gauntlet.

But come the end of the century, after the French Army had won many victories under Napoleon Bonaparte, there were indications that the Prussian Army was out-of-date generally as well as out of touch with revolutionary political and industrial changes: inadequacies which at Jena and Auerstadt in 1806 would be exposed all too disastrously.

CHAPTER 2

From Jena to Sedan

When Major Gerhard Scharnhorst, the taciturn, modest and incorruptible son of a Hanoverian tenant farmer, joined the Prussian Army in 1801, he realised that it was badly in need of modernisation. For already he had acquired experience in the French Revolutionary Wars and had been made a very progressive Chief of Staff to the Commander-in-Chief of the Hanoverian Army. Promoted lieutenant colonel and raised to the nobility by the King of Prussia, he formed the Berlin Militärische Gesellschaft, a society dedicated to organisational and doctrinal reform on French lines. Appointed Director of the Military Academy, he became the leader of a band of enthusiastic younger officers, but also a thorn in the side of dyed-in-the-wool leaders who assumed Frederick the Great's methods and rigidly trained long-service army would defeat Bonaparte's more flexible methods if it came to war.

Central to Scharnhorst's reforms was the creation of a General Staff of twenty-one selected officers (called the Quartermaster General's Staff), a proposal adopted by the King in 1803 at the suggestion of a maverick Colonel von Massenbach. Among the twenty-one was Scharnhorst, who, as Chief of Staff to the Duke of Brunswick, became engaged after 1804 in preparations for war. This task was fatally hampered by the machinations of senior officers, aged between seventy and eighty, and by the Adjutant General's Department which, as a complacent, secretive cabinet, advised the King. In the upshot, when Napoleon did invade Prussia in 1806, the nascent General Staff was side-tracked and the Army unready, outmoded and ineptly led.

At Jena and Auerstadt on 14 October 1806 the Prussian Army was outnumbered and routed by an enemy whose superiority in every department of the art of war, especially in speed of manoeuvre, was pronounced. It was sheer pace which enabled Napoleon (who managed without a General Staff) devastatingly to concentrate his forces at the decisive point and pursue the Prussians to destruction. But among the defeated were three men who soon would lay the foundations of a Prussian Army that would help bring France to her knees: Scharnhorst; the combative and sensible General Prince Gebhard Blücher; and the temperamental, fiery and ingenious Captain August von Gneisenau.

When freed from French captivity in 1807, Scharnhorst, Massenbach, Gneisenau and others, became members, under a new Adjutant General, of a committee appointed to purge the Army of some 800 officers who had failed in the recent debacle. More constructively important however was the committee's setting in motion of radical reform. Scharnhorst was the moving spirit of a plan creating a War Ministry in which a Great General Staff, subdivided into four sections dealing with strategy and tactics, administration, manpower, and weapons and munitions, would be set above the existing Adjutant General's and Quartermaster General's departments. The King's absolute power thus would be diminished and the old field formations replaced by all-arms divisions within corps, modelled on the French system. Corporal punishment and running the gauntlet were abolished. The old aristocratic officer corps would be retained but recruitment was to be by means of a combination of conscription and long-service regulars; and on the ingrained principle that the people had a duty to defend the state.

These changes did not occur all at once. There was strong opposition from the King, under pressure from Napoleon and the old school; acute shortage of funds; and always the threat, after the Peace of Tilsit in 1807, of further French interference. Mainly the newly created divisions existed only as skeletons. Only gradually were General Staff officers of the required merit trained in the Military Academy and posted to key appointments in the shadow army. The plan was far from complete when, in 1809, the Austrians attacked France. Sensibly rejecting calls by some General Staff officers to side with Austria, Frederick Wilhelm III clung to neutrality. French troops were lodged in Prussia. Furthermore the King was not insensitive to the fact that over 100,000 German soldiers of varying quality and loyalties from thirty-one states in the Confederation of the Rhine (including 47,000 Bavarians and 14,000 Württembergers) made up a high (and steadily increasing) proportion of Napoleon's Army.

Not that German unification was on the agenda of the states at that time, especially in the aftermath of Austria's crushing defeat by Napoleon at Wagram. Moreover, the realisation in 1811 that the insatiably ambitious Napoleon was bent on the conquest of Russia did little to promote nationalism or changes of alliances. On the contrary, there was more opportunist support than otherwise for the Emperor of Battles when in 1812 he launched his Grand Army (including a Prussian corps) into a European crusade against the feared Russian state.

This blatant act of aggression would stir key members of the Prussian General Staff to a political activity contrary to the King's self-serving desires. Already in 1808 Gneisenau had resigned in order, secretly in London, to negotiate a new alliance of Britain and Russia against France. Later Blücher was forced out of service by Napoleon, and Scharnhorst, ostensibly on leave, went to St Petersburg in an attempt to seal a treaty of alliance with Russia. Meanwhile some Germans, among them the brilliant Captain Karl von Clausewitz, who had been Scharnhorst's chief aide, had joined the Russians. In 1812 Clausewitz would play an important role in the Russian retreat to Moscow, the counterstroke which hurled Napoleon back in the depths of winter, and in the negotiations which, on 30 December, helped General Johann von Yorck to change sides by joining the Russians with the Prussian corps. This move encouraged the King to ally Prussia with Russia on 16 March 1813 and to sign an agreement with Tsar Alexander dissolving the Confederation of the Rhine while demanding that its states also should turn against France.

German nationalism thus was promoted by an army initiative in the midst of battle, although, in so far as Allied military strength was concerned, the gain was small. It was Prussia which supplied the bulk of the German forces under Blücher, with Scharnhorst as his chief of staff, to participate in the liberation of Germany from French occupation. And it was Gneisenau who took Scharnhorst's place when the latter died from wounds received in June 1813, thus forming the powerful duo which not only saw the Allies victorious in 1814, but also would lead a German Army into a crucial role in the final defeat of Napoleon at Waterloo in 1815.

*   *   *

In the aftermath of Waterloo, Europe was to enjoy an almost

unprecedented period of peace, lasting nearly forty years, before her armies engaged again in a major war – the Crimea. This epoch saw Germany grow strong with industrial prosperity, while adopting new technology in company with the evolving intellectual and liberating ideas of the so-called Romantic movement, to which the formation of the Kaiser Wilhelm University in 1809 significantly contributed.

Meanwhile European armies, including that of Prussia, drifted in the doldrums, unless urgently called upon (as in 1832 and 1848) to help contain revolutions in Poland or at home. Yet, beneath the calm, breezes of rising strength were generating future storms of unprecedented violence.

Stirring the coming vortex was the quiet, thoughtful and reserved Karl von Clausewitz who, while chief administrator of the Military Academy from 1818 until his death from cholera in 1831, compiled his indigestible, monumental, theoretical study *On War*. This was a work of political and military philosophy containing the celebrated statements that war is a continuation of politics by different means; that defence was militarily and politically stronger than attack; that every effort should be directed against the enemy's resources and will to fight; and that direction should be in the hands of the civil power.

On War, once described by the last Chief of the General Staff, General Heinz Guderian, as 'read by few, criticised by many', was not published until 1853. By this time a new generation of Prussians had edited out, among other things, the vital principle of political control. Nevertheless, as Guderian wrote: 'It had a large share in shaping the spirit of generations of general staff officers ... This book was also the fountainhead of all patriotism and idealism which inspired these same representatives of the General Staff.'

Probably it was no accident that the publication of *On War* followed shortly after a new Prussian Constitution, decreed by Frederick Wilhelm IV in 1850, was introduced in response to liberal pressures. It founded a flawed democratic parliamentary system elected by a constricted franchise, but retained for the King the appointment of ministers at a time when proposals to unify the German states were again in the air, and evidence of French bellicosity, driven by Napoleon III, was impossible to ignore. Nevertheless, until the death of Frederick Wilhelm in 1861, Prussian liberal policies survived, despite the arrival in government of four men, each of whom was opposed to democracy, and with military connections and orientation. There was the soldier Prince Wilhelm who became Regent in 1857 due to the insanity of his brother, the King; the aggressive General Albrecht von Roon (known as Ruffian) as War Minister in 1859; his friend the subtle and sophisticated Otto von Bismarck who became, at Roon's instigation, Minister-President in 1862; and an impoverished General Staff officer, Helmuth Karl von Moltke, a one-time aide-de-camp to Prince Wilhelm, as Chief of the General Staff.

These pragmatists believed in the inevitability of war, and unfortunately had no inhibitions about starting one if nobody else would oblige. They also were influenced (though not subjugated) by the writings of Clausewitz, and were concerned by looming threats from Austria, under the assertive Emperor Franz Joseph, and from Napoleon III's France, which, in the 1850s, had won two wars. They promoted the pre-eminence of the Army in government and favoured German unification – as long as it was dominated by Prussia. Under this autocratic quartet Prussia was instantly headed for rearmament, military reform and war – pre-emptive or otherwise.

Thus Bismarck (who stated publicly that great issues were 'decided by blood and iron'), supported by the newly enthroned Kaiser Wilhelm I, manipulated the Constitution in 1862 in order to bypass Parliament as the prologue to a new round of pre-emptive wars. This enabled Roon, a driving force ever at the King's elbow, and the intellectual Moltke, thoroughly to modernise the Army and successively overwhelm Denmark in 1864, Austria in 1866 and France in 1870.

*   *   *

In 1861 the Army was far from ready for war, even though it was ahead of other armies with a breech-loading rifle, would soon receive its first breech-loading artillery and was a leader in the development of the telegraph. Among Moltke's reforms the two most important were a shake-up of the General Staff and the integration of the railways, of which he was an enthusiastic protagonist, into the military system. Henceforward, under the eye of Moltke, General Staff officers were trained as an elite corps to use their initiative in accordance with 'General Directives' (present day 'Operation Instructions') instead of bureaucratically obeying detailed orders. With the collaboration of Roon, he created a Lines of Communication Department within the General Staff to bring the railways under War Ministry control in order to dovetail track and telegraph layouts with strategic and mobilisation schemes.

It was fortunate for Moltke that the war against Denmark (from which he was virtually excluded until the closing victorious stages by ennobled field commanders, who despised him) and the war against Austria (in which he played a decisive role) were of short duration against inept opponents. Shortcomings of the staff and defects in intelligence gathering and synthesis bred inefficiency and perpetrated serious errors. Victory at the Battle of Königgrätz might have been a lot less costly and more decisive if rail and road movements of troops and supplies had been better co-ordinated. Nevertheless, these campaigns as preludes to the Franco-Prussian War in 1870 provided for Germany the same service as did involvement, prior to World War II, in the Spanish Civil War and the bloodless invasions of Austria and Czechoslovakia. Moltke detected the rough edges and deficiencies and took remedial measures, though even he failed to eradicate the fundamental causes of serious breakdowns in communication and supply in 1870 such as would have fatal consequences when the German Army invaded Belgium and France in 1914.

Königgrätz, nevertheless, was a mighty catalyst in that it not only made politically feasible an enlarged North German Federation incorporating, under Prussian hegemony, Schleswig-Holstein and Hanover, but, with the exclusion of the South German states (including Bavaria and Württemberg), also made acceptable the creation of an Army which was 'the training school of the entire nation for war'. The Army was founded upon a drastically re-organised Prussian model in which men served for three years, plus four with the reserves; and in which the voluntary, democratic militia (Landwehr) was placed firmly under Army control, as an additional reserve with service reduced to five years.

Yet behind the polished execution of Moltke's plans by commanders and aristocratic staff officers lurked an arrogant snobbishness in relationships with mere engineers, communicators, railway troops and supply services. Although in 1870 the General Staff carried out its operational functions admirably by shutting up Marshal Bazaine's Army in Metz (where it later surrendered), and annihilated Marshal MacMahon's Army at Sedan as the culmination of Moltke's classic envelopment, it repeatedly overlooked or mis-employed non-combat troops. The embarrassing consequence was that, as in 1866, the fighting formations ran out of supplies and energy. These breakdowns, when they occurred in the concluding phase of the war, delayed by three months the positioning of heavy artillery and ammunition to support the politically crucial siege of Paris, and so delayed the victory which, among other things, at last secured the greatest prize of all. For Prussia's triumph in leadership of the North German Federation formed the corner-stone for Bismarck's diplomacy when negotiating the 1871 proclamation of a German Empire which at last included the South German States – plus Alsace and Lorraine wrested from France. Henceforward the schemes of Bismarck and Moltke and their successors would attain new and at times excessive dimensions.

Moltke, when asked by the Crown Prince what might happen if German strength was exhausted, had replied with political naivety and blinkered military arrogance: 'We must always win battles. We must throw France completely to the ground ... Then we can dictate the peace we want.'

'And if we ourselves bleed to death in the process?'

'We shall not bleed to death, but, if we do, we shall have got peace in return.'

This flawed doctrine contained the seeds of the disasters to come.

CHAPTER 3

Towards War on Two Fronts

History began to repeat itself a century after Prussia's rise to military prominence in the aftermath of the Seven Years' War. For following the humbling of France in 1871 there appeared two familiar and menacing manifestations: a yearning, on the French part, for revenge; and high-handedness and expansionism, alloyed with preparations for pre-emptive defensive measures on Germany's part. So while the French strove to restore their fortunes and rebuild their Army, the Germans, at Bismarck's prompting, looked beyond the continent of Europe in a belated desire to acquire overseas possessions in competition with the other colonial powers, such as Britain, France and Italy. Besides this Germany eagerly adopted new technology, growing its industrial base, building an ocean-going Navy and progressively improving and enlarging the standing army and its reserve formations against traditional opponents. Yet at the same time, also through Bismarck's diplomacy, it became a signatory to several elaborate treaties intended to retain a prudent balance between the European powers, especially France, Austro-Hungary and Russia, in order to maintain peace.

Like a colossus, Moltke held office until 1888, helped by Bismarck's pushing a generous military budget through Parliament every seventh year. He moulded the new Germany Army to Prussian ways and standards. With an open mind to the latest weapons, such as the machine-gun, motor vehicles, the telephone and radio, airships and aircraft, he trained to technical perfection the Great General Staff upon which the military (and therefore, according to his philosophy, the nation) depended in order to be ready for the two-front war against France and Russia which, to Parliament, he declared must be inevitable.

The Great General Staff, as selected and trained by Moltke and further developed by successive Chiefs of Staff prior to 1914, Alfred von Waldersee, Alfred von Schlieffen and Helmuth Johannes von

Moltke (the Younger), was a model for many another army to copy: an elite, comprising officers dedicated to a profession which took precedence over everything else.

Candidates were sometimes appointed directly after a successful spell at staff duty, or due to there being insufficient from their own arm of the service to achieve proportional balance on the course; such as in Guderian's class of 1913 when three cavalry officers with below average marks were admitted for this reason. Usually, however, it was the 168 officers who had undergone a period of very intensive study and scored top marks in a written examination who annually entered the Military Academy for a three-year course.

By 1914 the curriculum covered tactics up to the level of a reinforced infantry brigade, field craft, engineering, instruction in arms plus the (discretionary) study of languages, geography and history. But of these subjects tactics was favoured by a factor of five marks – which undoubtedly lay behind criticisms by the future Field Marshal Albert Kesselring when he held that 'training in some fields was inadequate' such as intelligence, supply services, air and naval warfare, applied science as a whole and 'anything to do with oil which soiled the fingers and hampered the tactician and strategist in the free flight of his ideas'. Such failings would impact crucially upon future wars.

Kesselring also commented on a divide between 'line officers' who, 'with satirical humour' in Imperial times, referred to General Staff officers as 'demi-gods'. There were also significant divisions due to tribe and caste. Kesselring, himself a Bavarian artillery officer, noted that 'the old Prussian nobility was given preferential treatment in the General Staff' which was 'also granted to the wealthy and capitalist class. It was a fact that the nobility predominated.' Whereas officers from states such as Bavaria had a different status because they 'lacked the typical military nobility and large estates'; with a resultant 'appearance in the General Staff of scions of the wealthy capitalist class', among whom 'the sons of parents in easy circumstances for most part tried to gain admission to the cavalry.' Whose '...lack of concern about the future,' he added, 'also saved his nervous energy ... so that he had an advantage over the officers in other branches of the service.'

Furthermore, there were snobbish differentiations between the guards, cavalry, light infantry, heavy infantry, artillery, engineers and the supply and technical services – in that pecking order. The order related to closeness, as well as honourable obedience, to the Emperor, to whom all ranks swore a very solemn and binding Oath of Loyalty. These emotional allegiances were stamped hard on the Army by a monastic General Staff whose standards of excellence and integrity won almost unchallenged approval from all ranks because they bore the authority of Moltke's thorough study of war in all its aspects.

'To me,' said General Hans von Seeckt (a future Chief of Staff), 'the best General Staff officer is just good enough to be a teacher for my officer students.' Central to teaching, as initiated by Moltke and elaborated by his successors, were staff rides and war-games, which also were tools for the solution of strategic, tactical, organisational and technical problems.

During staff rides, officers studied the lessons of history on the battlefields, for example, of the Seven Years', Napoleonic or Franco-Prussian wars and answered problems set by the directing staff. Moltke, indeed, made a practice whenever possible of conducting the culminating ride to decide for himself the qualities of each student.

But it was the war-games upon which most attention was focused for nigh-scientific studies in which, by no means incidentally, intuitive decision making was at a discount. Seated before a model or map displays players would consider organisations, doctrine, weapons and so on. At the Military Academy they were tested in tactics either during oral sessions or in papers written against time, which would demonstrate judgement, decision and ability to formulate orders. Once qualified and appointed to the War Ministry or a subordinate headquarters, they frequently would play war-games in winter, or attend staff rides in summer, to develop ideas, verify decisions and probe future plans and trends in every aspect of the military spectrum.

With the benefit, or otherwise, of these methods the Army which went to war in 1914 had a fairly clear vision of what the Chief of Staff considered the best strategy. His subordinates were thus able to translate his intentions into realistic operational procedures and tactics, making the best use of the latest weapons and facilities which had been provided after careful but, unavoidably, mainly theoretical study.

Realistic trials, short of war, were hard to perform. There was, for example, the artillery versus fortifications controversy of the mid-

1880s when France, Germany and Austria were undecided about the future of strong, fixed defences. Each carried out trials which demonstrated the inaccuracy of heavy guns and indicated the protection needed to defeat big projectiles – tests in which German observers, for the first time, used the telephone to send corrections to the guns. As a result the French and Austrians envisaged a continuing role for modernised forts. But in line with their ingrained aggressive strategies, the Germans, as well as the Austrians, concentrated upon developing much improved siege pieces for fort smashing.

The demand for increased firepower from quick-firing field artillery, like the French 75mm gun, and from the belt-fed Maxim machine-gun, fascinated the European Armies as they rearmed and expanded. Then there were the tactical implications of Alfred Nobel's smokeless powder to ponder upon; the advent of a practical internal combustion engine making feasible motor vehicles and aircraft; plus the invention of wireless telegraphy which promised a communications revolution. Yet, although there were those like Schlieffen who perceived some of the changes suggested by scientific marvels, nobody foresaw their full impact on current tactical formations and doctrine. Equip themselves as they would, as the result of war-gaming, with many new devices, they had only cloudy visions of the full operational potential of what they were creating. They realised massed manpower might be difficult to control and supply, but did not realistically grasp that once in battle mass could be destroyed or neutralised almost absolutely by highly intensive firepower.

Changes at the pinnacle of the German hierarchy also had a drastic effect on the Army as the nineteenth century drew to a close. The death of Wilhelm I in 1888, and that of his son Frederick III ninety days later, acted as a trigger. The ageing and weary Moltke, filled with serious doubts about the erratic and immature new Emperor, Wilhelm II (who declaimed 'I only want my Chief of Staff to be a sort of amanuensis') resigned. As successor he recommended his deputy, the ambitious and charming Waldersee, a favourite of Wilhelm II.

Waldersee, like most General Staff officers, was a warmonger, and no genius. He favoured lightning strokes in pre-emptive wars; but, unlike his erstwhile chief, had his sights set on being Chancellor. Henceforward at court and in government circles comparisons could be made with the disastrous, pre-Jena period – or even with Byzantium. Intrigue and corruption intruded and standards tended to slip. Bellicosity and immoderation were on the rise, in response, to some extent, to Wilhelm's love of war-games and flashy parades, along with boastful remarks such as 'I will lead you to glorious times' – though, in fact, he had little wish for actual combat.

When the conservative Bismarck threatened to change the Constitution by a putsch to establish a military dictatorship in order to get the militarily biased Budget past a liberally minded Parliament, it was Waldersee who in 1890 ultimately was instrumental in his fall – only to see the chancellorship given to the ineffectual General Leon von Caprivi. Waldersee rapidly fell from royal favour, to be replaced in 1891 by Schlieffen, a quiet, intellectual, cold and sarcastic bachelor who was an exponent of the theory of double envelopment to gain a quick victory. Henceforward his life's work would be the formulation of a plan to fight a lightning war on two fronts.

But, unlike Moltke, Schlieffen would no longer have at his disposal the entire military and industrial capacity and apparatus of the state. For Wilhelm, while playing soldiers at the head of the Army, had become enamoured also of the so-called 'new navalism' associated with colonialism; and enthralled by the brilliant, inexhaustible and aggressive Admiral Alfred von Tirpitz who, taking a leaf from the General Staff's book, preached pre-emptive naval warfare.

Backed by Wilhelm, Tirpitz, as Secretary of State for the Imperial Navy Department, pushed through the Naval Acts of 1898 and 1900 which, with subsequent supplements, were intended by 1917 to convert the small German Navy into the world's second largest naval power (after the British Royal Navy) with thirty-eight battleships and thirty-five cruisers supported by destroyer and submarine flotillas and airships. This was a dangerously provocative excess. Inevitably so vast a programme induced fundamental consequences, of which the diversion of enormous industrial and manpower resources from the Army was the least pernicious. For without fully understanding the ramifications of seapower and international trade, Germany embarked upon acquiring 'a luxury' (as Winston Churchill, the First Lord of the British Admiralty, called it) which distracted her from her traditional role as a very competent land power into a naval race with Britain – for whom command of the seas was a defensive necessity. Thus Wilhelm and

Tirpitz, quite deliberately and with the compliance of a submissive Parliament, seriously menaced a nation which, in the past, had been a staunch ally and friend in desperate times. Thereby Germany actually was weakened by introducing the likelihood of a war on three fronts, two on land and one at sea, as Britain allied herself with France and Russia to contain a formidable and uncalled-for threat.

Germany's Imperial Navy never matched Britain's. The latter kept the lead in the warship-building race; at the start of World War I German shipping was swept from the seas and her fleet, at Wilhelm's wish, was kept in port. This left the Army centre stage and, in accordance with the Schlieffen Plan, committed to knock out France while, in company with Austro-Hungary, holding Russia in check.

Governed by the underlying Napoleonic/Clausewitzian principle of concentrating overwhelming force at the decisive point, but bearing in mind another of Clausewitz's dicta, that the defensive was superior to the offensive, Schlieffen had concluded that France could not be defeated by a predictable direct approach into the teeth of her fortifications. Instead his very secret, strategic plan of 1906 embodied a wheel, pivoting on Metz, thrusting a heavily weighted right wing through neutral Belgium and Holland to outflank, envelop and paralyse the French Army by a descent, via Paris, upon its rear. Railways would enable the swift and efficient mobilisation of reservists to concentrate the armies behind the frontier and, along with horse-drawn transport, supply them deep into France in the achievement of a modern Cannae.

However, by the time his somewhat reluctant successor, the lacklustre but realistically-minded Helmuth Johannes von Moltke (the Younger), was fated to put the Schlieffen Plan into action, much had been modified. In 1912 he reprieved Holland, '... the last air-hole through which we can breathe.' He also weakened the right wing in order to strengthen the left against a predicted invasion of southern Germany and in order to launch a complementary, frontal assault through Lorraine. More creatively, however, he tried to enhance telephone communications with the widespread armies by the use of radio; had obtained 4,000 motor trucks to supplement supply columns; and had acquired airships and aircraft primarily for reconnaissance. But his preferred tactics of frontal attacks by massed infantry were frozen in the 1870 form.

As often has been remarked, the best laid plans, especially in war, rarely survive contact. When Europe stumbled into war in July 1914, the Emperor, egged on by his General Staff, fatalisticaly squared up for the two-front campaign so long anticipated. He was supported by Theobald von Bethmann Hollweg, the first Chancellor ever to rise from the civil bureaucracy, who managed, at the price of forfeiting complete surprise, to insist upon a formal declaration of war in accordance with the Hague Conventions. Other than that the Chancellor was incapable of withstanding General Erich von Falkenhayn, the War Minister, and Moltke when they insisted that to delay mobilisation would weaken Germany and to cancel it, when a last chance for peace was presented, would create chaos. The General Staff took charge. Mobilisation proceeded smoothly. Belgium's frontier fortresses were smashed by heavy guns and the armies thrust westwards on schedule. But then the flaws and miscalculations of the modified Schlieffen Plan appeared.

Britain, ostensibly in defence of Belgium by treaty, declared war and contributed her small Army which significantly extended the French left flank to, fortuitously, delay the German right wing, First Army of 320,000 men. The farther the Germans advanced the more difficult became maintenance, largely due to the inability of an ill-trained rail transport organisation to repair track and demolitions, and the reluctance of operational commanders and staffs to pay sufficient attention to logistics. Chaos at transfer points choked supply. Excessive demands on and exhaustion of horse-drawn transport throttled deliveries to the leading troops. There were insufficient motor lorries to make up these deficiencies. Also telephone communications failed because the lofty General Staff had not taken the lowly Signals Branch into its confidence, with the result that repairs to lines were improvised and haphazard; while radio telegraphy was misemployed and lacked sufficient capacity. Thus Moltke, verging on a nervous breakdown, lost close touch with his Army commanders, who therefore began to arrange unco-ordinated and erratic movements between themselves – which presented the French with victory at the Marne.

Come 8 September Moltke was largely in ignorance of the situation when the exposed right wing came under flank attack. Loss of confidence as well as control was inferred when, in a moment of Wagnerian fantasy, he sent Lieutenant Colonel Richard Hentsch of the General Staff Intelligence Branch by motor car to the front, authorised to co-ordinate a retreat 'should rearward movements have been initiated.' Whereupon this lowly staff officer, reflecting the gloom of some army commanders, inadvertently actuated the retirement Moltke intuitively desired. This encouraged Moltke, without bothering to consult his Commander-in-Chief, the Emperor, to be host to his fears and order a general retreat – unknowingly, at that moment, losing the war for the Central Powers.

For although a German Army under General Paul von Hindenburg by victory at Tannenberg already had thrown two Russian armies out of East Prussia, and the Austro-Hungarian Army was at least containing the mass of Russian armies elsewhere, all hope of bringing the victorious troops home 'before the leaves have fallen', as was officially said, was dead. A long war on two fronts in quite unprecedented form was unavoidable.

Moltke was replaced secretly as Chief of Staff in October by the strong-minded, energetic and clear-thinking Falkenhayn, who temporarily retained his position of Minister of War. His immediate aim was retrieval of the initiative in the West by means of a succession of outflanking attacks. But when this finally came to nought at Ypres at the end of October it suddenly had to be admitted that mounted men, who had been checked by armoured cars, were virtually obsolete and Moltke's doctrine of massed, frontal infantry attacks against even lightly entrenched positions bankrupt. Never again could men advance, as witnessed by a dismounted British cavalry regiment one calm evening, with '... a band playing "Deutschland über Alles", and then the charge sounded on the bugles and the Germans came through the hedge, advancing slowly in almost close formation, kettle drummers beating their drums as they advanced', to be shot down in droves.

A complete rethink of Central Powers strategy and tactics was overdue, and all Falkenhayn could come up with was a policy of wearing down the Allies in hope that they might become war-weary and negotiate a face-saving peace. The line of trenches dug from the North Sea to Switzerland was reckoned impregnable, and proven as such when, throughout the coming year, the French and British abetted Falkenhayn by futilely attacking them at immense cost in lives. Artillery was crowned king of the battlefield, but, paradoxically, unable sufficiently to rule since pre-war planning had neither foreseen immense ammunition expenditure nor the need for so many heavy guns. With both sides hampered by shell shortages, stalemate prevailed.

Meanwhile Turkey's joining with the Central Powers in October

1914 and Italy's siding with the Allies in 1915 added still more fronts to consume increasing quantities of men and materiel. Falkenhayn, given a blank cheque, called up more men in 1915, expanded the Army, stood on the defensive in the West, reinforced the Eastern Front and, with Austro-Hungarian collaboration, took the offensive in Galicia on 2 May. The vast breakthrough and subsequent sustained pursuit of the demoralised Russians by the German Austro-Hungarian forces was a tactical triumph not only for the courtly General August von Mackensen and his brilliant Chief of Staff, Hans von Seeckt, but also a great boost for Falkenhayn, who controlled everything with astute military sense and diplomacy. However, at the height of success, Falkenhayn now found himself at odds with Hindenburg, the national saviour of Prussia at Tannenberg, and the latter's rude, bullying but very able Chief of Staff, General Erich Ludendorff.

Hindenburg and Ludendorff, seeking further glory, now wished to attack on their northern front with the aim of knocking Russia out of the war. Falkenhayn demurred, in the belief that 'one cannot hope to strike a comprehensive and deadly blow ... at an enemy who is numerically stronger, who will stick at no sacrifices of territory and population, and in addition has the expanse of Russia and good railways behind him ...'. He permitted only a limited offensive because he intended to switch forces for further offensive action in the Balkans and the West. As a result the angered and obstinate Hindenburg's attack was only a partial success, although it contributed to Falkenhayn's aim '... to inflict quite enough damage ... for our purposes.'

The wrangle between Falkenhayn and Hindenburg would persist, but for the time being the former had the Emperor's confidence. Yet Wilhelm was closer to the mark when he estimated that the Russians would take only six months to recover, whereas Falkenhayn considered Russia's offensive strength to be indefinitely crippled. Nevertheless, Falkenhayn had attained a position which made it possible to put Serbia out of the war and, in 1916, turn directly on France and thus indirectly on Britain. Nevertheless, in his assessment of Russian power, Falkenhayn had supplied perfect due notice of Russian determination and endurance which, three decades later, his successors would have done well to recall and heed.

CHAPTER 4

Verdun to Compiègne

On the assumption that Russia could not be defeated, Falkenhayn was led to the logical conclusion that either the war must be ended or Britain and France knocked out. To adopt the first course was unthinkable since not only would it discredit the Emperor but also disparage the General Staff. Unavoidable as was the second course, Falkenhayn for once failed to have his way with Bethmann Hollweg since the Chancellor was able to persuade the Emperor that, following the outrage over the sinking of the liner *Lusitania* in 1915, blockade of Britain by unrestricted submarine warfare might drag the USA into war.

The alternative, therefore, was a land attack on the French; for which, however, there was no viable or orthodox way due to the neutralisation of infantry and the extinction of cavalry as the mobile arm of decision. So, because the artillery was incapable of taking and holding ground, Falkenhayn resorted to an experiment which no war-game could simulate: the bizarre attritional concept of 'bleeding white the French Army' in an artillery abattoir by applying pressure against Verdun, the strongly fortified, pivotal zone which, Falkenhayn correctly reasoned, the French would feel compelled to hold regardless of cost.

At Verdun, on 21 February 1916, the Germans opened fire with 1,400 guns, including twenty-six monster siege pieces, supplied with 2,500,000 high-explosive and gas shells for a six-day bombardment. Shortly, however, it became plain that the experiment was a failure which was costing the Germans almost as many casualties as the stubborn French. Falkenhayn wanted to call it off, but again was deterred by dread of the political repercussions of failure, since the titular German commander at Verdun was the Crown Prince. So piecemeal attacks by both sides continued while Russia, against predictions, launched relieving attacks; and the British, with French participation, began a very costly attritional offensive on the Somme

– giving Falkenhayn an excuse to put a stop to offensive action at Verdun.

Wilhelm, who by now was reduced by the dictatorial General Staff to little more than a figurehead, feared the worst. Not only were his armies under heavy pressure on all fronts, but his cherished Navy had been out-fought at the Battle of Jutland and again was locked up in port. The nation was overstretched. The Allied blockade was pinching, there was unrest and peace movements, which were anathema to Wilhelm, at home. When Romania sided with the Allies on 28 August, in support of the Russia offensive, it was the last straw. Seizing the opportunity by calling for Hindenburg's advice, he precipitated Falkenhayn's resignation next day.

To a paean of public ecstasy at the prospects of salvation, the idolised Hindenburg was appointed Chief of Staff, bringing with him the deeply patriotic, workaholic Ludendorff as assistant under the title of First Quartermaster General. Characteristically, Hindenburg delegated full power to Ludendorff who revelled in the task. As an organiser of genius the latter set about consolidation of the General Staff dictatorship already established by Falkenhayn. Guided by Hindenburg, who provided the necessary clear direction of strategy and inspiring leadership of the nation, Ludendorff, regardless of the Chancellor and Parliament, used what Guderian called 'His burning patriotism to fight with titanic force against the impending defeat of his people'. Progressively he employed General Staff officers to control the bureaucracy in the waging of what he called 'total war', in effect encouraging them to assume what Kesselring deprecated, as 'co-responsibility above the law' which sometimes generated '... unbecoming false pride.... What the General Staff officer needs is great personal modesty which finds its satisfaction in ability and knowledge and not the lust for power.' Now General Staff officers took to going over their commanders' heads not only in a shake up of the Army but also in the direction of labour (including women), food and industrial production for the war effort and to overcome the effects of blockade.

Already the duo realised that the Army was in dire straits. Many of the best leaders had been lost and not replaced. There was a deficiency of General Staff officers because the Military Academy, reasonably enough for a short war, had been closed in 1914. Reconstruction of the Army, they knew, would take at least a year and require something of a revolution in the selection of officers.

Against caste instinct, it suddenly became desirable to grant commissions to sergeants – with the proviso that they returned to the ranks after the war.

The training of high-class General Staff officers, drawing upon such future stars as Kesselring, Guderian and Walter Wever, was resumed. At the same time tactical doctrine and organisations were drastically revised. Led by Colonel Georg Bruchmüller, who grasped new technology well, the artillery developed practical firing of accurate concentrations to blast ways through the front, helping the infantry advance in relative safety. At the same time officers of the General Staff, such as Lieutenant Colonel Wetzell, and an infantry Captain Geyer, developed tactical drills whereby elite storm troopers infiltrated the enemy lines as spearheads of the main assault. Formed into ad hoc man- and horse-powered combat teams consisting of riflemen, light machine-guns, mortars and assault field guns fitted with shields for direct support by fire with movement, they were grouped within battlegroups commanded by vigorous officers moving behind the spearheads intuitively to exploit fleeting opportunities.

But for the immediate future, because renewed enemy offensives were expected, resources had to be concentrated on defence, especially in the West. Construction of self-supporting lines of resistance and strongpoints was begun in accordance with a doctrine of depth, which included instant local counter-attacks in the event of enemy penetration.

These German methods remain standard to this day, with one vital exception: tanks, the tracked, armoured fighting vehicles which the British had introduced with promising, if limited effect in September 1916. This omission is strange bearing in mind an immediate recognition of the tank's potential through commencement of a development programme by Colonel Bauer, head of the artillery technical department. Yet here lay a reflection of the General Staff's current tendency to cling overlong to proven technology and tactical doctrine; including an inertia concerning mechanisation which was to have dire consequences.

Abandonment of offensive action rankled as the admission of defeat it was – the more so since, in hunting for an immediate way to break the impasse, it was the Naval Staff which came up with the only apparent promising way ahead: the unrestricted submarine warfare which Falkenhayn had been persuaded to reject a year before. But this time the Navy, eager to make a contribution in justification of its ill-spent existence, and with twice the number of submarines as in 1915, was on firmer ground. Its staff had assembled statistics dubiously and over-optimistically indicating that the British could be blockaded and brought to their knees. They unwisely despised the enemy, being as dismissive of effective countermeasures as were their British opponents – until the convoy system was belatedly put into operation.

The land animal Ludendorff accepted the naval proposals at face value, perhaps because the wish was father to the thought. But in doing so he and Hindenburg exposed a political ineptitude which sent Germany downhill all the way. Arrogantly choosing to misread and dismiss American susceptibilities and warnings, he neither believed they would enter the war nor have much effect if they did. In this misconception he was supported by senior generals; including the normally prescient Seeckt, who, incidentally, held the opinion that the current war was only a phase which might end to Germany's disadvantage, but would be resumed at a later date as part of a continuing struggle.

This time Bethmann Hollweg was powerless to prevent the total submarine campaign which was launched with encouraging initial success early in 1917, setting in train a series of quite unforeseeable events. For, come 6 April, in response to the German propensity to anger other people, America had joined the Allies. This would eventually outweigh the outbreak in March of Russia's Revolution, and Russia's virtual withdrawal into a passive resistance that the Germans were careful not to provoke throughout 1917.

Equally unforeseeable was the serious breach of the German defences at Arras on 9 April, followed by the mutiny of the French Army in the aftermath of their disastrous, complementary attack on the Chemin des Dames. If Hindenburg and Ludendorff had been aware of this hushed-up debacle and the abandonment of future French offensive operations, they might have been even more sanguine than they were when, in July, they brought down Chancellor Bethmann Hollweg, on grounds of defeatism after Parliament had passed a resolution calling for peace, and appointed a succession of puppet chancellors in his place.

Henceforward the autocratic duo operated as an absolute dictatorship which badly needed victory before war weariness also afflicted their people and the Americans arrived in strength in 1918.

This was increasingly certain to happen since the submarine campaign was flagging as the result of improved enemy countermeasures, above all the convoy system which had been introduced in May. So once more they resorted to a dangerous political ploy, the secretive sending to Russia of the fanatical Bolshevik, Vladimir Ulianov (Lenin) to breathe fire into the Revolution and force Russia to sue for peace in November, thus releasing sufficient forces for the offensive action in the West which Ludendorff hoped might tip the scales to Germany's decisive advantage.

Yet the great so-called 'Hindenburg offensives' of 1918 were a desperate gamble upon which Ludendorff admitted he was prepared to lose a million men. For Operations Michael, Mars and their successors could not be calculated risks, since not only were there the usual military imponderables but also political factors in profusion beyond anybody's comprehension, let alone those of soldierly General Staff 'demi-gods'.

From the purely military angle the factors were indeed conflicting prior to the launching of Operation Michael against the British in Picardie on 21 March 1918. In 1917 the new infantry and artillery tactics had proved very effective in the capture of Riga in September, the rout of the Italians at Caporetto in October and the counterstroke at Cambrai in December. Riga, however, was only small scale; for logistic reasons the Caporetto breakthrough had proved impossible to exploit to bring about the collapse of Italy; and the Cambrai counterstroke (coming so soon after the devastating and completely unexpected British attack with 400 tanks and unregistered artillery fire which overwhelmed the strongest sector of the much-vaunted Siegfried Line) was only intended as a limited operation. Indeed, the Cambrai disaster did at last drum home to many General Staff officers an awful warning that they were confronted by an enemy weapon system which had revolutionised warfare and held a two-year technological lead beyond hope of overtaking. At best in 1918 Germany possessed only fifty tanks (of which thirty were captured British models) while the enemy had over a thousand. Moreover she was outnumbered by superior air forces.

The rest is a tale of disaster. Make initial breakthroughs as the Germans would in five successive offensives, each of which achieved less than its predecessor, they could never, as at Caporetto, sustain momentum. And always it was tank counterstrokes which checked them, until at Amiens on 8 August 1918, despite Ludendorff's insistence that German anti-tank tactics were adequate, 450 Allied tanks broke through and brought despair beside immense losses. For then it was that German reserves marching to the front were railed at by those retreating as 'blacklegs prolonging the war'. And then that Ludendorff lost his nerve and hope of victory and insisted the war must be ended.

He was indeed right, even though the obstinate Hindenburg in October refused to admit it because the Army showed signs of recovery until the impact of successive Allied blows forced it into a general retreat. For now, as each of Germany's allies lurched into collapse and piecemeal withdrawal from the conflict, mutiny broke out in the Fleet when it was told to prepare for a despairing sortie; and revolutionary Socialist activists raised the flag of revolt in Germany itself.

Amidst chaos at home, Hindenburg and Ludendorff parted over the proposed Allied peace terms which included a demand for the Emperor's abdication. The former, supported by the Chancellor, wanted to go down fighting. Ludendorff resigned and was replaced on 8 November by the brilliant, democratically inclined General Wilhelm Gröner.

As the son of a Württemberg non-commissioned officer, Gröner was a complete break from the old Prussian General Staff caste image, and one who did not always fit well with his peers. As officer responsible for rail transport in 1914 he had seen the failure of the logistic plans contributing to defeat at the Marne. From May 1916 to August 1917 he had run the personnel and supply departments in the War Ministry, until posted away because he sided with the munitions workers and fought against profiteers.

As he took over, the Red Flag of Communism, which Hindenburg and Ludendorff had injected into Russia, was already flying over many German cities, and the Great General Staff, in a political vacuum of its own creation, was alone capable of bringing home the Army and keeping order. Gröner, though bound by the Oath of Loyalty to the Emperor, put patriotism first, did what no Prussian would do and damned himself forever in their eyes. When Wilhelm reminded him of the oath, Gröner ended an epoch (and set a precedent others might much later have copied in desperate circumstances) by replying, 'Today oaths are but words.' At this Hindenburg said that since the Army would no longer obey the Emperor's orders, he should abdicate and seek asylum in Holland.

Two days later, in a railway coach at Compiègne, the Armistice was signed to enable Gröner, in Hindenburg's name, to lead home a humiliated and disintegrating Army whose General Staff was in a state of shock and, at Versailles the following June, would be abolished.

Moltke, the general who had dismissed such a possibility, must have turned in his grave.

CHAPTER 5

Seeckt to Hitler

In the immediate post-war period a field marshal, Paul von Hindenburg, retired to write the Memoirs (*Aus Meinem Leben*) in which he founded the legendary apologia that the Army had been 'stabbed in the back' by revolutionaries and the civil power. Meanwhile two far cleverer generals held the fate of the new German Republic in their hands as it writhed on the verge of civil war and against foreign armies on, or threatening, its soil.

As Wilhelm Gröner saw it, with only unreliable military forces at his disposal, natural stability was best achieved through firm diplomacy, and, when necessary, the application of brutal and at times excessive force. By telephone on 9 November, he had reached the vital agreement with the last Imperial Chancellor, Friedrich Ebert, committing the Army to support of the constitutional government which, in return, would assume responsibility for negotiating the Armistice and subsequent peace; and pledging the officer corps to 'preservation of law and order, suppression of Bolshevism and maintaining their traditional position as the ultimate guardians of the State.'

Very much due to Gröner's skilful handling of the dwindling number of disciplined troops and the ruthless Volunteer Bands (later known as the Freikorps and invented by Major Kurt Schleicher) this agreement, along with bloody suppression of some Bolshevik political activists and Soldiers and Sailors Councils, produced the desired result. Thus Gröner underwrote the creation of the shaky democratic Weimar Republic. But throughout those traumatic days members of the officer corps suffered unforgivable indignities at the hands of communistic revolutionaries which would shape their right wing leanings in the years to come.

The other general was Hans von Seeckt, once described by a member of his staff, Heinz Guderian, as '. . . an alert, reflective, cool and almost timid person. Equally gifted in the fields of strategy and organisation, he showed less understanding of technical matters, however, than Moltke and Schlieffen.' Seeckt spent the whole of World War I as a Chief of Staff at Army level. He never led a field force until after the Armistice when he took command of Frontier Force North, charged with defending the Baltic States and East Prussia against invasions by the Russian Red Army and the recently recreated Poland. Like Gröner, Seeckt also was a political realist with an eye to the future. He believed that an isolated Germany needed allies and that an equally isolated Russia fitted the role – a view reinforced when, as Military Member of the Peace Commission to Versailles, he discovered how, without negotiation, the victorious Western allies were bent on the neutralisation and punishment of Germany.

The Treaty of Versailles, as finally dictated, did indeed emasculate and infuriate Germany. Among forfeitures, her Navy would be slashed to 15,000 men and forbidden submarines and warships of over 10,000 tons. The Army would be reduced to 100,000 men and forbidden all offensive weapons such as heavy artillery, tanks, aircraft and gas. Surplus war material had to be handed over or destroyed, penal reparations paid in gold and foreign holdings eliminated so as to bankrupt the nation. And to rub salt into the wound, as far as the Army was concerned, the General Staff would be abolished and the War Academy and principal officer cadet school closed.

These draconian reductions, along with occasional putschs attempting to bring down the government and the subsequent need for sharp countermeasures, were what Seeckt had to cope with in November after he became Chief of the Troop Bureau (Truppenamt), whose sixty hand-picked, ex-General Staff officers, divided into four sections (Operations, Organisation, Intelligence and Training), served the newly created Reichswehr in the role of the late Great General Staff. Six months later he was appointed Army Commander-in-Chief, still with the task of defending the state against external and internal threats; but also with the more long-sighted recreation of the Army on modern lines. It is the latter task, with its brilliant, secretive evasion of the terms of Versailles, for which he is best remembered. Yet it must not be forgotten that, in accordance with his insistence upon detachment of the Army from politics, he disbanded the Freikorps, held dissidents in check and broke the 1923 Nazi Party putsch led by retired General Ludendorff and ex-corporal Adolf Hitler.

On 16 April 1922 Germany and Russia announced the secretly negotiated Treaty of Rapallo with its establishment of full diplomatic relations, reciprocal indemnification of war reparations and most-favoured-nation trade arrangements. Of most importance to Seeckt was a secret clause allowing Germany to develop and experiment in Russia with the latest weapons, including tanks, artillery, aircraft and poison gas; on the understanding that Russia would retain prototypes and be kept informed of results.

By then Seeckt had shaped both a master philosophy based on a return to the old values of 'severity for honour's sake', and a policy founded upon an assumption of the war's eventual resumption, though in the realisation that defence by old-fashioned, pre-emptive offensive action was currently impossible. Instead a strategy of yielding defence was adopted. In 1924 he laid the foundations of an air arm by setting up co-operation between the Truppenamt and the Civil Aviation Department, and, in 1926, Lufthansa, the civil airline run by Erhard Milch. A secret military flying training school was also established, in Russia at Lipetz, by Hugo Sperrle and Kurt Student, while in Germany, Student, Head of the Air Technical Branch, organised gliding instruction. Of the Army Seeckt demanded 'High mobility, to be attained by the employment of numerous and highly efficient cavalry, by the fullest possible use of motor transport and by the marching capacity of infantry; the most effective armament and continuous replacement of men and material'. A curious statement in its omission of tanks, which he envisaged only as 'a special troop' in support of infantry and cavalry, it was, however, of significance since it represented characteristic military conservatism in the face of radical change.

Training within combat units, to quote Edgar Röhricht, was guided by annual directives from the Truppenamt, concentrated on '... determined and bold action even in situations where, due to inferiority in numbers and equipment, the chances of success were not very great. Material was never overrated.' The system was founded on enlightened officer/man relationships and produced many excellent leaders among selected men who enlisted for twelve years.

There were many far-sighted and dynamic officers within and outside the Truppenamt who were busy identifying and analysing the flaws which had lost Germany the war and planning to put matters right. Arms and Services Inspectors were pushing hard for reform. Generals such as von Tschischwitz of the Transport Troops worked on mechanisation and encouraged those like Wever and Guderian who, until the former was detached to become the first Chief of Staff of the secret Air Force (Luftwaffe), expounded the concept of operations by aircraft and all-arms armoured (panzer) divisions in which tanks were dominant. Erich Fellgiebel was also encouraged and would become a driving force behind the latest 'quenched' radio sets, high speed teleprinters and the famous elec-tro-magnetic Enigma cypher machine which was claimed to be 'uncrackable'.

Seeckt, like Scharnhorst 125 years before, was forming a shadow army – a force of thirty-five divisions within the 100,000-man Army, which was rarely at more than ninety per cent strength but included a high proportion of officer and NCO material. Chiefly Seeckt worked through the Inspectorates which, Kesselring noted, 'influ-enced the development of the Reichswehr more, during their terms of office, than the Operations Staff.'

From Central Office in Berlin, where he spent eight years steering the reconstruction of the Reichswehr, Colonel Kesselring was ideally placed to watch evolution in a period when the image of General Staff 'demi-gods' was replaced by improved relationships with experienced line officers on the basis of professional ability – to the great advantage of the service. Kesselring, one of the greatest Ger-man administrators, recognised the interaction of evolving organi-sation, doctrine, rapidly developing technology, weapons procurement and sociology. He, in league with General Walther von Reichenau, strove successfully to prevent the reactionary Truppe-namt imposing its will across the board, while working for a central Department of National Defence which, in 1933, would emerge, in restricted form, as the Wehrmachtamt.

The elimination of the Military Academy meant that training of staff officers had to done 'in house' and by correspondence course. Past practices, including staff tours, and, at the Truppenamt, weekly war-games, were regular events. At the games, future stars such as Walther von Brauchitsch, Werner von Blomberg, Günther von Kluge and Wilhelm List, excelled; and, for future reference, took note of the most promising subordinate players. Seeckt and subsequent Army Commanders were never seen at the weekly games, nor except on occasion the Chiefs of Staff. Usually, how-ever, they put in an appearance at the Annual Strategic War Game when, for several days, current defence of the Reich was studied and, sometimes, what might happen 'if the Army etc were temporarily and intentionally expanded beyond the Reichswehr strength.'

Interwoven were lectures by ministers, politicians, scientists and economists, besides officers such as Schleicher, Reichenau and Wilhelm Keitel. And sometimes 'illegal' weapon systems and experimental rockets (seen as an alternative to the heavy artillery forbidden by the Versailles Treaty) were demonstrated secretly at Kummersdorf.

As Kesselring well knew, too much war-gaming could be '...prejudicial to practical command and too easily result in producing dangerous theoreticians'. But there was no choice until the shackles of Versailles were broken and sufficient hardware made available for large-scale trials and manoeuvres. Meanwhile plans for that day were discussed and matured as the Navy, through clandestine overseas contacts, and inspired by Karl Dönitz, developed submarines; as members of the air cadre in the Truppenamt, such as Kurt Student and Hans Jeschonnek, studied the Italian General Giulio Douhet's ideas for strategic bombing and promoted glider pilot training; and as reports of French and, above all, British experiments and demonstrations of highly mobile mechanised land forces came to hand. In 1929, there was encouragement in a speech in Parliament from the air ace and leading National Socialist (Nazi) Party representative, Hermann Göring, proclaiming that Germany must have an Air Force sooner or later: a view fully supported by Erhard Milch, the head of the airline, Lufthansa, and by Wever and Kesselring.

But 1929 also saw the commencement of the Great Depression and the train of events which, by 1932, persuaded nearly forty per cent of a desperate electorate to give the Nazi Party enough votes eventually to persuade President Hindenburg, against his true instincts and the fierce objections of Chancellor Kurt von Schleicher, to appoint a so-called 'saviour' as Chancellor whom the people hoped would cure their economic ailments. This leader, regardless of his obnoxious Party, was a lot more inspiring than the sly Franz von Papen who manipulated the selection of Adolf Hitler, thus opening the way for a revolution, the rejection of the Versailles Treaty, and the acquisition of everything that the Truppenamt yearned for, and much more.

Anybody trudging through Hitler's book *Mein Kampf* could read that he was bent on war. Likewise anybody who knew him should have realised that this extremely brave corporal, who had been wounded and shell-shocked during four years in the trenches, and held an Iron Cross First Class and other decorations, was a war lover. But although many officers from Hindenburg downwards despised him, there was no doubting his magnetism and popular following. Nor could the existence of the violent brown-shirted army of bullies and supporters (many ex-Freikorps) of the SA (Sturm Abteilung) under Ernst Röhm be ignored.

Nevertheless the officer corps, led by the Commander-in-Chief, Werner von Fritsch, and including such politically involved ex-General Staff officers as Defence Minister and temporary Chancellor Schleicher and Chancellor Papen, assumed that, as in the past, it could control the government. So they let the criminally minded Hitler and his gang loose, without realising that these people held a grudge owing to the several occasions Hitler's activities had been blocked. Nor did Hitler play by 'honourable' rules. But to begin with the officers concurred, partly because they were bamboozled by propaganda and mass-hysteria, but also because they were about to receive what they most desired: forces capable of defending Germany against two menacing neighbours – the well-armed France and a Communist Russia, hell-bent under Joseph Stalin on re-armament and the creation of a military economy.

CHAPTER 6

The Six Years' Revolution

Lacking a formal military and business education as Hitler did, there is no gainsaying his intuitive grasp of the basic Principles of War. Shrewdly applying his acute political instinct with calculating subterfuge and dishonesty, he repeatedly overcame strong opposition from both native and foreign opponents by lulling them into a sense of false security before striking decisively by surprise. During the first months of his chancellorship, these methods were revealed in all their complexity as he manoeuvred to convert an initially somewhat tenuous political position into one of impregnable strength. He trusted nobody completely, not even his closest colleagues and least of all the generals. Teamwork with Hitler, therefore, was at a premium.

Adept at setting peoples against peoples, Hitler was all things to all men, especially to the generals and the Reichswehr as they became increasingly worried by evidence that Röhm wanted to be Defence Minister and impose his roughneck SA on the Army. Hitler was against this. Winning military support by making a pliant General von Blomberg Minister of Defence at the Wehrmachtamt, and secretly promising rearmament, Hitler persuaded Hindenburg to call another election on 5 March 1933. Influenced by the dubious news that a Communist had burned down the Reichstag building, the electorate registered a forty-four per cent vote for the Nazis, who pushed through a bill giving full powers to Hitler two days later.

Tension with Röhm reached a climax in June 1934 when Hitler, realising the SA was a threat to himself, decided he must side with the generals rather than his old comrade. Mobilising his personal bodyguard, the Schutz Staffeln (SS), under the loyal Heinrich Himmler, he unleashed a plan to curb the SA. On 30 June Röhm, a number of his henchmen and, for sheer spite, some others, including Schleicher who had opposed Hitler, were murdered. This act of terror was approved next day by Hindenburg, Blomberg and some generals, including Fritsch, the Commander-in-Chief, but abhorred by Schleicher's friends, including thirty senior members of the General Staff, who tried feebly and ineffectually to persuade Hindenburg to purge the Reich Cabinet of leading Nazis, including Göring.

When Hindenburg died on 1 August, Hitler jumped at a priceless opportunity. Instantly announcing the combination of the Presidency with the Chancellorship, and making himself Leader (Führer) and Supreme Commander of the armed forces, he caught the Army so completely by surprise that it supinely obeyed an order to take an Oath of Loyalty to him, personally, instead of to the Constitution. Thus, on 2 August, Hitler had seized powers such as no emperor ever had enjoyed.

How some members of the Army felt at that moment appears in correspondence between Guderian and his wife. 'Pray God that both sides may abide by it equally for the welfare of Germany. The Army is accustomed to keeping its oaths', he wrote. To which she replied. 'We need unity more than ever, it is our strength abroad ... But sometimes we can become a little afraid about excessive elevation.'

With these startlingly dramatic events behind them, Hitler, his generals and admirals turned with increasing vigour to casting the Army in Seeckt's mould, and the Navy on a much more modest scale than in Wilhelm's time. By force of circumstances, they calculated, it would be 1943, at the earliest, before an offensive capability would be attained. Nevertheless the foundations were firmly laid in rapid succession.

Already Erhard Milch had been appointed assistant Secretary of State for Air under Göring and was creating a secret Air Force (Luftwaffe) and producing aircraft under cover of Lufthansa. In September 1933 a few hand-picked Truppenamt officers had been detached to form the nucleus of an Air Staff. Principal among them was the ex-infantry officer Wever, as Chief of Staff designate under the Commander-in-Chief, Göring; and Kesselring (who would have preferred the air arm to remain within the Army) but who now was put in charge of Luftwaffe Administration, Construction and Logistics. They would bring with them General Staff practices, including war-gaming, but find that most of their staff officers were Göring's 'old eagles' such as Student, Hugo Sperrle, Ernst Udet and Hellmuth Felmy.

Similarly in 1934 there were internal disagreements over the creation of a Panzer Command. In April, to avoid a row with the Cavalry, General Reichenau, who was in the process of developing the Wehrmachtamt, had, with Blomberg's approval, formed the Tank Troop (Panzertruppe) with General Oswald Lütz in command and Guderian as Chief of Staff. This move came about as a direct result of an earlier demonstration by Guderian to Hitler and Blomberg of mechanised infantry and a prototype light tank at Kummersdorf which had greatly enthused the dictator. But the innovation found no favour with the Chief of Staff, General Ludwig Beck, who disapproved of what would become known as OKW; feared the creation of an armoured army within the Army; and who preferred to integrate tanks as ancillary weapons within the Infantry.

Indeed, the able Fritsch of rigid outlook, and the quiet somewhat pedantic and hesitant Beck, the son of a leading iron manufacturer, already had their hands full. Not only had they, in March, to convert and enlarge the Truppenamt into an overt General Staff, they had also to proceed with the covert conversion of Seeckt's shadow army into a reality of thirty-six divisions, including a cavalry division to propitiate the horse lovers.

With six million unemployed and numerous semi-trained units of the SA to be incorporated into the Army and Luftwaffe, there was no manpower shortage, just a scarcity of generals and staff officers which could at once be rectified by recalling retired, old-fashioned officers. Inevitably, at this critical stage, the new General Staff was not what Kesselring called 'a finely tuned instrument'. Indeed that standard, under the pressure of rapid expansion and then war, was never achieved. Overstretch and overstress were the constant companions of the new General Staff and Army. The enormous influx of conscripts, many most unenthusiastic about the disruption of their lives, placed great pressure on instructors as they did what they could with limited training aids to churn out soldiers like sausages by repetitive drills and exercises. Kesselring noted how the officers '... passed their lives primarily in their own families and in the officer corps. Neither the pressure of their official duties nor their economic position generally permitted them to engage in much social life.'

It would be several years before the trickle of new equipment in 1935 increased to the flood required to equip and train the new divisions. So, at a moment when Göring was underwriting priority for 'his' Luftwaffe, when the Navy, under Admiral Erich Raeder, was ordering new ships and submarines, and when the Reichsbank was worrying about inflation, the arrival of the charismatic Guderian with a demand for two armoured (panzer) divisions and two thousand tanks, followed in due course by another eighteen divisions, was hardly welcome – especially since Beck, a gunner (as so many of the generals in OKW and the Army Command were) could not perceive the feasibility of unproven all-arms, mechanised divisions being commanded by radio from the front in fast-moving manoeuvre operations supported by aircraft.

There were fundamental controversies within the Luftwaffe too. Wever, an apostle of Douhet and therefore of strategic bombing and development of a heavy, so-called Ural bomber, was in disagreement with his gunner friend Kesselring who considered air power should be concentrated on the support of land operations. The debate would ultimately be settled by events, including the death of Wever in an air crash on 3 June 1936.

By that date Germany was challenging the world and creating consternation. Of course, before 9 March 1935 when Hitler revealed the existence of the Luftwaffe, rearmament was no longer a complete secret, if only because so much activity could not be concealed. But that announcement, followed a week later by the reintroduction of military conscription, shredded the Versailles Treaty and set alarm bells ringing throughout Europe, even though Hitler protested Germany's intention to respect its treaty obligations. Indeed, early in 1934 Hitler (tongue in cheek) had signed a Treaty of Friendship with Poland to compensate for a deliberate falling out with the Russians, who, in May 1935, responded by signing mutual assistance pacts with France and Czechoslovakia.

A few weeks later Blomberg issued his first planning directive to the Army, Navy and Luftwaffe and, at his suggestion, the over-ambitious but weak General Wilhelm Keitel (another gunner) took over from Reichenau at OKW to run the office for Hitler and become 'a recording of his master's voice'. Two more significant events followed on 15 October. At the reopening of the Military Academy to help rebuild a General Staff much shorn of its previous influence, Blomberg said that the Army '... must recognise where the sources of the nation's strength lie, and this created an obligation to political thinking leading to willing acknowledgement of Nazi ideology [Weltanschauung].'

That day, too, after a series of successful experimental exercises, watched by Blomberg and Fritsch, three panzer divisions were formed, but with only a handful of light training tanks.

Europe entered 1936 with a trepidation stimulated on 7 March by the sudden reoccupation by the Army of the demilitarised Rhineland on the pretext of the ratification on 27 February of the Franco-Russian Pact. Hitler's order filled Blomberg, Fritsch and Beck with concern. The Army was given only twenty-four hours' warning and reasoned that, militarily speaking, France could not permit Strasbourg and the Rhineland towns to be threatened by German artillery. Fully expecting a French reaction by force which the Army was in no state to resist, they protested loudly and sent forward only one ill-equipped division. But Hitler snubbed the generals, and got away with it since he had correctly judged French dread of another war. Taken as much by surprise as the German generals, all the French did, despite promises of support by Britain and Poland if France invaded Germany, was man the uncompleted Maginot Line and keep watch. But as Hitler later admitted, 'If the French had marched into the Rhineland then we should have had to retreat with ignominy'. And that might well have brought him down.

As it was he had won a crucial victory not only over France, whose infirmity stood revealed, but also over his generals, whose importance had never before been so reduced. Moreover Hitler characteristically, but privately, resolved on vengeance against those who had opposed him. In the meantime he soft-soaped them, made Blomberg a field marshal, revelled in success and acquired new allies. On 25 October 1936 Benito Mussolini, the Italian Fascist dictator, linked hands with Hitler. That day the Berlin–Rome Axis Agreement was signed, followed a month later by the German-Japanese anti-Comintern Agreement.

By then Germany and Italy were involved in somebody else's war in which they could experiment with new weapons and techniques and give notice to potential opponents of German strength – propaganda bluff though it was. Shortly after the outbreak of the Spanish Civil War in July 1936, the glory-seeking Göring won approval to send Ju52s, along with Italian transport aircraft, escorted by six fighters, to ferry troops from North Africa reinforcing General Franco's rebel fascist army in Spain. This was the prologue, also in company with Italian aircraft, to bombing missions and the eventual despatch of the Condor Legion, under Sperrle, whose Chief of Staff was Lieutenant Colonel Wolfram von Richt-hofen. This force was progressively equipped with the latest fighters, bomber and 88mm dual-purpose anti-aircraft/anti-tank guns. Kesselring feared the commitment might disrupt training and cause operational overstretch, but it enabled the Luftwaffe to steal thunder from the Army, which had no modern tanks and artillery to send and whose military advisor to Franco was a mere major, Wilhelm von Thoma.

As the political situation deteriorated the Luftwaffe began to overshadow the Army. On 2 December Milch and Kesselring abruptly were told by Göring that '. . . the Press all over the world is excited about the landing of 5,000 German volunteers in Spain. . . . The general situation is very serious. . . . We are already in a state of war. It is only that no shot has been fired. . . . Beginning 1 January 1937 all factories for aircraft production shall run as if mobilisation has been ordered.'

Kesselring was galvanised into action. He knew that, if war did break out, the Army would need all the air support it could obtain, and that recent war-games and technical information indicated that a mere increase in aircraft would not make the Luftwaffe fit for war. It was plain that a rationalisation of policy and change of priorities was essential. With the agreement of Milch, Wever's dream of a strategic bomber force was abandoned. The Ural bomber was beyond state-of the-art technology and Germany's manufacturing resources unequal to the effort without damaging vital projects. Above all amongst these was support for mobile Army operations, which war-games had shown to be impractical until a 'field' airfield system had been created; and the adoption of a dive-bomber which General Ernst Udet, when appointed Chief of the Technical Department at the Air Ministry, would promote.

Interwoven with this debate, however, was the delicate question of who should run the Luftwaffe on Göring's behalf. Wever had fought for a self-contained Luftwaffe, detached from Milch's Air Ministry, and was determined 'to strip State Secretary Milch of every vestige of power'. Kesselring agreed and now managed, by playing on Göring's suspicions of Milch behaving almost as if he was Commander-in-Chief, to clip Milch's wings. Additionally Kesselring, the General Staff officer par excellence, was determined, diplomatically, to side-track Göring's favoured 'old eagles', few of whom were properly staff trained. As he wrote, 'If the commander of Armed

Forces is not a trained soldier he cannot bear the responsibility for purely military actions.' The description could most certainly be applied to Göring (whose military ability was rated no better than a lieutenant colonel's) and Hitler.

Having eased Milch aside and won the support of Göring, Kesselring, the gunner turned airman, set about putting the Luftwaffe's house in order and giving priority to support of land operations. The reorientation was welcomed by the Army and made readily acceptable to Göring as lessons from Spain confirmed war-games theory. Neither there, nor anywhere else in the years to come on a grand scale, was strategic bombing seriously attempted. Instead the techniques of Army co-operation by reconnaissance, medium-level bombing, dive-bombing and air supply were brilliantly and unofficially developed in Spain by Richthofen, despite obstruction from the High Command. Inexorably the march of events dictated that the Luftwaffe would grow into a tactical air force. Its key Instructional Manual 16 was amended to place strategic bombing at low priority.

In June 1937 Kesselring rounded off his founding work in a legalistic policy document, drafted by himself and signed by Göring, which settled the future relationship of the Commander-in-Chief (Göring), the State Secretary (Milch) and the Chief of Staff. Henceforward Göring could delegate to Milch many functions, including co-ordination of the Budget. However, 'The Chief of the Luftwaffe General Staff is first military advisor to the Commander-in-Chief in all questions of preparation and conduct of war in the area of personnel, finance and material according to the instructions of the Reichsminister and Commander-in-Chief.' With that settled, Kesselring, with Göring's approval, resigned as Chief of Staff and was granted his wish to be given the plum command of Luftkreis III, making him responsible for the defence of the crucial East and Central Germany, covering Berlin and the Polish and Czech frontiers.

Important changes of Army doctrine and organisation were also made to the late Truppenamt's ideas in both strategic and tactical aspects. The new Battle Instructions Manual, written by Beck and General Karl von Stülpnagel, replaced the concept of strategic 'delaying defensive action' (what Fritsch derisively called 'organised flight') by reinstatement of traditional offensive action. But the long established combination of cavalry, marching infantry and horse-drawn artillery and transport, strengthened by as many motor vehicles and motorised antitank guns as could be produced, was being seriously challenged by the Panzertruppe.

Beck might hamper adoption of an official panzer doctrine, but Lütz, his new Chief of Staff, Colonel Friedrich von Paulus, and the three panzer divison commanders (including Guderian), were backed by Hitler and the High Command, and were disseminating one regardless. At Lütz's suggestion, Guderian's book *Achtung! Panzer!* was published. It outlined the history of armoured forces and their future employment, became a military bestseller and infiltrated new doctrine by the back door. Meanwhile the training of 187,000 tank and truck drivers between 1933 and 1939 by the Reich Motor Sport School, under SA leader Adolf Huhnlein, was of immense help to the Army, especially the Panzertruppe with its armoured fighting vehicles.

Meanwhile Colonel Erich Fellgiebel was making great progress assembling the fast and supposedly secure signal systems which would give the Wehrmacht a decided command and control superiority over future enemies.

Improvisation and self-help went hand-in-hand at a time when the traditional function of the General Staff was being called into question by Colonel Alfred Jodl and his assistant Walter Warlimont. In the near future Jodl would be head of operations under Keitel. He and Warlimont, among others, envisaged an intellectual General Staff concentrating on doctrine, planning and peacetime training, but in wartime becoming Assistants to Leaders such as Guderian. Jodl was a fervent admirer of Hitler and about to become a close confidant. This was his way of imposing Blomberg's 'acknowledgement of Nazi ideology' from the Wehrmachtamt. But what authority that office possessed in 1937 (staffed as it was by army officers only and therefore just an extension of the General Staff) was largely over the conservative Army. Raeder's independent-minded Navy and Göring's Nazi-orientated Luftwaffe continued to go their own ways.

What Jodl could not foresee was the effect of Hitler's 5 November 1937 announcement on Foreign Secretary Konstantine von Neurath, Defence Minister Blomberg and the three commanders-in-chief, of his resolve to gain more 'living room' ('Lebensraum') for Germany in Austria and Czechoslovakia – even at risk of war with France and Britain which, he sensed, had written off Central

Europe. At that meeting Raeder said nothing and Göring temporised, partly in the belief that 'his' Luftwaffe had almost reached parity with the French and British air forces, but mainly because of the involvement with 200 machines in Spain. But Neurath was sceptical of Hitler's political thesis and Blomberg and Fritsch objected strongly on the grounds that the Army was nowhere near ready for general war.

Afterwards, however, Blomberg (nicknamed the Rubber Lion) joined Göring and Raeder in supporting Hitler, thus isolating Fritsch who took counsel with Beck and Neurath on ways of dissuading the Führer. Two days later in an interview with Hitler, Fritsch was treated brusquely by the Führer who, revealing considerable knowledge of military history, brushed aside the military objections. Subsequent Army Commanders-in-Chief would experience the same treatment.

This was the crucial occasion when Hitler, for the first time, overrode the professional head of the Army in a technical matter and set course for war, triumph and ultimate disaster. He timed it, moreover, to within two months of another fateful event – the marriage on 12 January 1938 of the widowed Blomberg to Erna Gruhn, a secretary in the War Ministry, at a private ceremony with Hitler and Göring as witnesses.

A few days later the President of the Berlin police showed Keitel a file indicating that his Chief had married a member of the world's oldest profession. Keitel, aware of rumours already circulating and Army indignation, informed Göring who passed the documents to Hitler on 24 January. With some slight regret, it seems, Hitler hesitated before appointing a successor to Blomberg, although Fritsch was the natural choice. Himmler thereupon presented his Führer with a file accusing Fritsch, a bachelor without lady friends, of homosexual activity. Unhappily Fritsch, under interrogation by Hitler and, subsequently, the Gestapo, offered a defective defence.

Once more Fate and the generals had played into Hitler's hands. He had no alternative but to dismiss Blomberg, but caused considerable surprise by personally assuming the post of Defence Minister, in addition to President, Chancellor and Supreme Commander; and making the third-rate Keitel his Chief of Staff in what, henceforward, would be called Oberkommando der Wehrmacht (OKW).

Meanwhile Beck, incensed by Blomberg's behaviour and the

treatment of Fritsch, sowed seeds of resistance by endeavouring to persuade Fritsch to lead a putsch against Hitler. But Fritsch only had the strength to write out his resignation. So, as second best, Beck, with General Gerd von Rundstedt, the senior ranking officer, approached an excited Führer to request court-martial for Blomberg and investigation of Fritsch by a Court of Honour. To the latter (which in March exonerated Fritsch) Hitler reluctantly agreed. Meanwhile, however, he appointed as Army Commander-in-Chief the very able gunner, General von Brauchitsch, whose wife happened to be an enthusiastic Nazi.

Henceforward Hitler's Byzantine society would put those of imperial days in the shade. Striking while the iron was hot, he now culled the Army of a number of old-school generals, many of them Prussians, including Kluge, Kress von Kressenstein, Ewald von Kleist, Wilhelm von Leeb and Lütz. At the same time Göring was promoted field marshal and Guderian, by now well thought of by Hitler and who may have been considered as successor to Beck, was given the command of XVI Army Corps and promoted lieutenant general.

*   *   *

The pace quickened. On 11 March 1938, following a period of intense pressure by Austrian Nazis coupled with overbearing German support, the Austrian government wavered. At once Hitler not only ordered the occupation of the country but also took the opportunity to bolster prestige and overawe his neighbours by a demonstration of the power and might of the Luftwaffe and mechanised forces.

On 12 March over 400 German aircraft, including 160 Ju52s, some carrying paratroops, landed 2,000 men at Vienna while bomber formations flew menacingly overhead. Meanwhile 2nd Panzer Division and elements of the mechanised SS Division Leibstandarte in Guderian's XVI Corps led the occupation forces to Vienna via Linz. Although this first operational (though unopposed) employment of airborne and panzer spearheads exposed many logistic flaws in under-trained formations, it was also a remarkable success, bearing in mind that less than forty eight hours' notice was given and many of the latest aircraft and tanks were suffering from teething troubles. It was a considerable feat for the panzer division's tanks to cover 420 miles and the SS lorries 600 with relatively few breakdowns. Problems were noted and tackled, including those of signal communications, fuel supply, recovery and repair of broken-down vehicles and the need for improved traffic control in order to exploit the flexibility of these revolutionary formations and their ability to concentrate and advance with amazing speed. Even sceptics suddenly awoke to the potential of weapon systems capable of revolutionising war.

Nevertheless, the Army, including its dynamic Fast Troops, was very short of most weapons and equipment. Tanks were few in number due to excessive concentration on research and development (an advance on World War I practices, nevertheless) and inadequate priority for production, prompting Guderian to convince Brauchitsch that they should be issued only to the panzer and not spread among the infantry divisions. Moreover few of the vital medium battle tanks were ready for the existing three panzer divisions, let alone the six planned for August 1939, and there was a shortage of signal equipment. Therefore unhorsed cavalry units troops which were to be cadre of four additional so-called Light Divisions, could only have obsolete light tanks.

So the Luftwaffe was flourished as Germany's trump card, playing on the nerves of leaders and peoples who were convinced by propaganda and exaggerations from Spain of air power's decisive ability to win wars almost unassisted. Much-publicised reports of the notorious bombing of the town of Guernica in 1937, in tactical support of a land attack by Franco's Army, which was exploited by anti-German propagandists, forcibly reinforced the unscientific claims of strategic bombing enthusiasts. But these same enthusiasts overlooked the fact that the Condor Legion's latest Heinkel He111 and Dornier Do17 bombers and Messerschmitt Me109 fighters had met no real opposition. Warning voices from those like the sidetracked Milch, who visited Britain in 1938 and saw for himself the latest British aircraft and also sensed British resolve to fight if necessary, were ignored.

Behind a facade of strength, the Wehrmacht approached war in a haphazard manner. *Mein Kampf* was the only guide to Hitler's longterm strategy which, in practice, he tended to develop in one opportunist step after another. No sooner was Austria swallowed than he was preparing the secret Plan Green for the taking of Czechoslovakia, which he handed to Keitel on 28 May. Already a manufactured political crisis announced Hitler's intention. As usual

Beck, with sound reasoning when he read OKW's aim (dictated by Hitler with Jodl's assistance) of 'smashing Czechoslovakia by military action in the near future', foresaw a major war with France, Russia and Britain, in addition to the well-defended Czechoslovakia.

With the Condor Legion still engaged in Spain, a mere 1,600 serviceable aircraft with barely sufficient crews available, an Army only partially equipped with modern weapons and a Navy capable of little more than small-scale commerce raiding and coastal defence, Germany was headed for disaster. Aircraft, weapons and munitions production were increasing, but without effective co-ordination of industrial priorities or effort. As ever, despite the existence of OKW, each service fought its own corner and procured what it could afford from its own dedicated suppliers of long standing – a very wasteful process often barely related to a suspect strategy. Germany might just have been able to sustain a major war for six hectic weeks. Probably she would have been stopped by Czechoslovakia and then struck by the combined forces of that determined nation's treaty allies who would have penetrated the far from complete Siegfried Line, then under construction along the Rhine.

Again Beck tried to organise some sort of Army putsch, but his Commander-in-Chief, Brauchitsch (like many another general then and in the future), declined to help. He agreed with Beck's pessimistic military appreciation, but he lacked moral courage, was scared of the Führer, ruled by the Oath of Loyalty and his Nazi wife, and held the opinion that 'The German people had elected him [Hitler], and the workers, like all other Germans, were perfectly satisfied with his successful policy.' True as that was in a peacetime of increasing well-being, it was not to say that many people wanted war – few Germans did. Unfortunately, like the generals, they once more were bamboozled and overruled by a rampant War Lord.

As a last resort, when Hitler demanded 'unconditional obedience' from his generals and the Chief of Staff, Beck asked Brauchitsch to join him in resignation. But the Commander-in-Chief replied, 'I am a soldier; it is my duty to obey'. Beck resigned in solitude on 18 August.

Into Beck's shoes stepped Franz Halder, another gunner and the first Bavarian and Roman Catholic to become Chief of the General Staff. Quick, shrewd and witty, he was a brilliant specialist in operational and training matters and the son of a distinguished general. He supported Beck's resistance to Hitler, but when it came to a crunch was no real help. Flirt as he did, in September, with those opposed to Hitler, he toed the party line when extreme pressure was exerted for return of the Sudetenland and its German nationals by the Czechs to Germany.

Neither Brauchitsch, Halder nor their colleagues had much faith in Hitler's concept of a lightning ('Blitzkrieg') offensive over-whelming Czechoslovakia in four days before the French could mobilise and attack. Halder, indeed, was put out when Hitler lectured him on tank warfare. But the plans involving him and others, to depose Hitler, never bore fruit. This was partly because the plotters feared Nazi retribution and the people's anger; partly due to the plan being wishy-washy and unrealistic since the generals were tyros when it came to subversive activity; and not least because of ingrained respect for the Oath of Loyalty which, for most of them, was sacrosanct to the bitter end.

The conditions for launching a putsch never materialised because Czechoslovakia's allies, including Britain and France, shamefully deserted her, and, at Munich on 30 September 1938, bowed to Hitler's demands by agreeing to the sequestration of the Sudetenland. Peace had been preserved at a terrible price. The appeasement policy of the Allies again had vindicated Hitler's political judgement and made it almost impossible, henceforward, to prevent his relentless acquisitive designs. Not only had France and Britain been humbled but so too had the German General Staff. Never again would Brauchitsch and Halder take part in any form of resistance. Moreover, Czechoslovakia's complete engulfment was only temporarily deferred. At once Hitler ordered preparation of the plan which, on 14 March 1939 for spurious reasons and to the world's dismay, was accomplished by complete occupation.

Once more the Luftwaffe and the Army flaunted their burgeoning strength, but this time without the slightest chance of interference from within or outside Germany. Predictably Hitler, uplifted to classic Teutonic over-confidence and excess, turned his attention to Poland. Belatedly his neighbours began to take more serious defensive measures and all but the most incorrigible appeasers realised that war was the only way to stop Hitler's Germany.

CHAPTER 7

Blitzkrieg in Poland

Within three weeks of the occupation of Czechoslovakia Hitler handed out the first directive for Plan White – the invasion of Poland. At once, to the military and the outside world, he began to elaborate a customary tissue of lies to justify the intention. But not until 23 May 1939 did he reveal to the three Commanders-in-Chief and their Chiefs of Staff the full scope of the fatal design embodied in his intention to win 'living room' for Germany by seizing Poland at the earliest practical moment. The risk of war with France and Britain, entailing the occupation also of Holland and Belgium for air and naval bases, had to be accepted, he insisted. Only one ray of hope was offered: the possibility of Russia standing aside, thus avoiding another war on two fronts.

On military grounds those present were aghast. When Hitler spoke of 'a life and death struggle', they feared that their country, unready for general war, might perish. Yet the temptation to recover Poland was strong indeed among those who, because of the Versailles Treaty, had been dispossessed of their land by a despised and proud nation. Brauchitsch encouraged Hitler to believe that not only Poland, but also France and Britain, could be defeated – providing Russia stayed out. Yet the risks were tremendous. He calculated that forty-four divisions, including all the mechanised ones, would be needed for a quick, complete victory in the East, leaving in the West only six low-quality divisions which, due to lack of published doctrine for static defence, were unprepared for holding the incomplete Siegfried Line.

X Day was set for 20 August but postponed. On the 22nd Hitler treated his senior generals and admirals to a long harangue, causing one officer to fall asleep. He pleased them by announcing the completion of a German-Russian non-aggression pact, thus clearing the way for an invasion of Poland with much reduced chances of drift into general war. But he shook them, as never before, by revealing an unprincipled bestiality – the policy of genocide of 'inferior' people. He said 'I have ordered to the east my [SS] Death's Head Units with the mission to kill without pity or mercy all men, women and children of Polish race or language.'

Goodness knows what his audience was really thinking. Many were cultured men; only a handful totally inhuman. It may well have been that, in a state of incredulity, they dismissed from their minds an impending horror which lay beyond rational comprehension. In any case, caught in the web of Nazi power as long as they had been in accordance with their codes of obedience, they were powerless to prevent it.

Dutifully, and without demur, they returned to their posts. At 1430 hours on 25 August 1939 they received confirmation that X Day was fixed for dawn next day. Six hours later they were to pause in bewilderment when their Supreme Commander backtracked in a way no Moltke (Elder or Younger) would have countenanced at such a moment. For when, contrary to Hitler's expectations, the British and French made it plain they would fight, he suddenly lost his nerve and felt compelled to postpone X Day in order to fob them off with worthless promises. Moreover he gave vent to so much hysterical ranting and raving that, for a moment, Keitel among others thought peace might be saved.

The shaking of Hitler, even as troops were moving into position, was the immediate product of the news that a belated Anglo-Polish Alliance had been signed, coinciding as it did with a report from Italy that Mussolini would not stand at Hitler's side in war. But two days later, advised and egged on by Himmler and Foreign Minister Joachim von Ribbentrop, he recovered his nerve. Resolute once more for war, he chose the 31 August as X Day, and then, for spurious diplomatic reasons, postponed it yet again until, at midday on the 31st, he settled on dawn 1 September for the ultimate 'jump-off'.

Nobody except Hitler and a few cronies went to this war with enthusiasm. Unlike 1914 there were no spontaneous demonstrations as the soldiers marched to their task in grim silence. Naturally most of the Generals and officers put a bold face on it. Some, like Guderian, undoubtedly approached the contest with keen anticipation in hope of validating the new theory of mechanised manoeuvre warfare. Overhead thundered some 1,600 bombers and fighters of Kesselring's First and General Alexander Löhr's Fourth

Air Fleet, confidently tasked to strike overwhelmingly at military objectives in depth and give close support, respectively, to General Fedor von Bock's Army Group North and Rundstedt's Army Group South. This was Blitzkrieg in full force for the first time against an outmoded enemy deployed in static positions, whose mobile forces consisted of only a few light tanks and cavalry formations, and whose 400 aircraft were obsolete. The Germans, as Erich von Manstein, Rundstedt's Chief of Staff, said, were bound to win, providing the Western Powers did not render timely aid to the Poles.

General von Brauchitsch's plan, based on reasonably reliable intelligence of Polish dispositions and plans, was Clausewitzian in its aim of destroying the Polish Army, and Schlieffen-like in attempting it by a double envelopment. Apart from logistic requirements, it was almost incidental that the principal thrusts were directed on the communication centres of Danzig, Warsaw, Cracow, Lublin and Lwow.

Brauchitsch, whatever his weakness of personal resolve, was a very good commander who encouraged his subordinates to use their initiative to the full – a freedom which in a later campaign would have adverse effects. In the North, Bock had the easier task: to cut the Polish Corridor with the recalled General von Kluge's Fourth Army, spearheaded by Guderian's XIX Corps with a single panzer division and two motorised infantry divisions; then, in company with General Georg von Küchler's Third Army (reinforced by XIX Corps), to drive southwards from East Prussia and seize Brest Litovsk, far to the east of Warsaw. Meanwhile Rundstedt was to advance from Silesia in the direction of Warsaw with Eighth and Tenth Armies (each led by panzer divisions) at the same time as Fourteenth Army (spearheaded by XVII Corps) bypassed Cracow and struck north-eastwards at Lublin and Brest Litovsk. The aim was to complete the total envelopment of the entire Polish Army while simultaneously breaking apart and encircling the out-manoeuvred and outfought Polish armies, whose mobilisation was incomplete but whose soldiers did all they could in hopeless circumstances.

On 5 September Halder noted that the enemy was practically defeated. Both Army Groups were making fast progress as the mechanised formations demonstrated their speed, striking power and flexibility. Given an almost complete absence of Polish counter moves, Brauchitsch felt little need for adjustments to his initial plan. Army Group and Army commanders seized opportunities in their own special ways while collaborating comfortably with each other. When a threat by the Poznan Army to General Johannes von Blaskowitz's Eighth Army's left flank seemed possible on 4 September, he simply reinforced the flank by transferring two divisions from Reichenau's Tenth Army. He permitted General Georg-Hans Reinhardt's 4th Panzer Division to continue a solo charge for Warsaw in the hope that, on 9 September, he might take the city by a bold coup. Instead it was repelled in four hours with the loss of sixty-three out of the 120 tanks engaged, demonstrating that, in built-up areas, even all-arms panzer divisions had their limitations.

That same day, however, Brauchitsch took advantage of air and ground reconnaissance reports which revealed that the Poznan Army was concentrating twelve divisions and three cavalry brigades near Kutno, thus threatening Army Group South's left flank. Ordering Bock to form a blocking position in the north, he told Rundstedt to complete an encirclement of this Polish mass. Rundstedt and Manstein frequently visited Blaskowitz's headquarters (with Hitler present on one occasion) to co-ordinate operations by Eighth and Tenth Armies against the east, south and west perimeter of the Polish concentration. This was the genesis of the eight-day Battle of Bzura River, which became the model for many such concentric operations against enemy pockets in the years to come. By brilliant technique, eight infantry, one Panzer and a Light division, supported by intensive bombing against heroic Polish resistance, forged a steel ring against breakout attempts. Even so, two Polish divisions did manage to escape and join the defenders of Warsaw, but they left behind some 200,000 men and vast quantities of equipment. This catastrophe crippled the Poles for good.

On 10 September, Halder echoed Bock's boast that 'Performance of the troops is marvellous', yet also recorded serious misgivings when it was reported by Rundstedt that SS Leibstandarte Division, commanded by Hitler's favourite General Sepp Dietrich, was poorly trained and ill-disciplined. Its combat drills were slipshod; it fired indiscriminately and burned villages without cause. Küchler had refused to confirm the court-martial of SS men found guilty of herding Jews into a church and massacring them because he considered that the one-year prison sentence handed out was not severe enough. But, although further complaints of atrocities followed, in due course all SS men would be pardoned by Hitler – a whitewash giving notice to the Wehrmacht that Himmler's minions had abandoned the old codes of decency along with recognition of the Geneva Conventions.

Inevitably when the War Diaries, along with senior officers' reports, came to be studied by the General Staff, a number of technical and training defects throughout the Army and the Luftwaffe disturbed Halder.

The Luftwaffe's contribution had been less effective than expected or claimed, well led as it was by men with experience in Spain. Low cloud and poor visibility hampered initial operations, including attacks on Polish communication centres and the Air Force, which had been dispersed to satellite airfields. Air combat did not entirely go the German way; fear of raids against Berlin troubled Göring and Kesselring; and the Army had cause for complaint, not only about inadequate information from reconnaissance but also attacks upon them by their own bombers. To this the Luftwaffe would retort that many of their machines had been damaged or shot down by German army anti-aircraft guns.

Certainly there was poor liaison between the two services due to inadequate training, defective co-ordination and poor communications. Partly to blame was the arrogant unwillingness of Göring's Luftwaffe to collaborate with others, and OKW's inability to compel them to do so. For example, the training of young Army officers as observers had been blocked or neglected at Luftwaffe schools, and constant difficulties were made about the training of specialist artillery-spotting pilots.

It was ironic that the Army, not the Luftwaffe, brought about the final collapse of the Polish Air Force by overrunning enemy early warning systems on 7 September.

Like the Luftwaffe, the Army's problems stemmed mainly from inexperience, insufficient training and lack of vital equipment, especially of armoured vehicles with the right kind of armament. On the whole doctrine and the manuals had withstood their first test because the '. . . campaign had been fought in peacetime formation', as Röhricht put it. Faults among the staff and in units could only be corrected by intensive retraining once Poland was conquered. Halder would press the General Staff's Training Branch to issue a series of short directives drawing attention to lessons learnt and ways and means to apply them. But first the campaign had to be concluded and troops returned to German training areas, and also sent as reinforcements for the Western Front where, happily, despite a short-lived token French advance, no great pressure had been felt.

The elimination of the Bzura pocket on 17 September, coinciding with the closing of the strategic pincer movement projected by Army Group North from East Prussia and by Fourteenth Army from the south, and amplified by the unexpected invasion of east Poland by the Russians, ended the war of manoeuvre. Mopping up, including Warsaw as the toughest nut to crack, became the order of the day, and produced the only occasion Hitler intervened directly in operations. On 15 September he demanded a heavy, punitive air attack on the city. But next day, at Rundstedt's request, he agreed to its cancellation. As was seemingly habitual with this Supreme Commander, he saved face by ordering Brauchitsch to take Warsaw by 30 September.

Rundstedt and Manstein were determined to keep casualties low by avoiding large-scale street fighting against a big city garrison. They refused to attack until repairs to the railway were completed in sufficient time to assemble maximum artillery support. On 25 September fire was opened on the outer defences and on logistic targets while the besieging troops of Eighth Army closed in. The following day leaflets were dropped giving warning of heavy artillery fire and bombing. However, because the Poles continued to resist fiercely, a general bombardment by artillery and aircraft was opened that evening and continued unabated until midday on 27 September when two fortresses surrendered. A Polish request for capitulation followed shortly afterwards, and was chivalrously arranged by Rundstedt on the 28th. By 4 October all parts of the country were either in German or Russian hands.

Notable as the victory had been, it was already plain that time was needed to put right the Army's defects. But time would not be available if Hitler, dismissing suggestions for a patched-up peace with France and Britain, insisted upon a major offensive in the West by the end of October.

To every general this was sheer fantasy. Bock had changed his tune. He gave Halder his commanders' views: 'Infantry is far below 1914 calibre. The impetus given by the first line of attackers is lacking; all depends on the initiative of the commanders; hence high officer casualties. The light machine-guns in the advanced lines are silent for fear of giving themselves away.' In other words, prescribed fire-with-movement drills were set aside in the heat of action.

Manstein went closer to the point by asserting that lack of armoured support was a fundamental reason why the infantry (except those in the panzer divisions which alone had tanks) was weak. His proposal to reinforce infantry divisions with armoured assault guns was soon adopted. Artillery pieces with limited traverse were mounted on obsolete light tank and also modern tank hulls, thus enabling protected crews confidently to aim direct fire at the enemy.

More encouraging was Guderian's report. The fast divisions had functioned well and only rarely had been embarrassed by logistic problems. Medium tank losses had been relatively few and were almost replaced. All six panzer divisions would be refurbished within three weeks of their return to Germany. But the four light divisions had been a failure. Their light tanks, armed only with machine-guns, had hardly been fit for reconnaissance, let alone infantry and cavalry support; now that the German and Czech factories were producing more and better tanks, the time had come to convert them to panzer divisions. And this too was done. But his call for long-barrelled 50mm tank guns and a much higher priority for new tanks of up to forty tons (almost double the weight of the latest mediums) was ignored.

Hitler listened to these views and others at a great conference, on 27 September, at which it was misguidedly stated that 'Tanks and air forces are the keys to our success. If the Poles had possessed anti-tank weapons [which in fact they did], we would not have enjoyed a victory parade.' For there also were voices warning that 'The defences eliminate tanks.'

Two days later General Georg Thomas, head of OKW War Industries Department, was telling Halder about Germany's fundamental deficiencies. 'Demands of the three services by far exceed productive capacity.... Air Force in the east has used up fuel equivalent to production of one-half month. Major increase of powder production not before 1941.... monthly steel deficit of 600,000 tons. ... quotas of ammunition would be difficult to increase, even if we had the steel. If we start an offensive, production for the air force would have to be cut down.'

Yet preparations for the offensive went ahead, thus hampering major combat training. Panzer divisions, for example, could not be deployed to the necessary training areas and had to keep their vehicles in the open, where they deteriorated in bitter weather. It was found impossible to simulate co-operation of the ground and air forces because the Luftwaffe would not play. Some pontoon bridges were useless. The crossing of canals and rivers had to be simulated over roads. There was little fuel and ammunition – and so on.

Training of officers, however, was well managed at special training areas by experienced divisions, augmented by special so-called instruction groups of the different arms with corresponding units. Objections were raised against withdrawing combat-ready formations from the front. But the pay-off was two- and, later in the war, three-fold. Under this system it was possible in courses of four weeks' duration to train or update 1,200 officers, from battalion to platoon level, in the art of command, in how to educate their men and in how to care for welfare. The students took over from and were supervised by each unit's normal leader. Simultaneously the men's training was refreshed and battle weary troops benefited from a spell away from the front.

Specialist courses in signalling, gunnery and so on were held at central schools, as were 'crash' ten-week courses for staff officers until the Military Academy (which as in 1914 was closed at outbreak of war) was reopened in 1941. In these ways, when time was available in what came to be known as the Phoney War of winter 1939–40, the German Army made ready for the next round.

CHAPTER 8

Exultation and Errors in the West

As the guns fell silent and Poland sank under the rule of Gouverner General Hans Frank, the German generals entered the second phase of their emasculation by Hitler. Ordered on 9 October 1939 to mount a major offensive (Plan Yellow) on 25 November (later advanced to the 12th) against an enemy they deemed too strong to tackle, they could do no better, due to complete ignorance of enemy intentions, than come up with a very tentative plan which bore only a slight resemblance to Schlieffen's celebrated Plan employed in 1914. Above all it lacked his vision of total envelopment of the Allied Armies. But it did include his original, but subsequently abandoned, concept of an invasion of Holland as well as of Belgium.

Almost to a man, the generals, who had not contemplated this war starting until 1942, protested that they could not be ready for such a daunting task by mid-November, when the ground would become unsuitable for mechanised troops. Göring agreed, and voiced concern that the weather might restrict flying.

There was the usual talk of a revolt against Hitler in which Halder and Rundstedt may have been involved. But there were rational doubts that the Army would follow them, and a dread of being accused of mutiny and breaching a professional code. So Brauchitsch, exercising his traditional right 'to carry protest to the "King"', attempted to deter Hitler by presenting him with a summary of the generals' objections. The incensed Führer shouted him down and accused him, and the other generals, of disloyalty. The Commander-in-Chief had no option but, as always, to obey.

Stopping just short of sacking Brauchitsch (who had next to endure his Nazi wife's invective), Hitler then switched his channel of communication with the Army to OKW. But not even Keitel and OKW could control the elements. Twenty-nine times prior to 10 January 1940 the troops stood-to only to be recalled due to some of the vilest winter weather on record. Frustrating as this was, it did, on the other hand, provide time to develop intelligence sources and reveal the Allies' intentions when finally the balloon went up. They were to retain strong forces behind the frontier with Belgium until Germany had made its move – and thus make it impossible to calculate what those forces would do and how the campaign might develop.

Meanwhile Admiral Erich Raeder had put forward strategic ideas which, like Tirpitz's in the distant past, diverted attention and resources from the Army. Realising that his relatively few surface vessels and submarines could not impose an effective blockade on Britain, and having rejected any notion of invading England, he focused elsewhere. On the day Hitler issued Plan Yellow, he warned of British interest in Norway – without obtaining encouragement from a Supreme Commander who understood but little about the exercise of sea power.

But on 14 December 1939, three days after Raeder had introduced Hitler to Vidkun Quisling, the dissident Norwegian, the Führer, intuitively fearing the Allies might occupy Norway in connection with the Russo-Finnish War which had started on 30 November, instructed OKW to study an invasion of that country. Plan Yellow held centre stage – but only until 11 January 1940 when two unfortunate Luftwaffe officers accidentally landed in Belgium with a copy of Plan Yellow in their possession.

The inevitable outcome of this mishap was the calling off and radical recasting of an already suspect scheme. The change made essential the famous, sometimes vitriolic but eventually productive February war-games with their examination of Manstein's damning criticism of Yellow's shortcomings and his proposal for the inspiringly original Sickle Cut (*Sichelschnitt*) Plan. This shifted the *Schwerpunkt* of Yellow from the right to the left flank with emphasis on a massive thrust through and beyond the Ardennes by Rundstedt's Army Group A in a westerly direction. This Guderian supported from the start and Halder came to prefer once he felt sure the enemy's intentions reduced significantly the chances of a counter to a thrust through the Ardennes. Doubters remained, including Rundstedt, but Hitler approved the scheme after Manstein had been given the opportunity to explain it to him in private over breakfast on 17 February.

Two days later, however, Hitler ordered accelerated planning for Operation Weser Exercise, an invasion of Norway before Yellow.

Significantly, this was the first of many OKW controlled operations to come, an innovation which initiated the gradual relegation of the Army and Luftwaffe High Commands (respectively OKH and OKL), who were not even consulted, to a minor role. Reasonably enough, it led both OKH and OKL to object strongly for fear of jeopardising Plan Yellow. But the Führer and Jodl, his Chief of Operations, were adamant. General Nikolaus von Falkenhorst, with seven divisions in XXI Corps, was appointed to command the operation in conjunction with the Navy. The reluctant Luftwaffe contributed a parachute battalion of General Kurt Student's as yet unblooded 7th Air Division to spearhead the initial assault, and insisted that Denmark should be swallowed simultaneously in order to provide airfields for close-range support over Norway by fighters and dive-bombers.

Weser Exercise was the only large-scale combined amphibious operation ever undertaken by Germany. It was a complete success, notwithstanding the inherent weakness of the Danish and Norwegian defences, due to excellent planning and attainment of surprise. Within hours on 9 April Denmark was overrun as, simultaneously, parachutists seized Norwegian airfields in readiness for air-landed infantry, which were soon reinforced by seaborne forces landed against patchy opposition at Oslo, Arendal, Kristiansand, Stavanger, Trondheim and Narvik. Baffled by spurious orders from Quisling's adherents, Norwegian resistance was diffuse – although the sinking of a German cruiser in Oslo fjord and the failure, due to fog, of airborne troops to seize the airport, did enable the King and government to escape. By the end of the day the Germans had seized all their objectives and would secure them long before British and French land forces began arriving in strength nearly a week later.

Thereafter, from the German point of view, the situation was well under control, not least because the Allied Armies, hampered by air attacks, were unprepared as well as logistically ill-supplied. On 19 April Falkenhorst agreed to the return of some Luftwaffe units to Germany in readiness for the launching in May of Plan Yellow. By 10 June the last Allied units, those at Narvik, had been withdrawn because Plan Yellow had created a situation beyond all imagination. Several times the Führer exhibited acute nervousness, notably when the Narvik Group became isolated: he first wanted to evacuate it to Sweden but finally, persuaded by the iron-nerved Jodl, ordered it to fight to the last gasp. This it did, and survived, and in so doing created a precedent of great significance both operationally and with regard to Jodl's future role in dealing with his master's fear and depression in moments of crisis.

At the close, Hitler, OKW and Falkenhorst seized credit for the magnitude of success. They might have been less delighted, however, had they been aware of an event which portended disaster in the years to come. Between 15 April and 14 May, the British GC and CS organisation (Ultra), had used a Polish-invented electro-mechanical computer, known as a Bombe, to break the Enigma-machine code and gain access to all high-grade, special to Weser Exercise Army and Luftwaffe high-grade operational radio messages – some within an hour of their transmission. This bounty ceased when the traffic ended, only to be renewed by an even richer supply of priceless Signals Intelligence (Sigint) from Ultra as the Germans, especially the Luftwaffe, made extensive use of radio in France and all subsequent campaigns.

*   *   *

Ultra contributed but little during the offensive against Holland, Belgium, Luxembourg and France which began on 10 May 1940. This was not for lack of decryptions to read but chiefly because the British had yet to develop a suitable organisation to handle and securely disseminate a mass of material. As it was the Germans achieved tactical surprise because, on 1 May, they shrewdly changed all Enigma keys (except for Norway) and it was the 20th before Ultra read Enigma again. From this date, as the British Official History of Intelligence says, '. . . it broke [codes] virtually every day until the end of the war.'

Within forty-eight hours the Luftwaffe won air superiority as the airborne troops in Kesselring's Second Air Fleet seized strategic points in Holland and at the key Fort Eben Emael, guarding the Belgium frontier. Within four days Army Group B formations, including a panzer division, had linked up with the parachutists and the Dutch had laid down their arms. Meanwhile Halder was recording not only his pleasure at the performance and discipline of well-trained troops and at an advance going almost to plan, but also his satisfaction that the enemy was behaving as expected by moving strong forces into Belgium.

Army Group A, spearheaded by General Ewald von Kleist's

Armoured Group, consisting of two panzer corps (XIX commanded by Guderian and XXXXI commanded by Reinhardt) was making remarkable progress through the notoriously trackless Ardennes due to excellent traffic control and the immediate withdrawal of surprised and totally outmatched Belgian and French screening forces. Appearing suddenly on the banks of the Meuse between Sedan and Monthermé early on 13 May, Kleist, in accordance with war-games, ordered a crossing of the river that evening, overruling Guderian's objections that one of his panzer divisions might be late in position. Meanwhile to the north, General Hermann Hoth's XV Corps, led by General Erwin Rommel's 7th Panzer Division, already had reached the Meuse at Dinant and made a strongly opposed crossing with infantry supported by tanks and artillery.

At Monthermé Reinhardt's corps suffered badly under French fire from dominant ground and accidental bombing by the Luftwaffe as it struggled to make a crossing. Meanwhile, at Sedan, Guderian was in despair because the original war-game plan, of neutralising the French artillery by prolonged bombing, had been set aside in favour of a shorter and more complicated bombardment programme. In the event, however, the immense value of war-gaming was again demonstrated. Not only did Guderian's Chief of Staff save time and trouble by merely issuing the war-game's orders, with the times adjusted, but the staff of General Wolfram von Richthofen's VIII Air Corps decided to ignore the new orders and, to Guderian's relief, applied up-dated war-games orders.

A combination of audacity, surprise, firepower and luck, allied to an apparent collapse of French morale, saw Guderian's infantry across the Meuse by nightfall. Furthermore the air and artillery bombardment persuaded many French artillerymen to abandon their guns as rumours of German tanks approaching (when, in fact, none would be ferried across until the next morning) spread panic. Indeed, the arrival of French tanks in darkness, tasked to counter-attack the still vulnerable German bridgehead, had to be called off to check the flight of shaken French infantrymen.

Those on the spot came to realise that Hitler's insight into French decay, from top to bottom of society, was only too correct and that rich pickings were to be won by energetic exploitation. In consultation next day with the commander of 1st Panzer Division, Guderian dismissed his own doubts about the prospects of immense success. Those at the front recognised rout when they saw it. His dramatic orders to drive westwards ('For the right wheel, road map Rethel'), reflected an intention, as once stated to Hitler at a wargame, 'Unless I receive orders to the contrary I intend to drive for the Channel.'

Risks there were, but the inspired Guderian kept his nerve despite the danger that air attacks could wreck the Meuse pontoon bridges and prevent his tanks crossing to lead the pursuit and the approaching infantry formations' ability to secure the southern flank without delay. He was neither disappointed by events nor did he receive further orders, although the further his corps and those of Reinhardt and Hoth lunged at ever increasing speed, the more worried some superiors grew. Not that Brauchitsch, who constantly was on the move from one crucial place to another, was among them; nor Halder, whose calculations of enemy strengths and deployment based on excellent intelligence were likely to waver and throw away victory in the same way Moltke had in 1914.

Instead there was Rundstedt. On 15 May, when the thrust to the coast had barely started and evidence was accumulating that at least five of the seven French armoured divisions had been badly mauled, he wanted to halt on the River Oise and was fretting about '. . . the threat from the south and because the enemy must in no circumstances be allowed a success'.

Ironically next day when '. . . the spirited and ambitious' Bock (as Halder approvingly called him) '. . . took upon himself going beyond the mission assigned to him . . . the task of beating the Anglo-French forces alone', Hitler sent Keitel to him bearing 'Führer's urgent wish that motorised forces be moved to the front'. The highly aggressive commander of Army Group B suavely replied that 'they will be in line at the earliest'.

If at that moment the staff of OKW could have witnessed the defeatism permeating the French High Command (whose generals were older than their German counterparts), or taken proper account of Halder's confident assessments of the situation, they might, given better collaboration with OKH, have soothed Hitler's nerves. Halder had said to Hitler on 16 May that the southern attacks had been beaten off and the follow-up divisions were following closely. And on the 17th he stated unequivocally: 'On the southern flank of our breakthrough the enemy has moved up at least six divisions and tries to bolster his front. We have no intention of attacking in this area, and enemy is not strong enough to attack us.'

Yet that same day Kleist, in obedience to Rundstedt, was landing at Guderian's headquarters to reprimand him severely (without saying from whom the orders came) for turning a blind eye to instructions to pause for twenty-four hours. In high dudgeon, the commander of XIX Corps tendered his resignation on the spot – only to withdraw it a few hours later after General Wilhelm List had been sent forward to pour oil on the troubled waters and give Guderian permission to continue the main advance under the guise of 'a reconnaissance in force'. Guderian performed this with characteristic verve, but took care, henceforward, not to broadcast orders by radio.

Meanwhile Brauchitsch and Halder, far from complying with Hitler's wish to move the motorised units to Army Group B's front, switched them to Army Group A and told Army Group B only to contain the withdrawing Allies in Belgium by steady pressure. This took place against a background of sour disagreements with Hitler who, reflecting Rundstedt's illogical worries and his own memories of trench warfare, had little insight into the effects of the grandiose scythe cut. 'I see no threat at all at present [to the southern flank]' wrote Halder, adding that Hitler was causing 'confusion and doubt' through bypassing the established channels of command with direct, contradictory orders to Army Groups and Armies.

On 18 May, it was all go again when Halder, after unpleasant discussions, managed to convert the Führer to OKH's view. Kleist Group, meeting minimal resistance and with its communications and logistic support secure, shot ahead to reach the English Channel on the evening of the 20th. This completely severed Allied forces in the north from their logistic base in the south, and generated another bout of indecision.

Far-sighted and methodical, Halder urged the launching of a drive into metropolitan France at the earliest possible moment, to which Hitler now agreed. For the time being, however, Brauchitsch intended Army Group A, as the hammer, to combine with Army Group B, the anvil, in enveloping the Allied mass in the north. But again his plan was watered down by Kleist who, over-cautiously, withdrew 10th Panzer Division into Group reserve. This denied Guderian the mass of armour he counted upon to seal the fate of the Allied armies by preventing their evacuation by sea from Boulogne, Calais and Dunkirk. The weight from the hammer was thereby removed and further delay inflicted, exacerbated by the panic induced on 21 May when a medium-sized, poorly co-ordinated Allied armoured force struck southwards from Arras. This celebrated counterstroke inflicted considerable losses to Rommel's panzer division and an SS motorised division, but faded away in the evening.

Yet, on 23 May, the way to Dunkirk remained open for Guderian and Reinhardt to cut off every Channel port without necessarily seizing them. Both Halder and the German high commanders knew this; as did the British War Office when an Ultra decrypt of a Luftwaffe signal disclosed the rate and objectives of the German advance. Boulogne fell on 24 May to 2nd Panzer; 1st Panzer bypassed Calais and headed for Gravelines and Dunkirk, which were garrisoned by minor forces; and 10th Panzer, tardily released by Kleist, was motoring to Calais as Reinhardt's XXXXI Corps once more covered Guderian's right flank; and General Erich Hoepner's XVI Corps, switched from Army Group B, joined Army Group A reserve. Thus the fearful Rundstedt, allowing for a maximum deficiency of fifty per cent fit tanks, had in hand some 1,500 (soon reinforced by an ample stream of new and repaired machines), along with a stream of mechanised and marching infantry formations echeloned back to the Ardennes.

On 24 May Guderian reached the outskirts of Dunkirk where he was confronted by only light forces (since the mass of the Allied armies were still deployed well to the east). To his astonishment and without explanation, he was thereupon ordered to halt. 'We were speechless', he wrote.

After the war Rundstedt lied to Basil Liddell Hart when stating that the order came from Hitler. In fact, as the War Diary of Army Group A shows, it was he who gave the order, thus countermanding Brauchitsch's instruction that he should play hammer to Bock's anvil in the elimination of the gigantic pocket forming Flanders. In effect, all Hitler did was visit Rundstedt's HQ where, only too ready to assuage his fears and override OKH, to satisfy his own ego, he merely confirmed the order several hours after it had been issued. His greedy political deputy, Hermann Göring, leapt at the opportunity to polish 'his' Luftwaffe's image by assuming responsibily for preventing an Allied evacuation by sea. This left Army Group B the onerous task of mopping up the besieged pocket.

The Allies were let off the hook. Relieved of fatal pressure from Army Group A, they concentrated on delaying Army Group B (which had to manage without panzer divisions) while retreating to Dunkirk and establishing a strong enough perimeter to hold off the Germans. Meanwhile the Luftwaffe, still based mainly in Germany, was unable to give adequate cover against air attacks on Kleist's Group, let alone prevent the evacuation which already was under way.

Presciently neither Brauchitsch nor Halder believed the Luftwaffe capable of fulfilling its self-assumed task. Instead they foresaw Bock saddled with a prolonged and costly struggle to eliminate the pocket, thus imposing delay on Plan Red, the next phase of the campaign for the overrunning of France, for which Halder had issued instructions on 25 May. Rundstedt already was making preparations in connection with the plan. But belatedly, on 26 May, he conceded the error of his halt order by rescinding it. He found himself once more supported by Hitler who, performing a politician's game of playing off one faction against another, was slyly setting the pliant Rundstedt against Brauchitsch and Halder, to whom he was chillingly hostile. But the damage was done. It was too late to seize Dunkirk since substantial Allied reinforcements had retired into a perimeter which was being strengthened by inundations.

It was of almost minor consequence in the long run that the Belgians surrendered on 28 May. What mattered most at that moment was prevention of a British escape (less their equipment) – which already looked to be beyond German capability. Bad weather and stiff British fighter action frustrated the Luftwaffe. Kleist's renewed attack ran into a brick wall. On 1 June it was plain that many British would escape, although without their equipment. Still, the bulk of the French Seventh Army was trapped hopelessly, in part due to an apathetic unwillingness to break out. Halder proudly recorded on 1 June, '... the operation started on 10 May is now concluded'.

Already Army Group A and Kleist Group had been withdrawn for refurbishment in readiness for the conclusive offensive against France. The plan for this, despite somewhat weird procrastination by Hitler, was shaping the way Halder confidently desired. Indeed so confident was he that already he was busy planning the post-war strength of the Army at twenty-four panzer, twelve motorised and thirty or forty other divisions. But the antagonism of his Supreme Commander (who seems to have taken a perverse delight in patronising the Chief of Staff) and OKW rankled, not least because of their ill-concealed claim of most of the credit for a truly astonishing victory. On 4 June German troops entered Dunkirk to find but few enemy awaiting captivity.

Having recovered rapidly from its strenuous efforts since 10 May, the Wehrmacht was ready to strike again on 5 June. Long before then Halder was in possession of sufficient information to assess the strength and deployment of, he thought, some sixty Allied divisions strung out along 225 miles from the Channel to the Maginot Lines, with strong forces covering Paris. In fact it was only fifty and he seems to have been unaware that the best of the French mobile armoured forces were but a shadow of their former selves, as well as demoralised. The Germans, on the other hand, had 104 full-strength divisions and vastly outnumbered and outclassed their opponents in the air. A walkover looked certain.

In outline Halder planned to strike hard on both sides of Paris. Starting on 5 June, Army Group B, with three panzer corps, would attack on the right, heading for Rouen and the ports of Dieppe, Le Havre, Cherbourg, Brest and Bordeaux. It would be followed on the 9th on the left by Army Group A, with two panzer corps in Group Guderian, with its *Schwerpunkt* driving to Dijon, Vichy and Clermont Ferrand. This time, however, it was no walkover.

The French had established a position in depth, founded on fortified villages known as hedgehogs. There was nothing original about this system nor any chance of prolonged resistance unless mobile counter-attack forces were maintained and used with spirit. The real difference of battle, compared with what had gone before, was the spirit of the defenders who, too late for France, often fought to the death in the old spirit. Hoth's XV Panzer Corps, on the extreme right, had hard fighting before Rommel's 7th Panzer Division broke out. XIV and XVI Panzer Corps, suffering sixty per cent tank losses, had to be withdrawn, combined and switched to Bock's left flank behind infantry divisions.

For the first time, reports of random logistic breakdowns were coming in, caused mainly by a train derailment and higher ammunition expenditure than forecast. The problem was by no means crippling in the light of a decision on 20 May to mobilise several thousand Dutch and Belgian lorries in transport groups, to stock forward bases from the Ruhr until the railways were restored. However, it was an ominous portent for the future when an overstretched Wehrmacht, and the Army most of all, suffered from dependence on a bizarre collection of other nations' arms, equipment and munitions.

On 8 June the school-masterly Halder read Hitler a lesson on the principles of employment of armour. 'Tanks,' he said 'are operational assets only where they have open country to manoeuvre in. In slow-moving battles they only burn themselves out. Such fighting is the department of the infantry.... Panzer divisions which have gained a free field of movement must be followed up by motorised divisions (shaft of the spearhead).' Hitler's reaction to this lecture is unknown, but he could have seen it as tit-for-tat, an expression of the on-going struggle for intellectual leadership of the military profession. For Hitler had delivered a lecture on the same subject to the newly appointed Chief of Staff in 1938. Yet here too was implied criticism of the headstrong Bock who certainly had misemployed his armour with dire consequences.

Rundstedt and List (the commander of Twelfth Army), on the other hand, made no such mistake when crossing the River Aisne on 9 June. In order to conserve the panzer divisions, and contrary to Guderian's wishes, List insisted on employing infantry formations to break into the French defences in order to save the armour for the break-out and pursuit. The infantry, however, failed almost everywhere to cross the river. So Guderian immediately requested permission from List's Chief of Staff to pass his tanks at night through the only two small bridgeheads won – a sure sign of confidence in the high standard of training now attained by the Panzertruppe. At dawn this plan worked like clockwork when tanks and infantry advanced in unison; to be checked by French tank counter-attacks which were pushed home with great determination throughout the day. For sheer lack of numbers they faded away in the evening after close-range fighting during which, it is worth mentioning, Guderian himself was engaged personally in endeavouring, unsuccessfully, to penetrate a French heavy tank with a captured 47mm gun.

By 11 June the French were beaten and the Germans were advancing as they pleased. Halder revelled at the prospect of another 'Battle of Cannae' in the making, and gave final approval, seemingly for prestige purposes in the circumstances, for a long-planned, set-piece attack on the Maginot Line. But all it really achieved when it succeeded on 15 June was a demonstration of the line's inherent uselessness.

Hitler contributed a flow of instructions, now using General

Walter Warlimont of OKW as go-between, demanding changes of direction to seize prestige objectives and underline his self-assumed, superior knowledge of Grand Strategy. In the circumstances of free manoeuvre and certain victory, this display of irrational intuition was irrelevant. However he now went a stage further by including detailed orders for the use of specified SS divisions, no doubt for the greater glory of the Nazi regime. This tendency gave notice of the menace posed to the Army by Heinrich Himmler's organisation.

At 0135 hours on 25 June fighting ceased. France was prostrate, Germany triumphant and Italy, after declaring war on 10 June when Germany could not lose, stalled among French defences in the south.

But already on 22 June Halder had recorded disquieting thoughts about Britain, whose remaining forces in Norway and France had been withdrawn. 'The raids of the British Air Force are becoming bothersome. Now they are extending their attacks to Berlin and ObdL [Göring] therefore wants us to transfer army AA units. . . . The near future will show whether Britain will do the reasonable thing in the light of our victories, or will try to carry on the war single-handedly. In the latter case, the war will lead to Britain's destruction, and may last a long time.'

CHAPTER 9

Delusions and Delays

Taking advantage of the state of euphoria gripping Hitler and his Commanders-in-Chief on the morning of 21 May 1940, when it was clear that the campaign in France was all but won, Admiral Raeder sounded out the Führer's opinion concerning operations against Britain. For with the Channel in sight and possession of the Western Europe seaboard from North Cape to Spain a virtual certainty, many new options presented themselves. To the obvious question: 'Do you now consider this the moment to invade England? Or do we blockade?' he received the answer he hoped for: 'No! We blockade'. No doubt Hitler, the land animal, was unable to comprehend the full possibilities of that awe-inspiring moment; but also the political realist in him, like nearly everybody for the next few weeks, took it for granted that Britain would sue for peace. She might well have done so had not the BEF, by his and Rundstedt's lack of perception, been allowed to escape.

Yet there were those, like Kesselring and Admiral Kurt Fricke (Head of Naval Plans) and, to a lesser extent, Göring, who, within the next fortnight, did suggest that the British should be followed across the Channel without delay after the fall of Dunkirk, thus denying them the slightest opportunity to recover poise and prepare adequate defences. In hindsight, moreover, there are good reasons to believe that, even if the Germans had tried in mid-July, they would have succeded. Meanwhile the Navy, in case it was suddenly told to invade at short notice, took a few precautionary measures; and on 17 June two OKH staff officers were set to work by Halder on an outline scheme.

OKH meanwhile concentrated on the speedy occupation and securing of France, in addition to organisation of a Victory Parade. Halder studied reports concerning European and world affairs and concluded that 'Russia's attitude stands in the foreground'. It is a mistake to imagine the General Staff was ignorant of foreign affairs, as Hitler among others put about. It was as well informed as the reports reaching it allowed. By 30 June, Halder suspected that 'Britain still needs one more demonstration of our military might before she gives in and leaves us a free hand in the east.' Next day, therefore, he had an exploratory meeting with Admiral Otto Schniewind, Chief of Staff Naval Operations.

From this moment, and especially because it now dawned on them that Winston Churchill had no intention of making peace, the Wehrmacht's planners began to take an invasion of England seriously. At the same time, and paradoxically after three months of tolerably unified action in conquering Western Europe, it also began to split into the factions which Hitler's system of 'divide and rule' did little to discourage. For example, on 20 June, at a top-level conference, Raeder angrily raised the matter of an insulting message to him from Göring refusing strong air protection for the new naval base at Trondheim in Norway. Hitler adroitly side-stepped the matter, thus allowing a sore to fester and infect Navy–Luftwaffe relationships. This problem affected not only the preparation for the invasion (which in due course came to be called Sea Lion) but the entire strategic conduct of the war.

In essence on 20 June, Raeder, armed with a portfolio of imaginative ideas based on sea power, put the Luftwaffe and Army on the spot by pointing out that Britain had to be dealt with, and therefore it was now the Navy's war. Invasion was one option, he remarked, providing air supremacy was won and the Army was prepared to co-operate. But surely blockade was better – as Hitler had already conceded? This stung Göring, whose Luftwaffe had so recently failed to deliver victory at Dunkirk; and was the genesis of the Battle of Britain inspired by his determination to win lasting glory by defeating Britain with air power alone. But it also was the spur to a study by OKW's Chief of Operations, General Alfred Jodl. Keeping Hitler and all the others interested in Sea Lion, he began progressively diverting attention to other, peripheral Raeder-inspired moves at the very moment the Führer was contemplating the vast scheme on which his mind had long been set – the invasion of Russia.

Predictably, wide divergencies of doctrine, priorities and opinion clashed when the Army and Navy got down to joint planning and war-gaming for Sea Lion. For a start, because strategic surprise was impossible, Sea Lion bore no resemblance to Operation Weser

Exercise. Instinctively, therefore, OKH tended to underrate the difficulties by tackling it as a large-scale river crossing. The Navy, in trepidation, underlined the fundamental unpredictables of an amphibious operation, such as the need for smooth water and good weather, and the threat of an undiminished Royal Navy, despite its losses and damage incurred off Norway and Dunkirk. All agreed on the vital need for air superiority. But whereas the Navy insisted that it could cover only a narrow frontage across the shortest stretch of water (meaning the Straits of Dover), the Army demanded a very wide frontage, without cliffs to climb, in order to distract the enemy and give maximum room for manoeuvre.

Debate raged throughout July as preparation went ahead at top speed – including the conversion of 140 tanks for deep wading and the requisitioning of tugs, trawlers, coastal shipping and 2,000 barges. This, as Raeder told Hitler on 31 July, '... would lead to a thirty per cent reduction of Germany's inland shipping space and a serious curtailment of high sea fishing activities'. On 11 July Hitler had approved the initial plan (Directive No. 16 issued on 16 July), but remained filled with doubts about 'this dangerous operation' which was optimistically scheduled, initially, for 25 August.

Rundstedt's Army Group A was tasked to command the land forces, but its commander, now Field Marshal, stayed put in his comfortable St Germain headquarters ouside Paris; made no secret of his contempt for Sea Lion as 'an impossibility'; and never attended a single amphibious training exercise. Very likely he had in mind an amazing private conversation with Hitler, shortly before the start of Plan Red, when the Führer divulged that, since Britain must probably be ready for peace, 'Now ... he could begin his settling of accounts with Bolshevism.'

As the Army and Navy debated, improvised and gathered assets, the Luftwaffe opened its campaign against Britain by testing defences of which it knew remarkably little. The Wehrmacht's knowledge of the enemy from the Military Abwehr (Intelligence Service) was reminiscent of October 1939 when it unexpectedly prepared an invasion of the West. Nobody had envisaged the likelihood of invading Britain. Therefore, little had been done to develop an intelligence organisation. Mainly the Abwehr depended on neutral observers in Britain, who tended to denigrate the nation's morale and misreport the strength and location of defences.

Gerhard von Scharnhorst, the rebuilder of the Prussian Army

Gebhard von Blücher, the victor of the last battles against Napoleon

Karl von Clausewitz, the creator of a fatal war philosophy

Helmuth von Moltke the Elder, architect of the triumphs

Erich Ludendorff, an apostle of Total War

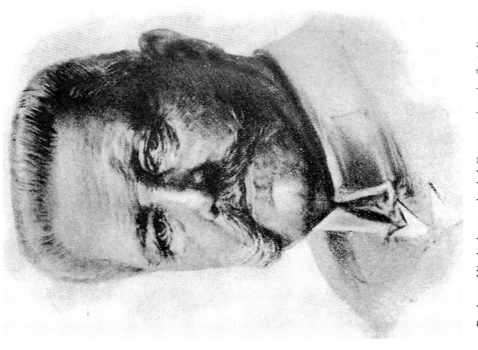

Paul von Hindenburg, who led Germany into its first disaster

Wilhelm Gröner, Germany's saviour in the first disaster

Hans von Seeckt, who remoulded the Reichswehr

Werner von Blomberg, the creator of the Wehrmacht

Franz Halder (*left*) and Walter von Brauchitsch

Creators of the Luftwaffe: (*left to right*) Erhard Milch; unknown; Albert Kesselring; and Hermann Göring

(*Left to right*) Albert Kesselring, master strategist; Erwin Rommel, tactical opportunist; and Adolf Hitler, demagogue

Leading actors in the triumphs and ultimate disasters: (*left to right, back row*) Alfred
Jodl, Walter von Brauchitsch, Erich Raeder and Wilhelm Keitel; (*seated*) Hermann
Göring (*left*) and Adolf Hitler

Victors of 1940 but defeated in 1945: Gerd von Rundstedt (*left*) and the last Chief of the General Staff, Heinz Guderian

Günther von Kluge, a victim of Hitler's fury

Kurt Zeitzler, a Chief of the General Staff in the shadows

Prussian field marshal Erich von Manstein

Walter Model, Hitler's baffled 'fireman'

Intelligence from England,' wrote Colonel Günther Blumentritt of Rundstedt's staff, 'was extremely meagre. No one knew whether there were any coast defences or field fortifications on the English coast, or where they were if they existed. It was not known which beaches were mined. No one could say exactly what forces the British had available for defence.... Our maps were inaccurate ... Naval charts were little better.'

Of the few spies in place in 1939, one already had been 'turned' into a double agent. Not until September 1940 were agents put ashore. Of the twenty-one amateurs who arrived between then and November, one committed suicide and the remainder either gave themselves up or were captured. Three of these agreed to work for the British, thus founding a British counter-intelligence operation which, as the war progressed, was significantly to mislead the Wehrmacht.

Wehrmacht opinions about British capability therefore varied widely. The Navy, gloomy in its safe assumption that the Royal Navy and Royal Air Force would intervene decisively, feared the worst unless the Luftwaffe achieved air superiority. This Göring, boastfully confident, supremely optimistic and arrogant as ever, loyally promised to deliver. After all, the Luftwaffe had suppressed the inferior air forces of Poland and France in two days. Against the stronger Royal Air Force, whose combat prowess was not held in high esteem by the more experienced Germans, it was assumed four days would suffice to defeat Fighter Command. It would then be possible for the bombers and their Me110 long-range fighter escorts to fly and bomb as they pleased and bring Britain to her knees.

Field Marshals Albert Kesselring and Hugo Sperrle, respectively the commanders of Second and Third Air Fleets and each a one-time member of the Army General Staff, held war-games to devise special tactics for a campaign without precedent. Unfortunately for them, however, certain false assumptions were injected by OKL's Intelligence Staff. Firstly, they believed that the Me110 could hold its own against British Hurricane and Spitfire fighters, which in fact already had out-fought the Me110. Secondly, they assumed that the British airfield-based fighter control system was inflexible and therefore incapable of concentrating against mass attacks, whereas in practice the Sector Control system (of which the Germans were in ignorance) created the opposite effect. Thirdly, some intelligence of those airfields said to belong to Fighter Command was wrong. Fourthly, radar early warning, linked to the control system, was underrated, and augmented an unwarranted belief that the radar sites' high masts could not be neutralised by bombing.

Most damaging of all, Göring and his (ex-cavalry) Chief of Staff, General Hans Jeschonnek, committed the military sin of stating two conflicting aims: to eliminate the RAF as a fighting force with its ground organisation; and to blockade Britain by attacking its ports and shipping.

This strategy dutifully and unwisely reflected Hitler's Directive No. 17, issued on 2 August, to set in motion an intensified naval and air offensive against Britain, for which the Navy had only fifty-five U-boats available. But the Luftwaffe, with ample reserves of air crew and machines, saw it as being within its compass, since it comfortably out-numbered an RAF suffering from a dire shortage of pilots and barely enough fighters.

The Army also was pursuing two operations. First priority went to Sea Lion, even though on 22 July there were broad hints that it might be postponed until May 1941, when the Navy would have ready four battleships, including the mighty *Bismarck* and *Tirpitz*. But concurrently looming ever larger was the Führer's expressed intention to attack Russia in Spring 1941. Or as Hitler put it when indicating his true priorities for action in the future: 'With Russia smashed, Britain's last hope would be shattered. Germany will then be master of Europe and the Balkans.'

The Abwehr and Army Intelligence officers, unlike those of the Luftwaffe, exaggerated the strength of enemy forces. Seemingly unaware that the vast quantity of equipment left behind in France had largely disarmed the British Army, they certainly were ignorant of the fact that the British Commander-in-Chief Home Forces, General Sir Edmund Ironside, had decided to abandon the thin coastal defences, once the Germans had obtained a foothold, and retire inland to a so-called GHQ Line. This feeble defensive strategy was made all the more vulnerable by a weird British Intelligence appreciation. This, without saying why, stated that the Germans would land on the east coast, instead of via the traditional route of the south coast – where, more than incidentally, German air support could most effectively be applied. Inevitably this thoroughly unsound bit of guesswork led to further dilution of the British defences exactly where the Germans intended to land. For, as rated by the commander of the almost immobile force defending Kent, his 1st (London) Division was 'ludicrous' and incapable of holding ground for more than a few hours.

The air battle of attrition over the Channel and ports which began in earnest on 17 July had risen to a new peak when Göring, in hope of three consecutive days of good weather, ordered Eagle Day – the concentrated attack on RAF airfields – to start on 10 August. It was postponed until the 13th, due to unfavourable meteorological reports. Yet for the next seventy-two hours the weather was good enough for more fighting over the Channel plus the first serious attacks on coastal airfields.

When at last Eagle Day did dawn, on 13 August, the offensive still went off at half-cock. Postponed until mid-afternoon, it mustered only 1,500 sorties and suffered heavy losses without much achievement. For no fewer than three non-Fighter Command airfields were bombed, along with many secondary targets which were easier to find. Next day was an anti-climax also, with fewer than 500 sorties; thus setting an inconsistency of activity which was to last the battle through. For example, 15 and 16 August would be so-called Big Days of maximum effort ending in the Germans' favour through the wreaking of large-scale damage to radar and airfields, and the shooting down of many RAF fighters. But, due to the need for recuperation and despite fair weather, the battle was not resumed at full tilt until 18 August, whereupon bad weather put a stop to major operations until the 24th.

Throughout this most incompetently conducted campaign, the Luftwaffe's commanders operated in a fool's paradise created by their air crews' excessive claims of enemy aircraft destroyed allied to the Staff's wishful thinking. On 18 August OKL deduced that Fighter Command had been reduced to half its actual strength. The misinformation had the cumulative effect of persuading Göring and Jeschonnek that victory was just round the corner. In reality, there was a long way to go since only a minority of well-directed attacks had hit the vital Sector airfields – thus, unbeknown to the Germans, threatening the fighter control system. These attacks might have been catastrophic if radar stations had not been left almost untouched. Not until the first week of September was Fighter Command brought to the brink of defeat, partly due to pilot shortage, but also because of severe damage to Sector Stations, which also carried out maintenance and light repairs to fighters. On 6 September, a little later than anticipated, OKL correctly detected indications that they were getting on top.

Yet also there were signs that the Luftwaffe was straying from its primary aim of destroying Fighter Command. Some raids, intended to provoke advantageous air to air combat, were merely fighter sweeps containing only a very few bombers. Day and night raids on ports further subtracted effort from airfields. On the night of 24/25 August the London suburbs had been bombed and a few bombs fell in the City. Churchill, by way of reprisal next day, ordered attacks on Berlin, thus damaging the reputation of Göring, who had boasted nothing of the sort would ever happen, and stinging Hitler to announce publicly on 4 September that vengeance would follow.

On the afternoon of 7 September (at the end of what for Air Marshal Dowding and Fighter Command had been a week of crisis) Göring, advised by Jeschonnek in the premature belief that the RAF was beaten, switched the bombers to London with a very effective daylight raid followed by an intense night attack. This was a psychological terror raid of the sort Luftwaffe pre-war doctrine reserved only for occasions when it was assumed beyond much doubt that the enemy was on the verge of collapse – which some neutral observers reported was the case.

Fighter Command profited decisively from the premature bombing of London and the simultaneous freedom from attacks on airfields. Granted a few days respite, its command, control and maintenance systems recovered. German bombers now flying on the fringe of cover by Me109 fighters suffered badly. All at once Hitler and his fellow doubters of all persuasions knew that Sea Lion was in jeopardy. Among them was Jodl at OKW, who was no enthusiast for attacking Russia before Britain was eliminated. He had taken shrewd note of a memorandum by Brauchitsch to OKW on 12 August analysing the difficulties encountered by OKH and OKM (Oberkommando der Kriegsmarine) in reaching agreement on how, let alone when, to launch Sea Lion. He had then prepared a well reasoned paper worthy of the old General Staff – whose role progressively was being usurped by OKW.

Jodl had outlined options, many of them copied from Raeder's perceptive, strategic mind. He assumed the Luftwaffe would win the Battle of Britain but that if the Navy and Army could not resolve their differences '. . . a landing in England must be regarded as an act of sheer desperation which need only be risked in a hopeless situation; but Germany at the present juncture has no reason to take such a risk, because Britain can be forced to her knees in another way, namely:

1. by continuation of air warfare until the entire armament industry in south England is destroyed;

2. by intensification of U-boat warfare, making fullest use of the French bases;

3. by the conquest of Egypt in an Italian offensive from Libya, if necessary with German support;

4. by the capture of Gibraltar in collaboration with Italy and Spain.'

At the end of August OKH and OKM, steered in conference by OKW, managed to resolve their differences through compromises none really liked. At that meeting Hitler continued to give lukewarm support to Sea Lion, hedged by the stipulation that arrangements must be completed by 21 September and making 11 September his day of decision to sail or not to sail. But the 11th came and went as British fighters, now benefiting from more time to concentrate, suddenly seemed to increase in number as Luftwaffe losses mounted dangerously: famously so on 15 September when it lost sixty machines to the RAF's twenty-six, set against claims of 170 by the Germans and 185 by the British. More to the point, the Luftwaffe had, since 7 September, lost more than 200 aircraft, many of them bombers, and on 15 September were forced by the number of interceptions by the enemy to the conclusion that they could not achieve their aim.

Thus on 17 September, after two more days' intermission due to bad weather, Hitler was left with no other option than to agree with Raeder that the time to disperse ships and barges, which were suffering heavy losses in ports from British bombers, had come. Finally, on 12 October after Raeder had pointed out that oncoming winter weather precluded the operation, Hitler called off Sea Lion indefinitely, although he ordered that, for deception, preparations were to be simulated.

Following the brilliance of Weser Exercise, Plan Yellow and Plan Red, defeat in the Battle of Britain and the Sea Lion debacle were a shock, especially to Göring and his Luftwaffe generals whose incompetence was revealed all too clearly by post battle recriminations and a search for scapegoats. In fact, all that had really occurred was a demonstration, due to technical shortcomings, of the inherent falsity of Douhet's theory of the omnipotence of air power. Kesselring had foreseen this in 1937, when debunking a strategic bomber force, and the Army General Staff had guessed it prior to Dunkirk.

All at once it was realised that the war was by no means won (as Hitler continued to claim), and this was allied to a belief that Russia was a threat and Britain likely to be a growing menace with American material aid. Hitler, however, once more lacked a plausible plan of action. This was unthinkable since, like all popular revolutionaries, he never could afford to stand still. Of course there was in hand the quickly maturing plan to invade Russia in May 1941, but of immediate concern were signs of Britain becoming aggressive in the Mediterranean.

Again it was Raeder, backed by Jodl, who offered a quick solution. Already on 14 September 1940, the day after the Italians had launched a short-lived invasion of Egypt from Libya, he had tendered a scheme to provide German forces, including a panzer corps, to help the Italians exploit their advance. He had in mind a link-up with Vichy-French forces in Syria to virtually deny British access to the eastern Mediterranean and to cut off Middle East oil supplies. Complementary to this imaginative strategy was Hitler's Raeder-inspired request on 16 September for Spanish collaboration in the capture of Gibraltar. Yet, at the same time, Foreign Minister Ribbentrop was accidentally creating dissent with Mussolini by unilaterally projecting German influence into Romania and the Balkans in order to secure Germany's southern flank ahead of the Russian venture. Ironically, he discovered on 19 September that Mussolini had unilateral designs of his own on Greece – of which Hitler strongly disapproved.

Inexorably Germany was being drawn by both Britain and Italy into the attritional Mediterranean commitments which ran contrary to Hitler's aim of attacking Russia, and being eased into that diversion of effort by those like Raeder, Jodl and members of OKW and the Army General Staff who held reservations about the Russian venture. Yet paradoxically the latter seemed to accept the inevitablilty of conflict in the East, even though all dreaded another two-front war – especially as it became plainer that President Roosevelt was bent on allying the USA with Britain.

In these circumstances Hitler turned to the sycophants who would give him most comfort: to the inept Ribbentrop; to a diminishing extent to the tarnished but still powerful Göring; to the third-rate

Keitel; and, most of all in operational matters, to the brilliant Jodl whose breadth of vision, alloyed with unreserved admiration of his Führer's genius, enjoyed a relationship with the Head of State not so very different in some respects to those of a Moltke to a Kaiser. The trend lent credibility to Jodl's earlier prediction that, in modern tri-service war, the Army General Staff would forfeit its political power and influence to the pioneering Central Defence Staff he intended OKW to become.

CHAPTER 10

Multi-Front War: Into the Mediterranean and Balkans

History has been harsh on the military reputation of the convicted war criminal General Alfred Jodl, to some extent because he was true to the General Staff tradition of 'Perform well without being conspicuous'. A Bavarian gunner of very strong personality from a highly intellectual family, he drew close to Hitler when, in 1937 in collaboration with the vibrant Colonel Walter Warlimont, he bypassed Blomberg and Fritsch to persuade Hitler of the necessity for OKW. Hitler saw this new group as a useful tool for clipping the General Staff's wings.

As a result, Jodl became the Führer's principal, manipulative advisor, and probably tutor too, on military matters from 1938 onwards. Usually he was present during conferences with the Commanders-in-Chief. At mealtimes, until September 1942 whenever Hitler was at OKW, he had the wearisome privilege of sitting on the Führer's right hand listening to dreary and contradictory monologues. A brilliant staff officer of strong nerve, who never held high command, he saw his mission as that of all Chiefs of Staff – to serve loyally a master whom he regarded as a genius. He did this with similar devotion to Alan Brooke's in serving Churchill and George Marshall's in serving Roosevelt; except that, unlike them, he failed to put loyalty to his country's best interests first.

Unhappily, the taciturn, reserved and devious Jodl, whom Guderian rated 'a basically decent man', became conditioned and subserviently blinded to his master's criminal iniquities. Losing touch with realities at the front, in due course he ceased to be qualified either to give sound military advice or able to minimise Hitler's illegal excesses which only a few members of the old General Staff would have condoned.

Jodl was central to the reshaping of German strategy in the heady winter of 1940–41 when Hitler believed the Third Reich capable of any task he set it. While OKH concentrated on preparing the Russia

operation (what became known as Barbarossa) and deemed anything else a distraction inducing dangerous overstretch, Hitler and
Jodl, at the mercy of evolving events, struggled to formulate a
piecemeal Mediterranean strategy forced upon them by people and
events. After the Italian invasion of Egypt came to a standstill well
short of Mersa Matruh and the Italians declined German troops,
plans for German involvement in North Africa went into abeyance.
Operation Felix, the assault on Gibraltar, also entered limbo when
Franco procrastinated and gave the impression of wanting far more
than he would give.

In complex negotiations with Mussolini, Franco and Vichy-
France's Marshal Pétain, Hitler grew to pin more hopes on an active
alliance with France than with Spain, especially since the former had
been infuriated and close to declaring war on the British after their
attacks on French warships in July. Indeed, during discussions with
Ribbentrop, Admiral Jean Darlan, Pétain's anti-British deputy,
gave permission for the inclusion in January of an Abwehr mission
within the Axis Armistice Commission in Syria, tasked to establish a
German–Italian base to support the fermentation of unrest
throughout Iraq and Persia.

Things went into the melting pot when, without Hitler's approval,
Italy invaded Greece on 28 October 1940. It was the Führer's
intention to deal diplomatically with the politically volatile Balkans
through economic measures and power politics. That policy now
was threatened, and, to make matters worse, the single Italian army
corps committed by Musssolini ran into difficulties as much due to
poor leadership and inferior motivation as lack of numbers and poor
equipment. In next to no time it was thrown back into Albania
whence it had come. The debacle was aggravated by the British
garrisoning Crete, sending bombers to Greece and, on 11 November
at Taranto, sinking or crippling three battleships by torpedo bomber
attack.

Typically Hitler became prey to exaggerated fears – this time a
threat to the Romanian oilfields by British bombers based in Lem-
nos. Interest in Gibraltar persisted, even though Raeder pointed out
the difficulties of seizing the Rock and the likelihood that Operation
Felix would only partially place the Mediterranean under Axis
control. Felix, however, was doomed when African involvement
again raised its head on 9 December after a surprise raid by British
armoured forces smashed the Tenth Italian Army in Egypt. On 21

December Halder learnt that four Italian divisions were surrounded in Bardia and only three left in Libya. 'Distress call for German tanks!' he recorded with slight irony before taking Christmas leave.

Upon his return on 16 January 1941 it was to find that matters in Cyrenaica had gone from bad to worse. Bardia had fallen, Tobruk was surrounded. There were fears Italy might collapse. 'The war in North Africa need not bother us much,' he casually wrote. Adding, almost as an afterthought, 'It will be necessary to send some help ... the force must combine mobility with a certain amount of offensive strength.'

Immediately, it was decided to send the Afrika Korps, commanded by General Erwin Rommel, with a Light Division as advanced guard; not to be reinforced until April, as shipping and logistics permitted, by a panzer division. But Afrika Korps would arrive far too late to prevent the annihilation of Tenth Army at Beda Fomm on 5 February; and the lines of communication to North Africa never were safe, even though the Luftwaffe had sent an Air Corps to Sicily to curb the depradations of British naval and air forces based on Malta. Nevertheless, the pending arrival of Afrika Korps at the beginning of March fitted into Raeder's concept of a link-up with Vichy-governed Syria, via Egypt. At last his desire to dominate the eastern Mediterranean seemed within reach, even though Rommel was instructed by OKH to abstain from offensive action for the time being.

Gradually, as the German initiative was loosened, diverse personalities superimposed Raeder's strategy upon Hitler and OKW. Step by step Hitler and Jodl, by now thoroughly committed to Barbarossa, had to bend to circumstances in order to secure that immense operation's southern flank. Additional air defence units had to be sent to Ploesti to protect oilfields. Italy had to be saved from her indiscretions by massive help, at the same time as Yugoslavia was 'persuaded' to throw in her lot with the Axis. But the arrival of the vanguard of a British–Australian corps in Greece on 7 March and the overthrow of the Yugoslavian government on the 27th, by a British-assisted plot, only two days after it had agreed to join the Axis alliance, created a mighty diversion. It was destined to have a crucial impact on the war by completely undermining Hitler's Grand Strategy.

First to upset the apple cart was Rommel, whose initial probing of British positions on the Cyrenaican border on 24 March met such

feeble resistance that he felt impelled to pursue a rapidly withdrawing enemy. One minor success followed another as probing
burgeoned into an offensive at the will of Rommel's tactical genius
and thrusting leadership. Abruptly the British, whose forces had
been extensively weakened by dispersal to Greece and Italian East
Africa, collapsed. On 10 April light German forces were near the
Egyptian frontier and Rommel, almost out of supplies, was checked
in a rash attack on the Tobruk defences. Yet this unorthodox leader,
contrary to OKH orders, was almost half way to the Suez Canal, as
well as in the process of establishing a propaganda reputation which
Kesselring, for one, came to believe hypnotised Hitler.

Meanwhile the coup d'état on 27 March in Belgrade galvanised
an infuriated Hitler into ordering Operation Punishment, the conquest of Yugoslavia, in conjunction with Operation Marita, the
invasion of Greece, which OKH had long ago prepared in readiness for execution on 10 April. The staff at OKW reacted with tremendous speed. Within twelve hours of news of the coup, an
outline plan in Directive 25 was issued to OKH and OKL. Inevitably this unexpected task diverted attention and resources from
Barbarossa, which Hitler conceded had to be postponed for '... up
to four weeks'. Speed was thus of the essence and fairly easy to
achieve since many of the ten corps allocated already were posi-
tioned in neighbouring countries for Barbarossa. Field Marshals
Maximillian von Weichs (Second Army) and List (Twelfth Army)
were needed as the core of the Axis invasions of Yugoslavia and
Greece, and included Kleist's Panzer Group of two panzer corps,
plus 22nd Air Landing Division. General Löhr's Fourth Air Fleet,
with nearly 600 aircraft, which had to be assembled from Sicily and
Western Europe, managed to concentrate with incredible speed as
an outstanding example of the Luftwaffe's efficiency and air
power's flexibility.

With hindsight it is clear that the Germans overrated Yugoslavian
strength and committed more resources than necessary to Operation
Punishment. But the mountainous terrain was daunting; they did
not know that the Yugoslavs would try to fight in the valleys instead
of the hills; nor did they place much trust in their reluctant Italian
and Hungarian allies. Above all they were anxious to finish the task
quickly in order to be ready for Barbarossa no later than mid-June.

Additionally, however, there was a growing danger that Rommel
might put himself out on a limb by plunging impulsively into

Cyrenaica with a single division and with few reinforcements in prospect from the much overstretched Italians. Moreover there was much uncertainty about British strength and intentions because, once more, the quality of German intelligence was inadequate. Furthermore, as in May 1940, there were generals who worried in case Germany became overstretched and therefore unable to withstand any setback.

In the event, of course, both Punishment and Marita were unqualified successes. Crossing the frontiers on 6 April, the converging Axis columns overwhelmed the Yugoslavs by sheer speed and weight, augmented by two days' terror bombing of Belgrade. The surprised Yugoslav army disintegrated. Halder noted that Croat and Macedonian troops were throwing away their arms, leaving the Serbs alone to offer what little resistance there was. Without much trouble Kleist's Panzer Group, spearheading List's Army, cut swathes from Bulgaria to Skopje, having already severed Yugoslavia from Greece and threatened the right flank of the entrenched Greek army in Albania, prior to turning south to reach Thessaloniki on 9 April to complete the first phase of Marita.

This was the Wehrmacht at the peak of its professionalism being made to appear, through astute propaganda, invincible under the generalship of Hitler and OKW. Underlining its prowess, it drove contemptuously into Albania and deep into Greece with stunning results. For the Greeks, with the bulk of their army in Albania, had exhausted themselves by their victories over the demoralised and ill-equipped Italians. Consequently the troops allocated to fight alongside the British corps in defence of central Greece had neither the strength nor mobility to check for long the well-drilled German combat teams.

The few crises that confronted OKH were usually manufactured by Hitler and OKW rather than by the enemy. Halder's diary (which mentions a protest from List about a Wehrmacht communiqué biased in the Lufwaffe's favour, 'which fails to do full justice to the achievements of the ground forces and the honour of the attacking troops') is the familiar recitation of his and Brauchitsch's objections to intolerable interference in operations by the Führer; and 'blasted squabbling' with Göring and OKL. But neither List, Weichs nor their corps commanders worried to the same extent as had some senior officers in France the previous year. So Halder, who, like Brauchitsch, frequently visited or flew over the combat zones, purred with contentment at the way senior army commanders' plans largely coincided with OKH's ideas.

The advance into central Greece proceeded smoothly to schedule. Only the British and Anzac troops offered strong resistance in a withdrawal forced on them by the encirclement and collapse of the Greeks. Successive lines of Allied resistance were overcome without undue trouble or loss to Germans infiltrating southwards through the mountains and valleys. Delaying too long their retreat from Albania, the surrounded Greek First Army was forced to surrender on 23 April after fierce fighting. Realising the hopelessness of the situation on 21 April, the Greek Commander-in-Chief had advised the British to evacuate while the going was good. Henceforward the Germans faced only a series of rearguard, delaying positions. Meanwhile the Luftwaffe did what it could to destroy shipping; but an attempt by its parachute troops on 26 April to seize the vital bridge over the Corinth Canal in order to cut off the British rear-guard was thwarted. As a result, once more, the British conducted a partially successful evacuation, though leaving much equipment behind.

The Germans could take much pride in their speedy conquests of Yugoslavia and Greece, even though they had been confronted largely by outclassed forces. So it is interesting, though hardly surprising, that at the moment of triumph the tone of Halder's diary is much more concerned for the future. Correctly he concentrated on the restoration of Barbarossa to full strength and the application of damage measures in connection with the peripheral operations in North Africa, Syria, Iraq and Crete, of which only North Africa was under OKH control.

For good reasons Halder had little confidence in the mercurial Rommel who, by General Staff standards, was rated second class. An officer with a splendid combat record in World War I, he had been turned down for staff training as unsuitable; and, on his own admission, was unhappy in staff appointments. Halder boiled over on 24 April when studying reports and a private letter from North Africa showing that '... Rommel is not up to his operational task. All day long he rushes about between the widely scattered units and stages reconnaissance raids in which he fritters away his forces. No one has a clear picture of their disposition and striking power.... The piecemeal thrust of weak armoured forces has been costly ... his motor vehicles are in poor condition.... Many of his tank engines need replacing. Air transport cannot meet his senseless demands, primarily from lack of fuel.' More in a similar vein indicated that in desert warfare quartermasters tended to rule and Rommel was no great logistician. Nor, he might have added, much of a diplomat with the Italians, whose theatre of war it was and who, like other German officers, he despised and bullied mercilessly.

Momentarily Halder considered flying in person to read the riot act, but instead sent General Friedrich Paulus, Deputy Chief of the General Staff, who had good personal relations with Rommel in days past when they had served together, observing: 'He is perhaps the only man with enough personal influence to head off this soldier gone stark mad.'

Paulus, an infantryman of country stock from Hesse who had commanded a mechanised battalion in 1934; was a disciple of Guderian. He was a brilliant staff officer with a passion for war-games and operational planning who, nevertheless, had once been described in a report as lacking in decisiveness. Halder valued him highly and made him responsible for planning Barbarossa. So before he arrived at Tobruk on 27 April he already had a vested interest in minimising the North Africa digression. Instantly he vetoed another attack on Tobruk scheduled for 30 April and put Rommel in the big picture. Rommel demurred. Elements of 15th Panzer Division and more supplies had arrived. By force of personality he managed to persuade Paulus to change his mind. The attack, monitored by Paulus, laid bare Afrika Korps' limitations in positional warfare. Inadequate training, poor morale, insufficient resources and stiff British resistance among minefields and artillery fire brought it to a halt on 1 May. These two generals of destiny now agreed that it would be several months before a renewal of offensive action would be possible.

Paulus returned to Berlin to report concern that the 'headstrong' Rommel might draw Germany into a campaign she could ill-afford when Barbarossa was pending. He also severely criticised Rommel's tactics and logistic management and recommended the appointment of strong-minded General Staff officers who would curb and steer him into safer channels.

At this very moment, however, other strong-minded leaders were propelling the Wehrmacht into commitments every bit as consuming as the North African sideshow. Ribbentrop's Foreign Ministry had obtained Luftwaffe support for the transport of 'tourists' and materials to Syria with a view to supporting Iraq in the ejection of the occupying British. Unwillingly Göring complied, but with little more than minimum transport aircraft since he too was bent on a diversionary operation which, like Ribbentrop's, fitted the Raeder–Jodl strategy through domination of the eastern Mediterranean.

During the Balkan campaign Jodl asked Warlimont to study, within the context of Mediterranean strategy, the pros and cons of invading either Malta or Crete. Warlimont and all the officers of OKW – Army, Navy and Luftwaffe – plumped solidly for Malta. But before Jodl had even seen their appreciation, Hitler had decided in favour of Crete as the result of a proposal by General Student to Löhr, commander of Fourth Air Fleet. He now commanded XI Air Corps (Parachute and Airborne Troops) and had first considered an airborne assault on the island in March; but whether or not he was aware of the OKW study or they of his is unclear. Together with Löhr, Student enthused both Göring and Hitler who, on 21 April, gave instant approval for an airborne assault on the island on 16 May. The Führer recognised the merits of seizing Crete, not only as a base and stepping-stone for control of the eastern Mediterranean and Middle East, but also to eliminate the threat to Romania from British air bases. His one stipulation was that the operation should be completed rapidly, presumably with a view to early intervention in Syria and Iraq, and in the interests of Barbarossa for which airborne troops would be needed.

Without consulting OKH, OKW allocated Operation Mercury to the Luftwaffe, although OKH heard about it indirectly on 22 April. The concentration on ten airfields of the 650 bombers and fighters in Richthofen's VIII Air Corps along with Student's 502 Ju52s and eighty-five gliders was relatively simple in comparison with the problem of planning. With so little time and the faulty information available about the enemy, this was little more than guesswork which underestimated British strength by a factor of four. Moreover it was unfortunate that the experienced 22nd Air Landing Division had to be replaced by the 5th Mountain Division because the former was inextricably deployed in Bulgaria. But Student reckoned the elite 7th Parachute Division would more than cope even if, as he correctly anticipated, the enemy chose to resist strongly.

On the assumption that the British would expect an airborne assault but would be unsure where, he decided, contrary to the Principle of Concentration, to seize three low-grade air strips

(Maleme, Heraklion and Retimo) instead of one; and also to land at Canea, where he thought the British reserve might be, and thus gain control of Suda Bay. The initial assault would be by parachute and glider, reinforced later by ferrying in by Ju52 the mountain division and supplies. As a supplement, and, on Hitler's sound insistence, tanks, heavy weapons, infantry and logistic support would be delivered by sea in caiques at night. It was a risky scheme which depended on boldness, surprise and considerable luck.

Unfortunately for the Germans, surprise was forfeited. The intense radio traffic associated with the concentration of forces and the planning of Mercury was well-monitored by the British Y Service and read by Ultra. By 17 May General Bernard Freyberg, British commander of Crete, was fully aware of the German objectives which were as strongly garrisoned as possible. In consequence the first waves of airborne troops dropped into a storm of fire from entrenched defenders. Few aircraft were lost, but many parachutists were scattered away from their objectives. To make matters worse, Ju52s returning to Greece for the next wave found chaotic conditions on the airfields. There were numerous crashes and subsquent delays which meant that the second wave arrived over Crete after the supporting bombers and fighters had departed.

Of the 8,000 troops delivered barely half had reached their objectives and only at Maleme was there a foothold. Disaster awaited the caique convoys too. They were intercepted by the Royal Navy which sank at least twelve and drove them back into port where they stayed for the remainder of the battle. On the first evening, therefore, Student had achieved virtually nothing and was counselled by those at Fourth Air Fleet who thought Mercury should be abandoned. This might have been inevitable if only Freyberg had taken a firm grip on the battle by launching counter-attacks which could hardly have failed. As it was troops holding vital ground commanding Maleme were withdrawn during the night when the courageously determined Student was deciding to persevere by concentrating on reinforcement of a tenuous success at Maleme.

Five days later it was clear that boldness had won the battle for the Germans. The British were retreating and, at heavy cost to the Royal Navy, being evacuated, leaving 13,000 men behind. But the cost to the Germans was not only high but also crucial. Some 170

Ju52s were either destroyed or badly damaged. About 4,500 out of 15,700 airborne troops were killed or missing, including a very high proportion of officers. More important, after the battle Hitler pontificated to Student that airborne troops had no future because the surprise factor, upon which they depended, had been lost. Time would reveal this as just another example of how wrong his intuitions could be.

If, on the other hand, Hitler had foreseen that Crete was the last of his absolute conquests, he might have been far more shattered than Student was. As it was, domination of the eastern Mediterranean and the Raeder strategy also was on its last legs for the time being. For although Rashid Ali's coup in Iraq on 3 April had succeeded and, on the 5th, the Axis agreed to supply him via Syria, it was the 17th before he actually appealed for help; and 30 April before, pressed by his generals, he took armed action against the British.

By then preparations for Crete and Barbarossa were in full spate, delaying a positive German response until 6 May, when Vichy gave belated permission for the delivery by rail of French arms to the Iraqis and use of a base in Syria. But the quantity of aid was never very large and quite insufficient to match even the relatively small-scale British land and air operations which overran the country and captured Baghdad on 30 May; by which time fuel shortage in a land rich with oil had crippled Axis air support. Yet next day, with a repeat of the last-gasp-stand formula initiated in connection with the Narvik Group in April 1940, Hitler called for a last-minute stand in Baghdad until relief supplies could be sent; a fantasy which was ignored by Foreign Ministry and Luftwaffe officers on the spot. On 1 June they withdrew and, in agreement with the Italians, concluded it was impossible to give further military support to Iraq.

This debacle left Vichy-governed Syria exposed at the very moment when the British, urged on by General Catroux of the Free French Forces, were assembling meagre forces for an invasion before German proposals (as indicated by Ultra) to reinforce the country could be implemented. Naturally the cessation of hostilities in Iraq assisted the British, as did the absence of Germans in any number. Yet, when they launched their attack on 8 June, the French put up such strong and prolonged resistance that their enemies were extremely relieved to learn, again via Ultra, that Vichy had banned any German participation, though it continued to request German support in the transport of reinforcements and material. With the fall of Damascus on 21 June the campaign was collapsing, though the Abwehr continued in residence until 4 July, pleading to the last for help which never appeared.

The pre-Barbarossa Mediterranean strategy was dead, the last nails in its coffin hammered home by British attacks on the Axis forces in Cyrenaica in May and June, which, although failing to achieve their aim by the relief of Tobruk, put an end to any renewal of aggression by Rommel in the near future. Moreover, this was just five days before the Wehrmacht struck Russia with nearly, but not quite, all the forces at its disposal.

The multi-front war thus created was of greater dimensions and further-reaching effect than even the sternest opponents of a two-front war had dreaded. For already, before Barbarossa created the vast Eastern Front, the Wehrmacht and the weakened Italian forces were too widely dispersed to hold down increasingly hostile possessions elsewhere.

In the West the Army stood guard on the coast and in the hinterland, while the German Navy demanded more air and logistic support for the Battle of the Atlantic and coastal defence. Meanwhile raiding by the Royal Air Force gradually mounted in intensity (if not accuracy) sufficient to force Göring to augment the defences, especially of Germany itself. To these commitments had now to be added anti-guerrilla warfare in Yugoslavia which, though as yet on a small scale, started under Josip Broz (later known as Tito) almost as soon as the main campaign ended. This fiery struggle would gradually spread thoughout the Balkans and would grow ever more bitter due to the savagery of the SS and the Army in its suppression.

At the same time too, of course, there was the land, sea and air struggle for North Africa which, notwithstanding OKH's desire to limit it for the time being, continued (owing to an abortive British attempt to recapture Tobruk in mid-June) to consume Axis effort, because of the vital necessity to prop up Italy.

These were the inevitable penalties of an unco-ordinated strategy, for which the squabbling hierarchies of OKW, OKH, OKM and OKL, due to their unwillingness to co-operate among themselves in the pursuit of a common aim, were as much to blame as Hitler. Indeed, underlying almost every aspect of this already overstretched and unstable structure were the familiar deadly sins of generals and admirals who had forgotten that, more than once in the past, their over-confidence and arrogance had fermented the excesses which led to Germany's downfall.

CHAPTER 11

Barbarossa and Degeneration

In a sealed railway train restaurant car on 29 July 1940, Jodl called a meeting of Warlimont and the three other most senior OKW staff officers to announce, without preamble, that Hitler had decided 'once and for all' to rid the world of Bolshevism by a surprise attack on Soviet Russia. To Warlimont the effect of his words was 'electric' – though why they should have been is also surprising since, at various moments during the past month or so, Hitler had mentioned the matter to a few senior officers including Jodl. The staff might have been even more astonished had they known that, to begin with, the ever impatient Führer had wanted to launch the invasion towards the end of that summer, but had been dissuaded from this lunacy by Keitel and Jodl with reasoned arguments of time, space and weather difficulties. This caused him to settle for May 1941.

Warlimont recalled the chorus of objections to Hitler's concept that, by knocking out Russia, Britain would then be brought to terms without an invasion. And although Jodl parried their protests, there is no doubt he too was worried – hence his subsequent strong support for Sea Lion, and efforts, in conjunction with Raeder, to undermine Britain by the Mediterranean strategy (see Chapter 10 above).

Unlike Jodl and the OKW staff, however, Brauchitsch and Halder were not nearly so concerned about the prospects of the operation which would be called Barbarossa. Not until the end of June 1940 did they learn from the Foreign Ministry that Hitler had his eye on Russia. Already, however, on 18 June before the end in France, Halder was a step ahead of Hitler when setting up under Major Reinhard Gehlen an Eastern Front Study Group. A week later he transferred Guderian's Panzer Group HQ to the East with panzer and mechanised divisions under command as a mobile striking force, as a precaution against Russian hostilities.

Already Halder was concerned at Russian military activity in the

Baltic states, Bessarabia and Bukhovina. For this reason, he formed additional General Staff groups to study 'how to deliver a military blow at Russia that will force her to recognise Germany's dominant role in Europe.' What he had in mind was, in effect, a preventative war should Russia show positive signs of aggressive intent. It seemed to him that it was well within Germany's capability to win such a war at this moment of supreme strength. It was therefore all the more desirable that it should occur at the earliest possible moment before her extremely anxious enemies and neighbours grew too strong.

Unfortunately the assessment of Russian strength by the Eastern Front General Staff Study Groups suffered from a fundamental weakness: the quality of intelligence available was characteristically and inevitably poor. As Clausewitz once wrote: 'The greater part of the information obtained in war is contradictory, a still greater part is false, and by far the greatest part is of doubtful character.' Even in peace the highly secretive Russia of Joseph Stalin was a most diffi-cult target for intelligence gathering by Germany, despite its enjoying, since the Treaty of Rapallo in 1922, a better relationship with Russia than other nations did.

In any case, since Soviet Russia was not a primary target in 1940, little effort had been allocated by the General Staff and Abwehr to the evaluation of the Red Army. Furthermore and to make matters worse, Lieutenant Colonel Eberhardt Kinzel, who ran the Foreign Armies East desk, not only was responsible for the armies of Scandinavia, some Balkan countries, China, Japan and the United States of America, besides the USSR, but also had little knowledge of the Soviet Union and could not speak Russian. It was scarcely surprising therefore that Kinzel was caught on the hop and pro-duced what turned out to be a gross underestimate of Russian strength and a false notion of Soviet will and capability. This assessment bolstered Halder's optimism, but, nevertheless, he told his wife that he '. . . trembled inwardly at the scale of events.' Kinzel's assessment may well have contributed to Hitler's low, and by no means false, opinion of the Slavic people's and Soviet regime's schisms when he remarked '. . . one good kick at the door will bring down the whole rotten structure'.

Moreover, regardless of this misinterpretation of Russian strength, Hitler and the entire German High Command should have been aware that, for so vast an enterprise as Barbarossa, they were projecting beyond the Reich's logistic capability, even though its manpower and industrial base had been enormously broadened by the conquest of Western Europe. Germany had yet to mobilise for Total War as waged by Ludendorff in World War I. In 1940 and, indeed, well into the future, her resources and production fell far short of the most modest estimates of requirements for a campaign lasting the mere ten weeks blithely assumed necessary for its completion. In any event it was folly to enter the vast Russian expanse. To do so with only three months' fuel reserves and variable shortages of other equipment and stores was imprudent to say the least; yet it was a product of inherited Teutonic arrogance and stupidity when dealing with eastern peoples.

The day Jodl was making his clandestine announcement to his staff, General Erich Marcks lunched with Halder and was briefed to prepare a report on an invasion of Russia. On 1 August he presented an outline of organisations and logistic requirements, proposing that one Operational Group should advance from Romania, south of the Pripet Marshes, to Kiev, and another should advance on Moscow. This scheme happened to coincide with Hitler's initial ideas but was rejected by Halder because he judged that Romania was 'insecure political ground'. Instead he wanted the principal effort aimed at Moscow, flanked by two subsidiary thrusts through the Baltic, towards Leningrad, and from Ukraine to Kiev.

Halder's concept, developed during intensive OKH war-gaming and internal debates throughout the autumn, was to be the basis of Barbarossa. Inevitably there was much chopping, changing and adjustment, along with dilution, as Hitler and OKW interfered and the Mediterranean involvement took its toll. Furthermore Grand Strategic doubts began to emerge when the Military Attaché in Moscow expressed concern about the feasibility of a decisive short campaign; and the War Mapping and Survey Branch confirmed this by pointing out the necesssity of making the Caucasus an objective – as Hitler wanted and Halder had set aside. Then came a Marcks follow-up study prophesying an Anglo-Russian-American alliance unless the campaign was over in 1941.

OKW became more deeply involved in September when Jodl asked Warlimont to prepare a study of 'the basic factors governing an operation against Russia. ... merely to familiarise him with the geographical and other military conditions before the Army leaders [who thus far had ignored him] presented their proposals to Hitler'.

It also was meant, as Jodl later testified at Nürnberg, to help 'carry out the staff work necessary to put Hitler's decisions into the proper military form to be used by the entire Wehrmacht machine'. This demonstrated, as Warlimont remarked, that the Supreme Headquarters in no way measured up to the requirements of real strategic direction (most of which was purely Army business) at a time when it was increasingly and directly engaged in a war of two fronts. When, for example, Warlimont pointed out that there was a fuel problem, all OKW did was issue instructions severely restricting the consumption of fuel prior to the start of major operations. This made a mockery of constructive planning.

Warlimont's study, which was not completed until 16 December 1940, turned out to be very similar to OKH's concept except that it placed greater emphasis on clearing the Baltic states. Meanwhile OKH's plan had been exhaustively war-gamed under Paulus's direction between 28 November and 3 December. Consequently, when Brauchitsch and Halder presented it to Hitler on 5 December, he approved it unconditionally, although he took the opportunity to patronise the professional heads of the Army. He scoffed at Halder's belief in traditional Russian sensitivity to the Smolensk–Moscow route, as fit only for 'ossified brains'; he deemed Moscow 'not so very important', and preferred the encirclement of the Baltic states, saying dismissively, 'Cut off the Baltic area! The rest can be done by Landwehr divisions'; and he announced Libya was 'no longer contemplated'.

These comments were registered by Warlimont who slavishly complied with his Führer's preference for concentration on the Baltic states and deferment of action against Moscow. As a result, OKW's Directive No. 21, when issued on 18 December, '... at the stroke of a pen', as Warlimont wrote after the war, changed Halder's concept, '... which the OKH had worked out as a result of months of painstaking examination and cross-checking from all angles by the best military brains available'.

It was Directive No. 21, therefore, which the Wehrmacht's top men discussed at two big conferences on 9 January and 5 February 1941. Then Hitler laid down the priorities of a strategy which must have made Clausewitz turn in his grave. There was to be no doctrinaire concentration on destruction of the enemy forces before all else, as studiously reflected in Halder's concept. Instead there were several aims couched to satisfy many purposes: a mishmash which would lie at the root of much undesirable confusion and fatal squabbling in the future. Now there were several equally vital missions: '... cutting off the Baltic area, annihilation of the Russian army, seizure of the most important industrial reasons, and destruction of the other industrial areas'.

Meanwhile the German government was engaged in large-scale deception measures in support of Barbarossa. These included the air attacks against Britain as an element of the Sea Lion cover plan; the positioning of troops for Felix and Marita as part of the strengthening of the Southern Front, but which the British interpreted only as a threat to themselves; the artifice that troop concentrations in the East were for training purposes only; and diplomatic subterfuge in pledges of friendship, linked to continuation of commerce with Russia, to prove that Germany had no designs on her intended victim. Amazingly this duplicity was largely successful, despite increasing evidence from many sources which gradually persuaded the British that Russia, not Britain, was the next major German target.

By no means every German senior officer was as sanguine as Jodl, Brauchitsch and Halder about Barbarossa's prospects, however. As the circle of those-in-the-know widened the number of apprehensive generals increased. There was a run on Caulaincourt's *Memoirs* (published in German in 1937) describing Napoleon's advance on Moscow in 1812. The fate of that campaign was hardly encouraging; nor, they might reflect, could their army even be compared with Napoleon's Grand Army since it comprised but few allies dedicated to the common cause.

Guderian, whose Panzer Group was to spearhead the drive on Moscow in Army Group Centre, was typically outspoken. He had bought a copy of Caulaincourt's *Memoirs* before the war, had heard about Barbarossa in November and possessed special knowledge about the Red Army. He hit the nail on the head when tendering his criticism to Halder through staff channels. 'Three army groups, each of approximately the same strength, were to attack diverging objectives; no single clear operational objective seemed to be envisaged.' Needless to say, he like most generals dreaded a two-front war.

Almost equally disturbing to Guderian was Soviet tank strength which, in *Achtung! Panzer!* in 1937 he had authoritatively put at 10,000 and now must be at least 17,000 – which also was quite

accurate. Against this number there were a mere 3,200 German
tanks plus 200 self-propelled guns, which, admittedly, were superior
to some 15,000 of the obsolete Russian machines (as General Wilhelm von Thoma confirmed to Halder), but very inferior to the latest
1,500 KV1 heavy and T34 mediums, of which the Germans were in
ignorance but the existence of which Guderian already suspected.

Field Marshal Milch and the entire top Luftwaffe staff were
against Barbarossa and strongly supported Göring who tried, in
vain, to dissuade Hitler. Kesselring, who at that time was conducting
the air war against England and was to command Second Air Fleet
in support of Army Group Centre, harboured reservations and,
right from the start, confronted Göring with a demand for additional resources – in which he was supported by 'my old friend
Jeschonnek'. He got his way after a struggle, but already it was plain
that the requirements of other fronts were overtaxing resources and
that work on the logistic base was behindhand, even though 'the
date proposed for the attack was pretty late'. At the same time he
was aware of the 'extravagant factory and armament programme' in
Russia and therefore shared Hitler's opinion that 'the Russians
would seize the first opportunity to attack us'. In due course, he too
would deprecate the Mediterranean diversions, in particular the
attack on Crete with its heavy losses of aircraft and ruination of the
parachute division.

No matter what apologists have said to the contrary, there is no
doubt that the month's delay inflicted by the Balkans campaign had
a damaging effect on Barbarossa, not only because it subtracted
resources but also because that much fine weather with good going
was wasted. Of course, within Halder's estimate of a ten-week
campaign, that did not matter, except that all generals worth their
salt should make allowance, if possible, for frictions, errors, surprise, contingencies and set-backs.

Against the background of events in the Balkans and Mediterranean, Barbarossa approached fulfilment against an enemy
whose Dictator, Joseph Stalin, steadfastly refused to admit the virtual certainty of attack. Evidence of the vast build-up of German
forces between the Baltic and the Black Sea was no more possible to
conceal or reject than the frequent flights by German reconnaissance
aircraft in Russian air space, or the spate of intelligence from diplomatic sources and clandestine agents. Among the many warnings
provided, those by Britain were the most authoritative, and all the

more so since their leaders continued to think they were next on the list for invasion. The truth dawned on 28 March 1941, when a report of German reactions to the Yugoslavian coup d'état revealed that a hitherto unimaginable event was imminent.

In a message to Stalin on 3 April (carefully guarded to conceal the existence of Ultra) Churchill spelled it out: 'I have sure information from a trusted agent that when the Germans thought they had got Yugoslavia in the net, that is to say after March 20, they began to move three out of the five Panzer divisions from Roumania to southern Poland. The moment they heard of the Serbian revolution this movement was countermanded. Your Excellency will readily appreciate the significance of these facts.'

Yet, despite this message and a mass of confirmatory reports from innumerable sources in the coming weeks, Stalin refused to change his stance until 21 June – when it was far too late to disseminate warnings in time for adequate defensive measures.

On 30 March Hitler summoned his 250 most senior commanders and staff officers of all three Services for a two-and-a-half-hour harangue on lines similar to those preceding the Polish and Western Europe campaigns. Except that on this occasion he lectured a completely silent and shocked audience on the need, since Communism was such a danger to the future, for the waging of an ideological war. Halder took notes of what his Supreme Commander said: 'This is a war of extermination ... of the Bolshevist commissars and of the Communist intelligentsia.... Formation of a new intellectual class must be prevented.... This is no job for military courts. The individual troop commanders must know the issues at stake.... This need not mean that the troops should get out of hand. Rather, the commander must give orders which express the common feelings of his men.' Thereupon, prior to writing 'All invited to lunch', Halder added the reminder: '*Embody in ObdH order*. This war will be very different from the war in the west. In the east, harshness today means lenience in the future. Commanders must make the sacrifice of overcoming their personal scruples.'

It is among the myths of World War II that many generals expressed resentment and dissent and that the Army was excused from shooting commissars, who were to be left to the mercies of Himmler's organisations. Some did protest to the cowed Brauchitsch, who chose not to transmit this to Hitler. In May Halder did send a draft OKH order embodying Hitler's policy to OKW which was not, as sometimes suggested, withdrawn. Moreover, Hitler's instructions of 31 March said, in effect, that in dealing with 'hostile inhabitants', the German soldier need not be bound by the letter of the laws of war or of disciplinary instructions; he could deal with any attack against the Wehrmacht '… with the utmost severity, including summary execution without court-martial procedure'.

It is another myth, therefore, that only the Waffen SS (and not the Wehrmacht) committed barbaric and criminal acts in the war zone. Some Army commanders watered down or ignored criminal orders, but many did not. Consequently the struggle which began on 22 June was to be fought with a pitilessness of almost unprecedented barbarity. Not even the Knights of the Teutonic Order and their followers in the Middle Ages sank to such depths as did the anti-Bolshevik Wehrmacht of 1941.

*   *   *

An hour after first light on Sunday 22 June the first wave of aircraft from the 2,770 belonging to the four Air Fleets allocated to Barbarossa climbed to maximum altitude on course to attack Russian airfields. In the crucial central sector Kesselring wanted to attack before daylight but had been forbidden by Bock to do so because the sound of so many engines would alert the enemy to the Army Group Centre's stealthy approach to the frontier. Neither need have worried.

When the bombers struck it was to find 'Row after row of reconnaissance planes, bombers and fighters lined up as if on parade.' The Germans were not to know, however, that poor serviceability and spares shortage grounded many obsolete machines, and that crews were sleeping off Saturday night revelries. On scores of airfields the mostly unopposed Germans wreaked havoc. At the end of the day, for the loss of only thirty-five German aircraft, 322 Russian machines had been shot down and 1,489 smashed on the ground. From this blow the Red Air Force would never fully recover, which disaster now enabled the Luftwaffe to give almost undistracted support to their Army.

The Red Army also was totally surprised as, from the Baltic coast to the Black Sea, Army Groups North, Centre and South advanced with the help of Abwehr-sponsored anti-Communist Lithuanians and Ukrainians, whose principal task was to wreck communications tentacles and centres. Here and there Russian troops resisted fiercely. But there was little co-ordination and a great many troops, along with many unserviceable tanks and guns, were rounded up in barracks.

The state of the Russian tanks epitomised the Red Army's poor condition that day. On average only twenty-seven per cent were fit, the remainder either in unit or second line workshops, often awaiting spares. These never got into action. Of those that did the vast majority were unequal tactically or technically to the experienced Germans who took a heavy toll. Most serious of all was the fate of the new and excellent KV1s and T34s, many lacking ammunition, and whose crews were as yet insufficiently trained. How effective these might have been if used properly was soon revealed by the few which did operate. They demonstrated the quality of their armour and deadliness of their 76mm gun; a combination which outmatched every German tank and almost every field gun, including, in the case of the KV1, the 88mm.

Coming into action piecemeal and, for the most part, with only twenty-four hours' fuel and ammunition in their supply echelons, units of the Red Army were offered up like sacrificial lambs. Vehicles ran out of fuel. Tanks ended their life as pill boxes. Entire divisions, caught out of position by air and ground attacks, were annihilated within the first twenty-four hours. With the Wehrmacht at the peak of its form (though with units, for the last time, at full establishment), the generals were in their element and brimful of confidence as they outmanoeuvred an outclassed opponent. At the end of a briefing by Paulus on 23 June, Brauchitsch asked how long the campaign might last. Paulus replied, after brief consideration, 'I think six to eight weeks, sir.' At which the Commander-in-Chief had nodded: 'Yes, Paulus, you may be right.'

On the left flank of the main thrust by Army Group Centre towards Smolensk, Hoepner's Panzer Group 4, which answered direct to Leeb's Army Group North (instead of being subordinated to either of the two infantry armies, as had been the practice in France) shattered the frontier defences and forged ahead. Its progress was only locally checked the following day when Russian armoured forces tried to counter-attack but were brushed aside and destroyed piece by piece. By 29 June this remorseless process of elimination inflicted ninety per cent Russian tank losses, due as much to mechanical breakdown as combat.

Riga was encircled after ten days in an advance of 155 miles.

Behind the spearheads lay ruined Russian divisions trapped in pockets and being mopped up by the slow infantry formations in co-operation with the fast mechanised formations they were tasked to supply and maintain. Often the fighting was fierce. Yet German losses were remarkably small, despite characteristic determination to sustain rapid momentum, often regardless of risks.

Nevertheless the appearance on this front of KV1 tanks, which proved extremely difficult to knock out, induced panic in some units – as it would elsewhere. Major J.A. von Kielmansegg, chief staff officer of 6th Panzer Division, detected signs of panic and danger of a serious defeat – 'one of the heaviest strains I ever experienced during the war'. It was mastered, he said, 'only by the attitude and discipline of the officers'. He might have added that another great help was the commitment of the clumsy 10cm gun well forward, in the anti-tank role, which proved a useful back-up for 88mm dual-purpose guns which sometimes failed to defeat the KV1's frontal armour. Yet 6th Panzer did manage, unaided in three days, to encircle and destroy 200 Russian tanks with barely a dozen casualties, except among some infantry which had been cut off, killed and mutilated.

Rundstedt's Army Group South, on the right flank, also made good progress on 22 June as it headed for Dubno and Kiev. In the lead on a narrow frontage, after the frontier defences had been overrun by two infantry divisions, was III Panzer Corps (from Kleist's Panzer Group 1) with two panzer and two motorised divisions and one of infantry. Typically, the Russians, lacking sound intelligence and communications, failed to co-ordinate their efforts when they began to counter-attack next day. Consequently they were either ambushed or split asunder and enmeshed. Within two days 267 Russian tanks and enormous quantities of men had been captured. And here too, as in the north, atrocities by the Russians were reported.

Kleist had not forgotten the lessons of France. No halts to let the infantry catch up this time, even though threats to his flanks were no less severe than in 1940. Rapidly General Eberhard von Mackensen's III Panzer Corps outstripped the marching infantry of Sixth, Seventeenth and Eleventh Armies and the Hungarian and Romanian troops following on. By 10 July he was 70 miles ahead of the marching infantry and had reached the outskirts of Kiev. At this point, to his and Rundstedt's surprise, he was stopped by a detailed

Hitler Order prior to helping the Eleventh Army encircle a small enemy pocket. Rundstedt, in the presence of Brauchitsch, rejected this after an analysis which showed there were richer pickings further East. Brauchitsch agreed, but was unwilling '... to make a decision that would not have the Führer's approval'. As now was routine, he left Halder (successfully on this occasion) to change Hitler's mind, after an hour's delay since Keitel had difficulty awakening the Supreme Commander and bringing him to the telephone.

Everybody was delighted with the outcome because the better part of three Russian armies were surrounded on 7 August by the other two panzer corps of Panzer Group 1, supported by Eleventh and Seventeenth Armies. But the incident not only highlighted once more Hitler's habit of abandoning proven General Staff methods (by handing down detailed orders instead of giving outline instructions), but also the Commander in-Chief's emasculation. By now Brauchitsch was virtually redundant, a mere shadow who left Halder to argue all the difficult matters with Hitler, Keitel and Jodl at OKW. Such was the Commander-in-Chief's decline in morale that his replacement, perhaps when the campaign ended in a few weeks' time, was now mooted.

This swift conclusion seemed more than ever likely, especially when the matter was viewed in the context of events on the front of Bock's exceptionally strong Army Group Centre. Parallel thrusts by General Adolf Strauss's Ninth Army from East Prussia, on the northern flank, and Field Marshal Günther von Kluge's Fourth Army from Brest Litovsk, on the southern flank, were to charge eastwards before turning inwards to meet at Minsk and form a pocket bulging with routed Russians. Or so Halder ordered, even though Bock had called, unsuccessfully, for a much more ambitious closing of the pincers at Smolensk. Both Armies were led from the start by Panzer Groups: Hoth's No. 3 of four panzer and three motorised infantry divisions in Ninth Army, and Guderian's No. 2 of five panzer and three motorised, plus the horsed cavalry division, with Fourth Army. They were supported by some 1,000 aircraft from Kesselring's Second Air Fleet.

The Panzer Groups led the crossing of the frontier and each made almost exactly the progress estimated in war-games. Hoth reached Minsk on 26 June and Guderian joined him on the 27th to seal the fate of the bulk of three Russian armies, including some 290,000 men, 2,500 tanks and 1,500 guns. Second Army took until 8 July to swallow these, leaving Ninth and Fourth Panzer Army (renamed on 28 June), headed by their Panzer Groups, to resume the advance on Smolensk on 1 July. By then Hoth and Guderian had held a co-ordinating conference to ensure close co-operation, regardless of what their Army Commanders asked for. Risks, they agreed, were warranted because of the magnitude of the prize. And indeed it was Guderian's crossing of the River Dnieper without great difficulty on 10 July (after overcoming Kluge's heated objections and his sour comment, 'Your operations always hang on a thread'), which prompted Halder, on the basis of what appeared to be reliable intelligence from Russian sources, to crow that, to all intents and purposes, the campaign was won. Guderian reached Smolensk on 17 July, nearly 400 miles beyond the starting point. This time he was just ahead of Hoth, forming another enormous, though, as events would show, leaky pocket teeming with Russians.

This was victory, on time, on a massive scale: an event which, in accordance with the Barbarossa plan, should smash the Red Army beyond repair. But, quite apart from the fact that the enemy continued to resist and counter-attack with desperation, multiple frictions were mounting within the Wehrmacht, and they were not only to do with strategy and what to do next. For also arising were problems of logistics, politics and morale, which would shape future strategy and take their toll.

Because the Wehrmacht, and the Army chiefly, launched Barbarossa on the assumption that the campaign would be won in little more than ten weeks the General Staff's logisticians planned on that basis. This meant that, from September onwards, certain commodities and equipment (such as fuel, spare parts and winter clothing) might only be available on a hand-to-mouth basis. Shortages would be exacerbated by delays and difficulties on the lines of communication, many of which actually had been foreseen.

For one thing there was traffic indiscipline, such as the choking of main supply routes by the unauthorised movement of Luftwaffe transport. For another, it was found that roads and tracks were even worse than expected, prone to collapse under heavy vehicles and conversion to quagmires when it rained. Moreover, because the Russian maps were out-of-date and unreliable, route finding was often haphazard. Due to these combined factors, staff estimates of fuel consumption proved too low, wear and tear on vehicles excessive and repair services, beset by shortages of spares, over-loaded. A complicated situation was made all the worse by Hitler's original insistence on giving priority to the manufacture of tanks and self-propelled guns, thus inducing a multiplicity of German vehicle types along with a motley collection of Swiss and captured enemy vehicles. Most of these were poor cross-country performers because they were not multi-wheel drive.

Then there was the bottleneck caused by the different Russian railway gauge. Of this too the Germans were well aware. Yet they had denied the railway troops adequate training by employing them on other tasks prior to S Day. Thus history repeated itself when, as in 1914, the Germans became enthralled by their operational plans to the detriment of vital logistic necessity. Moreover they para-doxically deluded themselves that they would capture sufficient Russian rolling stock and supplies, but did not make adequate arrangements to utilise vast stocks of vehicles, equipment and supplies left abandoned in depots and at the roadside.

When the prospects of victory shone brightly, the early logistic shortcomings were merely irritants. Morale stood high as char-acteristic arrogance stimulated extremism and, most damaging of all, the doctrinal barbarism and criminality encouraged by Nazi as well as Communist policies. It is a toss-up which side initiated the atrocities which were perpetrated within a day of the commencement of hostilities. The Russians already possessed an unenviable repu-tation for brutality in peace, let alone war, which recently had been highlighted during their occupation of Poland and the Baltic states. Knowledge of this very likely affected many Germans (especially ex-Freikorps) who had fought against the Communists in the post-World War I civil war when appalling crimes were committed. Furthermore, the Germans were urged to corruption and depravity by orders to the SS murder squads (Einsatzgruppen), operating under Reinhard Heydrich, in army controlled areas; by Wehrmacht instructions for curtailment of military jurisdiction; and by orders and guidelines for the extermination of 'Bolshevik agitators, guer-rillas, saboteurs and Jews'.

In one form or another these instructions reached the troops, despite protestations by many generals, such as Guderian, who tried to circumvent them. Already on 25 June, for example, General J. Lemelsen, commander of XXXXVIII Panzer Corps in Guderian's Panzer Group 2, was complaining about 'senseless shooting of both

POWs and civilians' he had observed. 'We want to free the civilian population from the yoke of Bolshevism and we need their labour force', he wrote. 'This instruction does not change anything regarding the Führer's order on the ruthless action to be taken against partisans and Bolshevik commissars.' Yet five days later he felt compelled to repeat himself about the shootings of POWs and deserters '... conducted in an irresponsible, senseless and criminal manner. This is murder!' Precious little good was achieved by Lemelsen or any of a number of very senior officers such as Manstein and Reichenau who, also in writing, condemned such methods. This was firstly because of what Omer Bartov calls 'the strange mixture of arguments for good against barbarism failing to produce a coherent whole', which simply led to further brutality. And secondly, the seeds of wholesale massacre had been sown and would grow like weeds out of control.

Setting aside the flummery of interpretations of controversial instructions, there now seethed in the minds of combatants on both sides a bitter mutual hatred and terror spread by word of mouth. The cult of atrocity and murder already was deeply implanted and nothing could expel it, not even recantation by Hitler if he had in some unguarded moment relented. Soon the oppressed Slav peoples, most of all the Ukrainians, who hated the Greater Russians and welcomed the Germans as liberators from tyranny, were disillusioned by the barbaric behaviour of the SS and Wehrmacht.

CHAPTER 12

III-Met at Moscow

It took the Germans three weeks to constrict and eliminate the vast Smolensk pocket with the capture of 3,100 guns, 3,200 tanks and 310,000 prisoners. The total might have been higher if only a gap had been plugged earlier, as Kesselring (who flew over the gap to see for himself) believed would have been possible if the 7th Airborne Division had been available instead of ruined in Crete. Yet determined Russian relief attempts from the South played their part by distracting the Germans, while Hitler and the High Command dilly-dallied and squabbled.

Losses had been remarkably light and morale was good. OKH and the Army Group commanders were convinced that an immediate drive to take Moscow would finish the war at a stroke. Unfortunately for them neither Hitler nor OKW agreed. They were committed to the original Warlimont–Jodl plan which laid down that, once Smolensk was reached, Army Group Centre would consolidate and the main efforts should be directed against Leningrad, the Ukraine, the Crimea and the Caucasus. Indeed, a pause was necessary for logistic reasons: to rest the motorised troops, bring up replacements and supplies and carry out maintenance.

The ensuing debate, however, took nearly a month to resolve and symbolised the wide schism between OKH and OKW in the latter's fantasy world. Directive No. 33, plus a supplement issued on 23 July 1941, did order Army Group Centre to advance on Moscow, but without its two Panzer Groups. Hoth's Panzer Group 3 was to join Army Group North to outflank Leningrad before returning to Bock's Army Group Centre when Hoepner's Panzer Group 4 was brought home to Germany.

Guderian's Panzer Group 2 was to strike southwards towards Kiev to help Rundstedt's delayed Army Group South complete the envelopment of the Russians in the Ukraine.

Pig-in-the-middle of various meetings was Jodl, who now thought

Hitler was wrong but was unable to change his master's mind. When Halder, with Clausewitzian logic, asked Jodl if Hitler's aim was military conquest or economic expansion, Jodl replied they were of equal importance. On 21 August Hitler finally rejected a last plea from Brauchitsch and Halder in favour of an immediate advance on Moscow. Once more Halder asked Brauchitsch to join him in a protest resignation. As usual the cowed Commander-in-Chief refused, this time on the defeatist grounds that Hitler would refuse that too. Meanwhile Bock had so outstretched himself by playing what Halder called 'an all out gamble with the superior enemy', that he now calculated that only by resuming the offensive could he avoid serious trouble on the defensive.

Following a meeting at Army Group Centre in which Guderian argued brilliantly that logistic difficulties and the men's weariness precluded diverting his Panzer Group to the South, Halder in desperation arranged a meeting for himself and Guderian with Hitler on 23 August. He and Bock had been impressed by Guderian's reasoning that, although the southward diversion was just feasible, it would prevent the taking of Moscow before winter set in. No doubt too, Halder had in mind that Guderian, the one man who could possibly change Hitler's mind, might very soon replace the broken Brauchitsch – who instructed Guderian not to raise the Moscow issue, but omitted to mention that OKH orders for the southward attack had already been signed.

On 23 August they reached Rastenberg by air, where, for some unexplained reason, Halder did not accompany Guderian to the meeting. So Guderian found himself alone, confronted by Hitler, Keitel, Jodl and Colonel Rudolf Schmundt, Hitler's military assistant. Inevitably the conversation got round to Moscow and Guderian opposed the move on Kiev. Predictably Hitler, with his entourage nodding assent, patronisingly overrode Guderian, saying, 'My generals know nothing of the economic aspects of war.' Tamely, and perhaps because he did not want to spoil his chance of becoming C-in-C, '... he could not debate a resolved issue with the Head of State in the presence of all his company'. Now, as an embittered and disenchanted Halder put it, Guderian felt it his duty '... to make the impossible possible' in order to put OKH's orders into effect.

In concert with Army Group South, this is what he devastatingly did, although leaving little strength to spare in bad weather at the end of crumbling roads. On 16 September he linked with Kleist's

Panzer Group 1 at Lochvitsa, closing a pocket which would yield some 500,000 prisoners, 3,500 guns and 800 tanks – the greatest haul from any pocket. As far as Guderian was concerned this was a miracle since Halder had withheld a panzer corps from his group and spread a tale that Guderian was acting contrary to Hitler's orders. The intrigue misfired when the truth was revealed to Hitler, reinforcements were prised out of Army Group Centre, and Bock and Kesselring told Guderian's Chief of Staff that there 'had been mistakes'.

At last Hitler consented to a drive on Moscow, Operation Typhoon, although not the concentrated blow first deemed feasible in August. Time and resources had to be diverted to clearing the Kiev pocket and fending off attacks by newly arrived Russian divisions. Hoepner's Panzer Group 4 had to be brought back from Army Group North to rejoin Army Group Centre. Guderian took command of XXXXVIII Panzer Corps from Kleist's group. And a few days later all the panzer groups would be upgraded to panzer armies, enhanced by whatever signal and administrative resources might accrue and granted direct access to an army group instead of via an army headquarters.

None of these changes saved the fighting formations from impending chaos. The necessity for haste in striking on 2 October, before the weather broke, denied sufficient time for rest and maintenance. Logistic services were in disarray. From Berlin came news that 'We are on the verge of catastrophe.... There is a shortage of steel, therefore the production of several kinds of vehicle has had to be cut by as much as forty per cent.' Even tank engines, let alone tanks, were being withheld, on Hitler's personal order, for future tasks. Whereas the Luftwaffe had already placed orders for winter clothing, no such firm action had been taken by the Army's inflexibly bureaucratic logistics department, even though OKH had mooted the necessity.

Nevertheless when Guderian played the overture to Typhoon on 30 September, two days before Ninth and Fourth Armies on Army Group Centre's left flank, his Second Panzer Army immediately broke through. Its XXIV Panzer Corps covered eighty-five miles in a single day. Orel was reached on 3 October as his left flank curled northwards to cut off Bryansk and, in concert with Second Army, encircle with another vast haul of Russian men and materiel. Meanwhile Third and Fourth Panzer Armies had attacked on 2

October, broken the Russian Front on each side of Vyazma and created yet another pocket on the 7th. The combined captures from these two pockets was put at 673,000 men, 1,240 tanks and 5,400 guns. Thus the door to Moscow had been thrown open on two axes when Army Group South also broke through in Ukraine and, on Hitler's insistence, headed for Rostov to seize that region's important coal and industrial complexes.

On 5 October the High Command was chanting victory. Five days later it was singing another song. Advancing against light opposition towards Mtsensk, 4th Panzer Division was suddenly struck by more than 50 KV1 and T34 tanks and thrown back with heavy losses in an encounter which shook commanders and rank and file. Listening to them, Guderian noted how the enemy was 'learning', how this was 'telling' on his soldiers and how damage to the enemy tanks was less than to his. Next day it started to snow. It was another eighteen days before he could advance again.

On all fronts it became a winter's tale with alternating spells of freeze, thaw and rain which converted the roads to morass and ruts. Now, too, manpower shortages and logistic shortcomings took their toll. Even Halder admitted this,with concern yet without being able to do much about it since railheads were still far behind the front. In extreme conditions of frost (−34 degrees were recorded) and wet, men deprived of adequate rations, winter clothing and good boots suffered terribly.

Morale declined. Heated shelter was at a premium and only a few stoves available. Horses died by the thousand, besides finding it difficult, due to lack of proper shoes, to keep their feet, thus hampering movement of artillery and transport. Tanks as well as two-wheel drive trucks floundered in mud, skidded on ice, often would not start and frequently suffered engine damage for want of anti-freeze. Firearms froze and broke down through lack of proper lubricants. Conditions deteriorated savagely in a nightmare snowscape. The Luftwaffe was also in difficulties – not only at the front but at home where General Ernst Udet committed suicide in knowledge of impending disaster due to mismanagement of technical developments and production.

Yet, in fits and starts on all fronts whenever the ground froze solid, great progress was made even against stiffening opposition. On 25 October Bock called a halt to stabilise the line and bring up reinforcements and supplies. On 15 November he started again and once more broke through, Guderian's Second Panzer Army covering twenty-five miles in a day to reach the outskirts of Tula; and Hoepner's Third Panzer Army, despite local enemy counter-attacks which drained resources, coming to within nineteen miles of Moscow on the 27th – and then sticking in a perilously exposed position. At that Bock told Halder that unless the enemy broke soon a withdrawal to safety was essential.

The energetic but cautious Kluge, commanding Fourth Army, was in two minds about renewal of the offensive planned for 2 December and was accused of indecision. Eventually he went forward to consult the junior front line officers, who told him they believed it possible to reach the city and that an attempt should be made. Kluge relented. A few troops did enter the suburbs, but then were checked by stiff opposition.

Two days later the first retrograde German move of the war was ordered by Bock. As Fourth and Ninth Armies took up defensive positions, he pulled back the weakened spearheads of Third and Second Panzer Armies, a decision which, General Günther Blumentritt wrote after the war, 'was just in time to avert the worst consequences of the general counter-offensive that the Russians now unleashed, into which Marshal Zhukov threw a hundred divisions'.

Meanwhile Kleist's First Panzer Army had reached Rostov. But there too desperate enemy resistance and a threat of envelopment checked further advance and compelled Rundstedt to order a retreat for safety's sake. The order was countermanded by Brauchitsch after a routine bullying by Hitler.

At that an enraged Hitler began a culling of generals. To begin with he brought Keitel to the verge of resignation and suicide by calling him a *Strohkopf* (blockhead): it was Jodl who removed a pistol from his chief and persuaded him meekly to serve on. On 1 December he relieved Rundstedt of command and replaced him with Field Marshal Reichenau – who died of a heart attack in January. On 19 December Brauchitsch, suffering from heart trouble and on the verge of a nervous breakdown, was rudely sent into retirement without award or a word of thanks. He was followed within hours, on sick leave, by Bock who was suffering from stomach ulcers.

Hitler then appointed himself Army Commander-in-Chief (in addition to all his other duties). Halder was left 'to carry on the business functions' on the Eastern Front, while Keitel took over the administrative part. This formalised what already prevailed: a partial merging of OKH with OKW and, in effect, the pairing of Jodl with Halder as Army Chief of Staff. At the same time Kluge took command of Army Group Centre from Bock, tasked by Hitler's panacea orders (drawing on his Western Front experience in World War I, but originating specifically from their success at Narvik in 1940) to stand and fight with 'fanatical resistance' and not retreat without specific permission.

Willy-nilly, regardless of convention, Hitler and OKW repeatedly bypassed Halder and dealt direct not only with Army Group but also Army commanders. On 17 December, as it happened, Bock had granted Guderian permission to seek a personal meeting with Hitler in the belief that Hitler had faith in his judgement and in the hope of making him understand the truly disastrous situation at the front. During a five-hour meeting on the 20th, in which he attempted also to persuade Hitler to replace OKW officers with experienced front line generals, Guderian got nowhere. Hitler only felt comfortable with the yes-men in place.

So Guderian returned to his Panzer Army and continued, despite Hitler, to conduct local withdrawals, as the doctrine of manoeuvre warfare, hammered out in Truppenamt days, demanded but which Fritsch had called 'organised flight'. This Kluge permitted – with qualifications. For whereas Guderian's disobedience of orders was habitually undisguised, Kluge (who agreed with Guderian's tactics) was more subtle by way of psychological attrition and persistence. One day, for example, he rang up OKW no less than fourteen times to squeeze minor withdrawals from a harassed Führer.

Between Guderian and Kluge, however, there was bad blood caused by earlier disagreements when Kluge had disapproved of the former's risk taking. Moreover, Kluge was watching his own back and anxious not to fall foul of Hitler. So when on Christmas Day it seemed to Kluge that Guderian had flouted one of his own standstill orders, there was an almighty row. Guderian telegraphed a request to be relieved of his command – only to find that Kluge had already referred the matter to Hitler, who instantly gave permission to sack his best panzer leader.

At this time, as Blumentritt was later to comment, Hitler was intuitively correct in insisting on stand and fight. If the old Truppenamt defensive doctrine of manoeuvre warfare had been employed in ice and snow, 'the Wehrmacht would have suffered the same fate that had befallen the [French] *Grande Armée*'.

Nevertheless, almost on the nod, thirty-five other generals, among them many of the best combat leaders, were removed – some, including Hoepner, to join the ranks of the disaffected who were plotting Hitler's removal. Like Guderian, they had lost faith in Hitler's much vaunted intuition and foresaw the nation's doom at the hands of a maniac. Nevertheless, they deserve blame for initially backing their Führer's resolve to attack Russia. They were now lambasted by Goebbels' propagandists for having thwarted the Führer's strategy by imposing, against the Führer's wishes, the drive to Moscow, although naturally no mention was made of how he had fatally delayed it by two months.

*   *   *

There was indeed a desperate crisis of confidence at the top and at the front, in which Hitler floundered when the Russian counter-offensive began on 6 December. It seemed even worse as it became apparent that the Axis armies in North Africa were in trouble and suffering heavy losses against the British, with no way to ship replacements. Halder was aware that the eastern armies were 340,000 men short (with infantry companies under appalling stress at half strength); only 33,000 men were available in Germany and most of them under-trained; truck serviceability was only sixty per cent; six months were required to rehabilitate the panzer divisions; and industrial production was actually falling. Small wonder, therefore, that Hitler's wisdom was in question by those in the know.

Yet next day the gloom lifted when, without the slightest hint to the Germans of its imminence, the Japanese attacked Pearl Harbor and the Philippines, along with British and Dutch possessions in the Far East. Warlimont described how officers 'seemed to be caught up in an ecstasy of rejoicing'; how the event was toasted in champagne (even by the teetotal Hitler); and how the Führer, Keitel and Jodl immediately took the train to Berlin.

Warlimont also recorded astonishment when he heard on 11 December that Hitler, in the absence of careful consideration, had declared war on America. Once more the Wehrmacht was caught short without a strategy, let alone a joint plan with Japan. As Jodl said to Warlimont, '... so far we have never even considered a war against the United States and so have no data on which to base this examination.... See what you can do. When we get back to-morrow we will talk about this in more detail.'

In practice both Hitler and his advisors tended to take the easy way out. However, Warlimont correctly appreciated that, in the light of the USA's hostility to the Germans, the Americans would give priority to attack on Germany. OKW then went on to assume (without proper calculation) that it would be a year before the Americans could contribute much; that by then Russia would be beaten; and that the U-boats would prevent large-scale transatlantic movement. Furthermore, just like their predecessors in World War I, they (and Hitler especially) tended to dismiss American fighting qualities and industrial capability. 'He regarded anybody who tried to show him such information [about growing American strength] as defeatist.'

As for Hitler's lapse in breaking his oft-stated intention '. . . never to be so foolish as the old Kaiser and declare war on anybody', this quite unnecessary and very stupid action (which disposed of several awkward matters of Allied protocol) Warlimont could only ascribe to:

'1. Fidelity to his part of the treaty with Japan [which in fact obliged Germany to participation only if attacked].

2. His romantic feeling of wanting to support a soldierly nation such as Japan.

3. The continued hostile attitude of the United States.'

CHAPTER 13

Mediterranean Diversions and Strategic Flaws

The gigantic drama played on the Russian stage in 1941 coincided with the mutual exhaustion of the Axis and British forces in North Africa after the June battle for Tobruk sidelined the Mediterranean war. Even so OKW did note, in its mid-September review of the overall strategic situation, that as Britain's position in the Middle East was strengthened, she would, with American aid, build up strong offensive forces. Therefore 'The situation of the German–Italian forces in Libya will become increasingly difficult unless we succeed in greatly stepping up the scale of supply shipments across the Mediterranean, or take Tobruk before the British launch an offensive (impossible before October).' But as Halder was studying this paper, Rommel was in the act of committing an error which would disturb the balance of forces.

Fearing an imminent British offensive, he launched 21st Panzer Division on a raid in mid-September (Operation Sommernacht-straum) upon a non-existent British supply dump. Thwarted, he intuitively struck at British light forces on the frontier – and hit thin air as his enemy took evasive action. The Germans then ran out of petrol, were shelled and heavily bombed and had their tank strength reduced from 110 to forty-three (with the total loss of five tanks and many trucks). 'Caused by our own fault', this was a blow from which, due to sinkings at sea, Afrika Korps, within what now was called Panzer Group Afrika, did not recover until mid-November. This set-back, which deeply depressed the mercurial Rommel, was hushed up.

For argument's sake there can be discerned, in microcosm, a resemblance between the Wehrmacht's combat performance in Africa and in Europe. Here was Rommel, the propaganda hero who, rather like Hitler, was strong-minded, charismatic, ruthless and intuitive. He was a general who, supported by an elite staff he treated none too well, had initially won public adulation by defeating outclassed enemies whose generals were incompetent, whose tactical doctrine was faulty or non-existent, and whose training and weapons were inferior. Yet gradually Rommel and his staff were being worn down and defeated by opponents who, as Kesselring had warned in 1940, would gather superior strength and gradually learn hard lessons.

Of course, neither Hitler, his generals nor the Wehrmacht as a whole would admit this. Rommel planned to capture Tobruk in November 1941 and, myopically, initially refused to believe that the British offensive (Operation Crusader), launched on the 18th, was a major operation by a numerically larger enemy whose logistic situation then, as always, was better than his. So poor was Axis intelligence, it was not until 21 November that Rommel was convinced something more than a raid was in progress. By that time the British had seized vital ground and a breakout from Tobruk was imminent. Rommel became personally involved in a wild mêlée between rapidly manoeuvring armoured formations groping for each other in clouds of sand and smoke. On 23 November the struggle went the Germans' way because their tactics, combat techniques and equipment were better than those of the British. However, Rommel then forfeited this local victory on the 25th. For instead of completing his enemy's destruction near Tobruk, he led an ill-considered and poorly executed raid into Egypt which, instead of achieving the strategic result he envisaged, awarded the British time enough to recover and threaten the envelopment of the Panzer Group.

From this impulsive and rash act Rommel was saved in the nick of time by overriding orders from his Operations Officer, Lieutenant Colonel Siegfried Westphal, acting in the finest traditions of the General Staff. But he had thrown away a chance of victory and, henceforward despite a few more local successes, was condemned to annihilation or retreat as irreplaceable equipment, fuel, ammunition and supplies ran short. Retreat it had to be, and all the more ignominious in the light of Rommel's loss of nerve when talking crazily to the Italian Commander-in-Chief, Marshal Bastico, about a retreat to Tunisia in order to have his forces interned by the French. This time, however, he was saved from his own folly by the arrival of sufficient reinforcements, tanks and supplies to enable him to deal the British a few bloody noses on the way back to El Agheila, which he reached on 10 January 1942.

News of the upsets to this propaganda hero was most unwelcome in Germany when events were so adverse in Russia. But it was typical of Rommel's luck that he bounced back on 20 January. Helped enormously this time by the outstanding perception of his chief intelligence officer, Major Friedrich von Mellenthin, he was provided with insight into a momentary enemy weakness. With characteristic alacrity, he completely surprised the British and drove them back, with heavy losses, to Gazala.

By then, however, a very great General Field Marshal had appeared on the scene to inject a new dimension into the Mediterranean campaign. In response to OKW's September staff study, Hitler, persuaded by Göring and Jeschonnek, had appointed Kesselring as Commander-in-Chief South. His task, while remaining commander of Second Air Fleet, was to override the Italian High Command and neutralise Malta through air power, thereby securing the frail lines of communication to North Africa. The diplomatically urbane and energetic Kesselring had arrived in Rome on 28 November 1941 and, typically, ignored Hitler's orders by choosing, instead, to work on an equal footing with the Italians. At the same time, he was formulating a plan to invade Malta because he realised that air power alone would not achieve the stated military aim. Meanwhile he endeavoured also to improve relations between Rommel (over whom he had somewhat tenuous command and whom he disliked), Bastico and the other Italians. But this was a forlorn hope since the arrogant Rommel, with some reason, despised and mistrusted the Italians whose hearts were not in the war.

Kesselring swiftly produced good results as he gathered more and more strings into his own hands and eliminated Rommel's control of the Luftwaffe in Tripolitania. Having strongly reinforced the Sicily air base, from which attacks on Malta were launched, he rapidly reduced losses at sea to the marked benefit of the Axis forces in Cyrenaica where Rommel, habitually underestimating the logistic factor, again set his sights on the capture of Tobruk (Operation Theseus). But Kesselring knew that Malta, not Tobruk, held the key to logistic plenty in what he called 'a poor man's war'. So, having obtained Rommel's support for what became known as Operation Hercules, he broached the subject with Hitler and OKW and, in February 1942 at a bad-tempered interview with the Führer, won approval for an Axis invasion of the island.

Not until after the war did Kesselring discover that he was

treading in the 1940 footsteps of Raeder and Jodl. For by seizing both Malta and Tobruk, an invasion of Egypt became feasible as the first step for control of the Middle East in conjunction with the planned German advance from Russia into the Caucasus in 1942. Moreover, this latest scheme contained a new dimension since it dovetailed with Plan Orient, a half-hearted Grand Strategy (first mooted in June 1941) to consider joint moves with Japan in the Indian Ocean, the Indian sub-continent and the Persian Gulf if and when the Japanese entered the conflict.

Hitler's granting of approval in principle for Hercules still left it standing on shifting sands. With memories of Crete to the forefront, both he and Mussolini agonised about another major airborne operation, while at OKW Jodl ambivalently made no attempt to initiate a staff study and kept very much in the background. Meanwhile German airborne forces under Student were making ready and Rommel, with Kesselring's approval, had calculated that Theseus could be launched in May. But the reluctant Italians prevaricated about Hercules and stated they could not be ready until August. To stiffen their resolve, and that of Hitler, Kesselring staged an all-out air offensive against Malta. The island was all but neutralised until mid-May when the supply of bombs ran short and Hitler, in consultation with Göring (who also disliked Hercules), authorised an essential transfer of part of Second Air Fleet to Russia for the forthcoming summer offensive.

Nevertheless, in Rome a unique joint Italo-German air and naval staff was at work and Kesselring and Student (with Jeschonnek's support at OKL) were confident that Hercules would work. But on 21 May, five days before Theseus was scheduled to start, Student was called to report to Hitler, who brushed aside Hercules, proclaiming Malta was of no significance once Tobruk was taken. Jodl shared this opinion, and although he was not consulted at that moment he may have inserted the notion in Hitler's mind. Thus, to all intents and purposes, Hercules was slain, along with any chance of Plan Orient's adoption as a war-winning strategy, which the Allies dreaded.

In point of fact a true German–Italian–Japanese Grand Strategy was never in prospect, if only because the Germans and Japanese were unwilling to overcome their respective national pride and inherent, mutual mistrust. There had been no disclosure on Germany's part of Operation Barbarossa, or on Japan's of her plans in the Far East. Hitler, Ribbentrop and OKW lived in hope of Japan attacking Russia, but the Japanese were too scared to do so. After Pearl Harbor the main channel of communication between Berlin and Tokyo was on the encoded diplomatic link. And the majority of this high-grade radio traffic was read, with enormous benefit, by the American Magic and British Ultra deciphering organisations.

OKW created nothing like the highly sophisticated Anglo-American system of military sharing and co-operation governed by a well-thought-out global strategy. From 1942 onwards, Axis strategy increasingly evolved piecemeal as possession of the initiative was lost. Meanwhile, however, when the Germans recovered from their set-backs in Russia and North Africa, they and the Italians stood poised to resume the offensive in both theatres. Their navies scored heavily in the Battle of the Atlantic and in the Mediterranean; and the Japanese continued to exploit their massive victories in the Far East and Pacific, but no dynamic impulse to collaborate emerged. Instinctively each nation preferred to conquer in splendid isolation from each other.

So, when Rommel struck at Gazala on 26 May, German confidence was strong – and made exuberant when, after a month-long ding-dong battle with the British, Tobruk fell. Yet that confidence was ill-founded, as Hitler and Jodl might have learnt from studying Warlimont's paper of 6 June, *War Potential 1942*. For he concluded, along with figures showing serious deficiencies in manpower, materiel and supplies, that 'Our war potential is lower than in Spring 1941. It must be compensated by the infliction of increased losses on the enemy, superior leadership and increased efforts on the part of the troops, quality of weapons and increased emphasis on anti-tank weapons. By these means we can ensure superiority at those decisive points where we decide to concentrate.'

According to Warlimont, Hitler probably never saw this comprehensive analysis, nor would he have welcomed it. 'Jodl took little interest in this aspect of command activity and Keitel would hardly have dared to send it on' (again quoting Warlimont). In any case the document, coming from a supposedly tri-service department, had a fundamental flaw. It contained only passing mention of the Navy's or the Luftwaffe's role. After the war, Kesselring wrote: 'The intricacies of the overseas theatre of war were not understood by the German command, educated to think in continental dimensions. It was not conscious of the importance of that area, overlooked the difficulties and did not lead with initiative and with proper consideration of focal points, but rather intermittently when forced to do so and when the situation finally did not permit any other solution.'

A moment such as this occurred the day after Rommel had seized Tobruk with its immense haul of prisoners, enemy equipment, fuel and supplies. Until then he had not contemplated pursuit to the Nile and Cairo. But on 22 June, buoyed up by a victory beyond his dreams, promoted field marshal on the spot and revelling in the limelight of public adulation, he saw fit to suggest to Hitler that conquest of Egypt would match splendidly with the forthcoming drive into the Caucasus (Operation Blue which started on 28 June: see Chapter 14 below). To Mussolini he suggested the triumph of riding through Cairo on a white charger.

Rommel, correctly sensing the demoralisation of a defeated enemy but without sparing time for war-gaming or a staff study, got his way because, as Kesselring believed, he '... exercised an almost hypnotic influence on Hitler, which practically precluded an objective estimate of the situation on the part of the latter'. Kesselring was not consulted. The Panzer Army shot forward, driving back the British to an un-outflankable defensive position at El Alamein. There, between 1 and 26 July, a costly battle of attrition, ending in stalemate, raged. It became obvious, to those prepared to admit it, that Rommel urgently needed reinforcements and supplies because the enemy was much stronger than supposed, and that possession of Tobruk did not eliminate the need to possess or neutralise Malta.

Kesselring, who doubted if Axis possession of Alexandria and lower Egypt would bring the British to their knees, supported renewal of the offensive because 'The situation in the Mediterranean and North Africa had become very unfavourable.' With the approval of OKW and OKL, despite the needs of the Russian Front and home defence, he played what he called 'the last trump card which might temporarily improve the supply position': another exhausting air offensive against Malta as cover for delivery to Rommel of what seemed like sufficient men and material for a new offensive at the end of August. But Rommel's knowledge of his enemy had been seriously weakened by the loss in battle of his principal intelligence gathering unit (with all its records). The British, in fact, were much stronger than estimated and on the eve of better leadership by Generals Harold Alexander and Bernard Montgomery.

The decisive defeat of Rommel at the Second Battle of El Alamein permanently deprived the Axis of the initiative both in North Africa and the Mediterranean. Moreover, it brought a disillusioned Rommel into collision, for the first time, with Hitlerian embargoes on withdrawals. Although Kesselring and the Italians did all in their power to reinforce the Alamein position, it was in the fear that the supply lines could never be secured and in the presence of strong intelligence that a new, yet undefined threat from the West was pending.

Prior to 23 October, when Montgomery attacked at El Alamein after careful preparation, Kesselring dismissed the danger of an amphibious invasion of Sicily, though realising such an event might cause 'a catastrophe'. But when Rommel was routed at the beginning of November, and Anglo-American forces (catching the Axis by surprise, off balance and with their command and control systems in a tangle) invaded North West Africa on 10 November and began advancing into Tunisia, the sudden emergence of a threat of that magnitude coincided with very bad news from every other front. Stalemate in Russia; ever more damaging air raids on Germany; and every indication that the Japanese, after the naval defeat at Midway in June and the American invasion of Guadalcanal in August, were in trouble, combined to bring the realisation that, for the first time, the Axis was forced onto a Grand Strategic defensive.

Henceforward an atmosphere of frenetic desperation disturbed the functioning of the High Command. Already on 8 September a serious row erupted between Hitler and Jodl. Warlimont said it 'shook Supreme Headquarters to its foundations' and seemed to paralyse the organisation. Indeed, it preceded the dismissal of Field Marshal List on 9 September and the removal of a played-out Halder on the 24th. In Warlimont's judgement, Hitler's confidence lapsed as he realised 'his wanton arbitrary activities will grind the Reich to powder.... He could no longer bear to have around him the Generals who have so often been witnesses of his faults, his errors, his illusions and his day dreams.'

Hitler now toyed with the idea of replacing Halder by the soldier-cum-airman Kesselring, whose ability he regarded very highly. But with crisis looming in the Mediterranean, this was not the moment for change. So the choice, backed by Göring, fell on Kurt Zeitzler.

He was a Brandenburger, an infantryman who had risen from platoon to regimental commander in World War I and become a member of the Truppenamt in 1927. A one-time subordinate of Jodl and supporter of unified Wehrmacht command, he now was a very experienced Chief of Staff of armoured formations, who had worked for Kleist and Rundstedt. Moreover, he was a close friend of Rudolf Schmundt, Hitler's chief military aide, who now played the part of king-maker within the Führer's entourage.

To begin with, from Hitler's point of view, this appointment looked as comfortable as Keitel's had proved, especially when Zeitzler issued a sensationally placatory edict demanding that every staff officer '... must believe in the Führer and in his method of command'. Tradition, however, would tell. Zeitzler, whose tasks were now confined to the East Front only, wasted little time in attempting the elimination of the continual assumption of authority by Jodl and OKW over matters which once were the province of OKH.

Meanwhile in Africa Rommel was on the run. His retreat, thought Kesselring, '... more or less takes the form, apart from rearguard actions, of an administrative march with little enemy pressure on the the ground and in the air'. This was far too precipitate for Kesselring's liking. He needed time, as well as reinforcements, to prepare Tunisia for a long siege. His strategic aim, which evolved into Germany's for the rest of the war, was to hold the enemy at maximum range from the Reich in order to sustain the Axis and mitigate air attacks.

'It is an old experience of siege warfare that the main chance of a successful defence lies in the battles in the outpost area,' he wrote. 'It was the mission of the Panzer Army in Tripolitania to create the necessary time [to construct fortifications] by appropriate conduct of battle.'

Rommel intended the opposite. He aimed to prevent the destruction of his army by retiring, as a first step, to Sicily before abandoning Italy and retreating to the Alps. He tried to impose his strategy by stealthily staged amendments to his earlier intentions. Having told OKW and Kesselring he would stand on the south Tunisian frontier, '... when everything would be in order', he subsequently proposed withdrawal to a small bridgehead when 'everything will go well'.

But although Kesselring, by adroit diplomacy and firmness had his way by having General Jürgen von Arnim's Fifth Panzer Army launch attacks in the north and centre and compelling Rommel to hold the Mareth Line in the south and counter-attack, OKW was unable to send adequate forces to hold Tunisia for any length of time. In the prelude to the fall of Stalingrad and the subsequent Russian drive into the Ukraine in February and March 1943, central reserves and resources were at a premium. Furthermore, much despatched to Tunisia went to the bottom of the sea as the Allied sea and air blockade tightened into a stranglehold.

Yet when, post-war, Kesselring blamed OKW for acting 'very late, often too late and in insufficient measure', he must surely, as an airman, have realised, as he later said, that 'A single position cannot be permanently held against the modern means of attack of ground and air forces. The most favourable prospects for defence will be found in a defence zone which is sub-divided into several positions.' Tunisia only marginally fitted this description. Moreover, he must surely have realised that defeat was unavoidable in the face of the devastating Anglo-American air offensive which, prior to his being recalled to Germany in March, had plunged Rommel into gloom.

The naturally optimistic Kesselring also was acquiring, with some at OKW and OKL, a reputation for pessimism by frequently, and realistically, reporting to the Führer and Göring 'by radio [read by Ultra], in writing and verbally', that the enemy had gained air superiority; and proposing measures 'to anticipate the enemy development in number, type and ability'. His submissions were intended to strengthen Jeschonnek's hand at a moment when the indolent Göring was attempting to get rid of a Chief of Air Staff whose criticism of himself was becoming intolerable.

At the beginning of April 1943 the desert war entered its closing phase. The Axis spoiling attacks of February and March had been defeated and the mobile forces driven back to be penned within the mountainous 'keep' shielding Tunis and Bizerta. Now, while Kesselring strove mightily to hang on and the troops, as they nearly always did, fought splendidly, thoughts turned sensibly to saving as many highly experienced officers and men as possible to form cadres for the defence of Europe. But Hitler would have none of that and obsessively took vengeance on all whom he now frequently accused of betrayal, by rejecting all such pleas.

The end came on 13 May after a crushing Anglo–American–French offensive had overwhelmed the strongholds and caused mobile forces without fuel to disintegrate. Along with piles of equipment and munitions, all the top generals among an estimated 275,000 prisoners had been captured. Total Axis casualties since 1940 came to something in the region of 620,000, of whom about 200,000 were Germans. It was a disaster the equal of Stalingrad. Henceforward nothing on earth could save Germany as long as Hitler and OKW continued to pursue flawed strategies and refused to consider overtures for peace.

CHAPTER 14

Suicide in Russia

It was indicative of Germany's declining capability in 1942 to wage war, as described in Warlimont's paper *War Potential 1942*, that it was impossible that year to attack simultaneously along the entire length of the Eastern Front. For one thing Russian strength, as still underestimated by OKH in December 1941 at 200 rifle and thirty-five cavalry divisions, plus forty tank brigades, remained a formidable force despite many operational and equipment shortcomings. In the dual role of Army Commander-in-Chief and Supreme Commander, Hitler (chiefly advised by Jodl who often did not bother to consult his staff) ran almost roughshod over Halder and OKH throughout the winter months when his standfast strategy proved remarkably sound. He not only re-established confidence at the front but also gave it a most welcome boost. Strategy now evolved out of his intuition at Jodl's prompting. Halder was left to implement it. War-gaming, never seriously practised at OKW, became a thing of the past as OKH was progressively confined to running the Eastern Front only. Furthermore, without a pause between campaigns as fighting went on continuously, there was very little time for such leisurely activities.

In these conditions training suffered. Halder noted (22 June 1942) 'The non-commissioned officer situation remains difficult.' General Edgar Röhricht pointed out: '... the constant engagements left the troops no time for periods of rest.... The immediate influence of the Army Training Branch decreased in consequence. The geographical, climatic and other combat conditions were so varied on the different fronts, and even the different sectors on the Eastern front, that uniform training directives could no longer be issued. Troop training was more and more taken over by the army group and army headquarters which slowly developed tactical systems of their own.' This was a phenomenom compounded by the independence and special privileges of Himmler's ever expanding Waffen SS formations.

The practice of rotating divisions between the Eastern and Western Fronts further diffused doctrine. But in one crucial respect there was uniformity of attitude among the combat units: the merciless savagery of fighting on the Eastern Front and in those theatres (such as the Balkans) where guerrilla warfare was rampant, left no room for chivalry. In combat it was frequently kill or be killed for survival. A rising mood of apathy impelled men to fight in sheer desperation in order to prevent vengeful and rapacious Russians reaching their homeland.

Against this background in February, Hitler laid ambitious plans for 1942. He still intended to seize the Caucasus and Leningrad – but in sequence since even he realised the Army was far below strength, especially in infantry. Indeed he displayed acute realism by no longer talking about knocking Russia out of the war.

Directive No. 41 was founded on OKH's well-thought-out draft plans. These were discussed at a major conference on 28 March and then handed for final drafting to OKW's staff. According to Warlimont, they 'made a special effort to limit the contents of the directive to "tasks" and eliminate any unnecessary restrictions on OKH'. On 4 April Jodl presented this document to Hitler, who, to burnish his ego, spent several hours amending its form and vital operational passages. 'It was,' criticised Warlimont, 'long and repetitive . . .; in general it was unclear and in detail it was complicated.' In other words, Directive No. 41 was the antithesis of the sort of mission instructions General Staff officers had long been trained to produce, and was therefore a tiresome recipe for misunderstanding and error.

As preliminaries to the deep thrust intended to deny Russia her Caucasian oilfields (which Halder thought beyond German capability), it was essential first to seize the Crimea and wipe out the so-called Izyum Salient to the south of Kharkov. These operations succeeded beyond expectation. By 21 May, after a massive concentration of firepower, Manstein's Eleventh Army had inflicted enormous losses on the Russians while clearing the Crimea; less the besieged port of Sevastopol. Meanwhile on 12 May, the Russians, spurred on by Stalin, attacked Kharkov in strength. But, after making some progress, which brought suggestions (instantly squashed by Hitler and Halder) that the Izyum attack on 17 May should be cancelled, they were brought to a halt with crippling losses. Come the 28th the Russians had been stopped by Paulus's

Sixth Army before Kharkov and encircled in classic manner by Group von Kleist at Izyum. This boded well for Operation Blue. Nevertheless Halder was disturbed to find, ominously, 'The enemy anticipated our attack. Reports in the enemy press reveal information about our strategic intentions for the entire front ...'.

Brimful of confidence, Hitler approved Operation Blue at a conference on 1 June which included Keitel, Bock (Army Group South), List (Army Group A), Weichs (Second Army), Kleist (First Panzer Army), Paulus (Sixth Army) and Hoth (Fourth Panzer Army). Blue's prime aim was destruction of the Soviet forces as a preliminary to seizing the oilfields at Maikop and Grozny. 'If we don't get them', Hitler is reported to have flippantly remarked, 'I shall have to pack in this war.' The focus was on the Caucasus. There was neither mention of Stalingrad nor Moscow. But, no sooner had Manstein taken Sevastopol on 2 July, than Halder (who saw no further need for the siege artillery in the South) was opposing, unsuccessfully, Hitler's order for Manstein (promoted field marshal) to repeat his siege warfare triumph at Leningrad. Ever inconsistent in strategic ideas, this simply was Hitler's overture to forthcoming fundamental changes to Directive No. 41.

Meanwhile Blue won immediate success when launched on 28 June. By 6 July Voronezh had been taken and there was evidence, as the two Panzer Armies surged forward against sporadic resistance, that the enemy was in poor shape: except that 80,000 prisoners were taken during three weeks' fighting was meagre to say the least. When on 13 July Halder was crowing that 'The southern operation has now really got going', Hitler, unwilling to be upstaged, seemed bent on thwarting it by throwing his weight about by imposing a sequence of changes to deployment, plan and generals. That day, with Halder's approval, he 'retired' Bock for dilatoriness at Voronezh; and would also have removed Bock's Chief of Staff had not Halder pointed out that General von Södenstern had opposed Bock's decisions and to remove them both at once would create chaos.

More crucial that day, however, was Hitler's decision to manoeuvre for a great encirclement of an unlocated enemy west of the River Don. This split Army Group South in two by directing Army Group B (now commanded by Weichs) towards Stalingrad (Operation Heron) while List's Army Group A plunged into the Caucasus (Operation Edelweiss). In France tinkering of this sort in

1940 had not mattered against a collapsing enemy with no territory to spare. Here, in Russia, it did matter because the Russians were by no means beaten (despite Hitler's guess that they were) and had vast spaces in rear to trade.

Divergence of effort and repeated changes of mind flew in the face of common sense and the Principles of War. In due course both Weichs and List, despite further initial successes as they neared Stalingrad and Maikop respectively, complained about manpower and logistic shortages at the end of extended lines of communication which, occasionally, were made impassible by torrential rain. Naturally, too, they worried about lengthening flanks which, for the most part, were protected by inferior Romanian, Hungarian and Italian troops.

These difficulties Halder (and many another officer) perceived without being able to do much to resolve them. He recorded the Führer's '... terrible excitement. Intolerable language used about other people's mistakes when they are merely carrying out orders which he himself has issued.' Jodl too had similar difficulties but, intent on maintaining his influence and his aim of downgrading OKH, pandered to his master's wishes. Fatally in mid-July he stimulated the drift of opinion that led Hitler, and many another, to feature Stalingrad as an essential flank guard to the main drive into the Caucasus. Compliantly, therefore, Halder proposed strengthening the left wing to the detriment of List in the Caucasus. Hitler perversely rejected the redistribution until 30 July when, to Halder's amazement, Jodl without warning 'In solemn tones stated that the fate of the Caucasus would be decided at Stalingrad. Forces must be diverted from Army Group A to Army Group B.'

Thus the Germans and their allies, at a moment when the Russians were extremely worried, blundered, virtually by default, to their fate and into the September leadership crisis mentioned in Chapter 13 above. By 22 August Paulus's Sixth Army, spearheaded by a panzer and an infantry corps from Hoth's Fourth Panzer Army, was within striking distance of Stalingrad. As a result, on 31 August, List told Hitler to his face that without Hoth's Panzer Army he lacked the resources to retain momentum in the Caucasus. Moreover he followed that up on 6 September by telling Halder 'he would not be responsible for a further advance'. Hitler, most unusually, sent Jodl to investigate. He received an unexpected answer from his most favoured Chief of Operations to the effect that List was right since (a) he was abiding by Hitler's instructions and (b) a local withdrawal was necessary.

The resultant Führer explosion did more than skake OKW 'to its foundations'. It induced yet another purge of the Old Guard Generals who had won so many victories since 1939 and who, admittedly, were wearied by the strain of fighting the Russians as well as Hitler. And socially too it estranged Hitler from the OKW staff. Never again would he take meals with them. Henceforward his closest military colleagues were personal military assistants of the likes of Schmundt, whose influence increased significantly.

Keitel told Halder that List must resign and hinted that he too might soon lose his job. For the time being Hitler would command Army Group A in addition to the Wehrmacht and the Army. Jodl assumed he would be replaced because he had shaken the self-confidence of a dictator by pointing out 'where he has gone wrong'. But he stayed on and gradually repaired the rift with his revered Führer. Halder, to his relief, bade farewell to Hitler on 24 September: 'My nerves are worn out; also his are no longer fresh. Necessity for educating the General Staff in fanatical faith in The Idea. He is determined to enforce his will also into the army.'

At Schmundt's suggestion, Zeitzler was appointed. He brought with him an overt policy of 'enforcing' the Führer's will and a covert one of resisting Jodl by eliminating 'OKW's theatres of war' and excluding OKW from anything (including information) to do with the Eastern Front. Frictions and a schism at the top thus became inevitable at a moment of stalemate in the Mediterranean and Russia.

As at El Alamein, in the desert, there now evolved a virtual standstill in the Caucasus and very costly fighting in the built-up area of Stalingrad. There the Russians held out grimly among the ruins while they prepared a counterstroke in open country. The Caucasus campaign most certainly was being decided at Stalingrad, but not on OKW's terms since Army Group A's advance, hampered by lack of resources and Hitler's personal commands from a distance, had petered out. Of a sudden victorious fluidity of movement had been superseded by deadlock. The stalemates were broken in cataclysmic succession when Rommel admitted defeat at El Alamein on 3 November; the Allies landed in North West Africa on the 8th; and the Russians launched their Stalingrad counterstroke on 19 November which, by the 23rd, had encircled Paulus's Sixth Army.

The Allied triumphs highlighted to perfection Kesselring's dread of the day when Germany's enemies would have learned sufficiently from their mistakes and experience to make better use of their enormous industrial potential. Despite continuing German successes in the Battle of the Atlantic, Allied sea and air power had made feasible the Mediterranean victories. Russian armoured and artillery tactics on the German model were the keys to the defeat at Stalingrad where their tank columns, well equipped with T34 tanks, swiftly broke through the extended northern and southern flanks of the salient to achieve victory by concentrating strength against weakness; and then, in the classic Blitzkrieg manner, logistically maintaining deep thrusts as never thought possible by the astonished Germans. The German intelligence staff, yet again, had failed the Army by underestimating the enemy's strength and intentions, and not even acknowledging the threat to the southern flank.

As was his way when faced with the need for a difficult decision, Hitler the politician procrastinated and bent to the wind of change, yet retained a determination to fight on. He dismissed Mussolini's suggestion that 'The war against Russia ... must now somehow be closed', in order to fight against England. Warlimont was not alone in realising that Hitler knew the war could not be won and right when he wrote 'His every thought and action became increasingly centred on holding what he had won ... and never giving up anything anywhere ... any thought of being forced on the strategic defensive never entered his head. Though this is what happened, no word of it ever appeared in the string of OKW directives which we prepared with such urgency.'

Amid the turmoil of that cataclysmic November the lives, let alone the jobs, of those at OKW were cheap to Hitler. One unfortunate Army major, after passing unwelcome news from North Africa to Hitler, was only saved from summary execution on Schmundt's personal intercession. In connection with the same incident, Warlimont too was sacked but, also at the behest of Schmundt in response to strong objections by OKW staff, restored within twenty-four hours for 'unjust treatment'.

The Stalingrad crisis forcibly imposed immediate organisational changes. Although Zeitzler managed to persuade Hitler to hand over command of Army Group A (whose role now was of secondary importance) to Kleist, he made no positive proposals. Only Jodl, it seems, thought clearly and rationally when proposing that conduct of the battle should be left to Weichs at Army Group B. Instead Hitler devised a characteristically diversified improvisation which further complicated command and control. He called on Manstein's Eleventh Army to form a new Army Group Don, tasked to fill the gap opened up in Army Group B on either side of Stalingrad. He was seeking a miracle from his latest, favourite field marshal, who indeed had a reputation for working them. If similar to Napoleon in no other respect, Hitler certainly liked backing commanders with lucky stars.

Since, at this moment, Hitler was conducting operations by telephone from Bavaria, something akin to paralysis again afflicted OKW and OKH. It was not unlike that which had paralysed the Younger Moltke's distant HQ in Luxembourg at the crisis of the battle of the Marne in 1914. But whereas, in 1914, Moltke had at least made the clear-cut decision to withdraw from danger, Hitler, when asked on 23 November by Paulus, Weichs and Zeitzler for permission to withdraw, only gave approval in principle. He withdrew it next day because, meanwhile, he had committed himself publicly to standing fast on the Volga – and had been supported in this instinctive intention by Keitel and Jodl.

It was plain to the General Staffs that Stalingrad was not sufficiently stocked for a prolonged siege. Nor was Göring's bombastic promise that his Luftwaffe transport fleet, mostly committed to the support of Kesselring in North Africa, backed up by sufficient resources to supply some 200,000 men, 8,000 horses and 10,000 vehicles for an indeterminate length of time in winter weather. It was also plain to Manstein that, even with the relatively small force of two panzer and four or five infantry divisions at his disposal, he could not launch a relief operation until 3 December, later postponed until the 12th. And he was less likely to succeed if Paulus persisted in obeying Hitler's repeated orders to stand fast and make no attempt to link up with Manstein's advancing columns.

For sixteen days Manstein persisted with great skill and determination, yet predictably failed to break through a well-informed enemy whose strength was unimpaired, morale high and resolve absolute. There is very little doubt that if Paulus had been allowed to break out immediately after 23 November, or had the courage to disobey Hitler's ludicrous command (as one corps commander, General Walter von Seydlitz-Kurzbach, strongly urged upon him), the crisis would have been solved. But neither the weaker-willed

Paulus nor his other four corps commanders had the moral courage to disobey. Thus they doomed themselves and their men to extinction or captivity.

How was it that well-trained, brave and, by their lights, principled commanders and leaders such as these lacked the character of a Guderian or Kesselring to disobey and risk the consequences? The excuse normally offered hinges on traditional values of discipline and compliance with the Oath to the Head of State and Supreme Commander; and includes the sort of overweening behaviour of men such as Keitel and Jodl who clung to power for ambition's sake. Moreover, it is sometimes suggested, the fact that the mass of the Wehrmacht, deluded by propaganda to believe in the Führer's military genius (without knowing his incompetence and fallibility), was sufficient reason to sustain hope in victory.

To some extent these motivations were valid and, undeniably, they were extremely difficult to throw overboard without notice. But also there resided among the generals, until it was too late, an innate complacency and over-confidence in the Wehrmacht's much vaunted tactical and technical prowess – compounded by misinformation, underestimation of a despised enemy, poor security and overstretch. Their pronounced irrationality was similar to that which, throughout history, had wrecked earlier Germanic states due to a propensity to ignore reality and pin hopes on a miraculous salvation from desperate situations.

The fact remains that, once Manstein had been brought to a halt and it became plain that the airlift could not possibly maintain a garrison of such size as that at Stalingrad, the ruined city's extended defence became a strategic absurdity. At best it might only temporarily divert a few enemy formations from operations elsewhere. Indeed, it was not only the success of Russian forces in stopping Manstein which brought an end to his offensive operations on 28 December, but also the deadly menace of an enemy thrust into the Ukraine. This was a stroke which threatened the entire southern front from Voronezh to the Caucasus, thus imperilling Army Groups A, B and Don. If they were to survive, Sixth Army at Stalingrad had to be abandoned.

The surrender of Paulus at Stalingrad on 2 February 1943 ushered in what might be called the Suicide Syndrome and a new phase of the war as far as the generals were concerned. Henceforward, to an ever increasing extent, they and the Wehrmacht were driven by dread of

the consequences of defeat along with terror of the Führer's excesses. Hanging over their heads was the threat of execution and, in due
course, torture inflicted by Himmler's SS minions, whose motif and
badge was a death's head. Frequently, as Hitler persisted in issuing
orders which were tantamount to suicide for formations and units
thrown into hopeless situations, he spoke of suicide and summary
executions. To quote from conference notes of his reaction to the
capture of Paulus and fellow generals at Stalingrad and their failure
to shoot themselves: 'Here is a man who sees 45,000 to 60,000 of his
soldiers die defending themselves bravely to the end – how can he
give himself up to the Bolsheviks?' Then, referring to General Ernst
Udet's suicide in November 1941 for having failed the Luftwaffe
(and Göring): 'He did it easily enough! . . . A revolver makes it easy.
. . . When one's nerves break down there is nothing to do but say "I
can't go on" and shoot oneself. . . . Just as in the old days commanders who saw that all was lost used to fall on their swords.'

Already battle casualties among the generals proportionately were
higher than in World War I. At one meeting with the Führer at this
time, Zeitzler reported the death of three generals on a single day. In
the years to come they would rise to unprecedented numbers in
combat and from executions and suicide.

CHAPTER 15

Change of Course

The publication of Warlimont's *War Potential 1942* naturally reflected the inadequacy of Germany's industrial output. At the root of the trouble lay raw material shortages, inefficiency and labour problems. The causes were equally diffuse but boiled down to lack of central direction exacerbated by Göring's Four Year Plan Organisation; intervention by the Wehrmacht in policy matters; by the direct influence of each of the three services with their 'own' exclusive manufacturing concerns; and Hitler's unwillingness to conscript women. It is a myth that German women did not put on uniform or work in the factory, although the fact remains that the majority worked as housewives or joined branches of such organisations as the Young Maidens with its important role in the war effort.

Of course the factories of conquered countries contributed significantly, though insufficiently to meet rapidly expanding requirements. And needless to say attempts to centralise control and reduce waste were made by Dr Fritz Todt, after February 1940 when he became Minister for Armaments. But very little was achieved until, in February 1942, he was killed in an air crash and was succeeded by Hitler's architect, the very able and dynamic Dr Albert Speer.

Taking over during the winter crisis in Russia, Speer benefited by being granted direct access to Hitler with the advantage of as near to a free hand as was possible in the Third Reich; thus enabling him to bypass the Four Year Plan Organisation and bring the Wehrmacht's purchasing agencies under centralised control. In April he set up a Central Planning Organisation which, in consultation with the Wehrmacht and three services, decided priorities of raw materials, industrial distribution and research and development of new weapons. Most important of all, he brought industrialists, engineers and inventors into the committees (Rings) which functioned on the principle of 'industrial self-responsibility'.

Solving the labour problem was more difficult. Already a steadily increasing proportion was drawn from the inmates of concentration camps and prisoners of war. But from 1942 onwards these slave labourers were supplemented by the forcible transportation to Germany of citizens from the occupied countries in the West. This practice induced a backlash in that, to begin with, these conscripts often worked slowly and inefficiently; and, in due course, either indulged in factory sabotage or lesser acts of resistance in addition to providing intelligence to the enemy.

Far more pernicious in a military sense, as well as counter-productive in other ways, was the number of people who evaded transportation by going 'underground' or joining partisan bands to perpetrate guerrilla warfare. From 1942 onwards, supported by the British Special Operations Executive (SOE), active resistance to the Wehrmacht spiralled in frequency and ferocity. In consequence German relations with the conquered nations worsened whenever they felt impelled to mount repressive operations, including the taking and killing of hostages under the direction of orders approved by Hitler, Keitel and Jodl.

The disasters in Russia and North Africa seriously depleted the Wehrmacht, especially the Army and Luftwaffe. Banking on a short war of their own creation, the Germans in September 1939 repeated the mistake of August 1914 by closing the War Academy. They then compounded the error by waiting three years before reopening it in 1942, when a shortage of staff officers became apparent due to the wastage of casualties and promotion in what, from 1940 onwards, bore the hallmarks of a long war.

Thus an old mistake, indicating an endemic inability to learn from history, now had to be rectified as before by the institution of short General Staff courses – run this time at Potsdam and not Sedan.

Designed to train division operations officers, the instructors were battle-experienced operations officers and chiefs of staff. The candidates, recommended by unit commanders on the grounds of talent and combat behaviour, initially spent four weeks with either an infantry, artillery or panzer unit; then three weeks with engineers; followed by two with signals and a further three with a division staff. Finally they spent four (but later six and nine) months at the Academy. Pre-war General Staff officers tended to criticise the brevity of the course, but it was practical and sufficed – just.

Also at the end of 1942, four-week courses for potential division commanders were run. They consisted of war-games, lectures and demonstrations, plus introductions to the latest weapon systems. And, later in 1943, one out of three of these Senior Officers Courses were held for potential corps commanders. They did more than instruct and give weary officers a break from duty at the front along with a chance to take leave and enjoy Berlin, despite the air raids. For, by bringing together groups of very experienced officers from all fronts, valuable exchanges of ideas occurred which, in the absence of adequate manuals, contributed, among other things, to the development of tactical doctrine for the latest weapon systems.

As a background to these courses there loomed inevitably the vital change from a strategy of offence to one of defence. It was a fact that in Field Service Regulations only one short paragraph dealt with defence. But now, regardless of Hitler's objections to this enemy-imposed change, both OKH and, most of all, army group head-quarters wrote their own tactical doctrine of Fighting from Fortified Positions, covering layout of main positions, hedgehogs, counter-attack, artillery reserve positions, tank intercept lines and so on. After the war General Röhricht commented on imperfections: 'Even the instructions issued by OKH contained contradictions dependent upon whether the memo had been compiled by a tactician or a technician.' But, like the short staff courses, these improvised instructions were reasonably coherent and served their purpose well enough.

Special treatment was needed by the two key combat arms, the Luftwaffe and the Panzerwaffe, both of which, pre-Stalingrad, had fallen on hard times. Come 1 January 1943 the Luftwaffe's opera-tional strength had been reduced to only 4,000 aircraft with no reserves. Moreover, as Field Marshal Milch (who took over from Udet as its Director General of Equipment) earlier had recognised, the Allied strategic bomber offensive could only be defeated by fighters – and that current production of 300 a month was hopelessly inadequate for a task requiring 1,000. Blocked by Göring, Hitler and Jeschonnek, who thought production of that magnitude impossible, but strongly helped by Speer, Milch managed to achieve his target by June 1943, barely in time to check temporarily both the heavy Allied night and daytime attacks.

As for the Panzerwaffe, it was now that Hitler's king-maker, General Rudolf Schmundt, came to the rescue by recalling Guderian to reorganise and revitalise the armoured forces. To do so Schmundt needed all the tact at his disposal. For Hitler at first was unhappy about dealing with somebody he had previously distrusted and sacked. Guderian was meanwhile willing only to tackle the task of Inspector General of Armoured Troops under a Charter of his own drafting, approved by the Führer. At Guderian's virtual dictation, Hitler made Guderian 'immediately responsible to me for the future development of armoured troops along the lines that will make that Arm of the Service into a decisive weapon for winning the war'. He was given the status of a Commander-in-Chief of an Army and the Senior Officer of the Panzer Command, responsible for organisation and training not only of Army units but also, where appropriate, of the Luftwaffe and Waffen SS. He was authorised to issue regulations and create new formations and doctrine, and was to work closely with Speer in technical and procurement matters.

Guderian's Charter was unprecedented in that it created an army within the Army and cut across long-established lines of responsibility running the military bureaucracy. For example, the issue of panzer training manuals (blocked since before the war by the Training Branch on the grounds of unorthodoxy) was resented and alleged to have induced confusion. But the situation was desperate (on average panzer divisions had only thirty-two tanks each), time was short (for the Russians already were deep into Ukraine) and so the niceties of protocol could no longer be preserved. Moreover, timing of the revolution was imperative to success coinciding, as it did, with the Führer's fleeting loss of self-confidence in the aftermath of another severe defeat. When Hitler stated his regret to Guderian for their past misunderstandings and said, 'I need you', he may even have meant it. And certainly Guderian believed that a special relationship had been re-established. For the signing of the Charter took place on 28 February 1943, a week after Hitler also had given a temporary free hand to a renowned commander in the field, Field Marshal von Manstein.

On 24 December 1942, Manstein had warned OKH that the Russian offensive into Ukraine not only threatened Kleist's Army Group A in the Caucasus but also his own Army Group Don, near Stalingrad, which guarded Kleist's rear. In the days to come Manstein repeatedly pressed for Army Group South to be reconstituted to include both army groups under his command – on condition that Hitler's interference was barred. Indeed, on 5 January 1943, Manstein took a most unusual step by asking to be relieved of command if his proposals were not approved. This Hitler refused to do until the next crisis arrived, during a meeting on 6 February with Zeitzler and Kluge, when Manstein virtually forced Hitler to agree to further withdrawals, or face the consequences of rout at Rzhev – the shortening of the line to release troops for a long-conceived counterstroke in the vicinity of Kharkov.

At that meeting, too, Manstein (described by his aide-de-camp as almost carefree) managed to raise the subject of unified high command (or rather lack of it). Hitler acted as if he had not heard the question. Nevertheless Manstein did at last succeed in having Army Group Don become Army Group South, thus absorbing, in due course, elements from Army Group A (as, despite Hitler's repeated objections, it pulled back skilfully from the Caucasus) and B as it progressively became redundant.

Manstein was regarded by many officers as Germany's greatest strategist, although there are other contenders for that distinction. Nevertheless, his conduct of the withdrawal into Ukraine and subsequent counterstroke do rate as a masterpiece of manoeuvre warfare against a numerically superior enemy – and were all the more masterful in that he managed to dominate Hitler during a crucial three-day meeting at Zaporozhe, starting on 17 February, at which Zeitzler and Kleist were present. Unavailingly the two Army Group commanders tried to obtain Hitler's views on the future course of the war, at the same time endeavouring to prevent him from meddling with current plans for the counterstroke. Again, Manstein (who, according to Goebbels, was unaware that Hitler had come to sack him, or that, as shown by a facial tic, the Führer was not at ease when in the Field Marshal's presence) dominated the strategic debate. But Manstein survived and actually managed to achieve as free an operational hand as any field marshal was likely to enjoy.

The difference in strategic grasp of the two men was obvious. Whereas Hitler was concerned only that the city of Kharkov, the fall of which on 16 February had triggered the conference, should be recaptured, Manstein was intent on destroying enemy spearheads which radio intercept had revealed to be even weaker and shorter of fuel than Army Group South. The sheer scope of the co-ordinated attacks Manstein launched on 20 February against the enfeebled Russian spearheads, and his progressive exploitation in rolling up the Russian Sixth Army and Third Tank Army, with the loss of some 40,000 men, 600 tanks and 500 guns, seems to have impressed Hitler less than the recapture of Kharkov on 14 March.

Unfortunately, Manstein's victory was not, due to bad weather and debilitated logistics, complete. For when the front stabilised on 26 March, the strategic route centre of Kursk still stood in the midst of a great Russian salient which just begged to be pinched out.

CHAPTER 16

The Long Rearguard Action

'A war is not lost until one is forced to admit to oneself that it is', wrote Manstein to General Ludwig Beck at the time of the 1943 Kharkov counterstroke and at a moment when he became aware of the liquidation of Jews by the SS. In the aftermath of the counterstroke Manstein still felt, as did Guderian and many another German who realised Germany's underlying weakness, that 'we would be able – under reasonable leadership – at least to fight our way to a stalemate'. At that moment too, of course, Beck was up to his neck in plans to remove Hitler, by assassination if necessary. These plans were as repugnant to Manstein, when he got to hear about them, as to several others, including Guderian.

Just then Zeitzler (who was by now disenchanted with Hitler) and Manstein (who had to put up with Hitler claiming all the credit for the Kharkov success) were concentrating almost exclusively on the Eastern Front. Hitler and Jodl, however, taking the broader view as the end in North Africa drew near, began to focus on the imminence of an invasion in the West and the need to transfer troops away from Russia to meet that threat. Nevertheless, because Hitler had persuaded himself (quite erroneously) that the German war economy would collapse if the Donetz basin and Ukraine were lost, sided with Zeitzler and Manstein in their belief that offensive action in the East was desirable as soon as the ground had dried out in May. So, while tacitly admitting that a strategic strategy prevailed and therefore preferring to distribute forces evenly along the length of the front, he nevertheless came to favour what Manstein regarded as a limited and pre-emptive offensive: the elimination of the Kursk salient.

This did not satisfy Manstein. Risky though it might seem, but with the conviction that the depleted German mobile forces were still superior to the larger, improving Russian Army, he preferred manoeuvre warfare of a sophisticated kind. His idea was to allow the Russians 'the upper hand' by inveigling them into driving a characteristically deep advance prior to catching them at the apposite moment in the flanks, then enveloping and destroying them. This would promote the sort of disaster which might present further profitable opportunities leading to the stalemate he sought in Germany's favour.

This grandiose scheme was, of course, contentious, involving five armies and requiring much imagination. Not unreasonably, it was rejected by Hitler. Yet it is worth pointing out that, even as low as at corps level, the concept of counterstroke in depth by mobile, armoured forces became standard and very effective German practice for the remainder of the war. This was in fact an adaptation of the Reichswehr's 'delaying defensive action' once decried by Fritsch as 'organised flight'.

Thus the celebrated Operation Citadel, the so-called greatest clash of armour of the entire war and the last major German offensive on the Eastern Front, was born, although its delivery was two months later than Manstein desired. For once more Manstein and Hitler were at loggerheads about the aim of the operation. Manstein sought to destroy a large Russian force and capture a strategic route centre, while Hitler reached for a propaganda success to further restore his tarnished prestige.

Be that as it may, the repeated postponements of Citadel until 5 July 1943 in order to have available the maximum number of unproven Tiger and Panther tanks, along with heavy tank destroyers, gave the Russians ample time to prepare a hot reception. Fully informed from a wide variety of sources of what was impending, they had fortified the 120-mile-wide Kursk salient in depth with four lines of resistance, backed by mobile reserves in the centre and on the flanks. Additionally, starting on 15 April, they launched co-ordinated guerrilla attacks upon German lines of communication to the Citadel area. The Germans were forced to counter with five separate, major anti-guerrilla operations, between 16 May and 6 June, which absorbed two panzer and four infantry divisions besides ancillary police.

In the knowledge that strategic surprise would be non-existent, the generals disagreed among themselves over Citadel. Jodl shook Hitler by envisaging nothing better than a local success. Manstein and Kluge were satisfied with the original pincer movement plan whereby the former's Army Group tackled the southern and the latter's the northern sides of the salient, but deprecated the long delay. Guderian, whose participation in the debate was resented by Manstein, objected strongly because he dreaded the heavy tank losses of the latest, underdeveloped armoured vehicles that would set back his rebuilding of the Armoured Forces. Neither Zeitzler nor the army commanders were enthusiastic and all had serious reservations. But Hitler, despite his expressed fears, remained unmoved.

The pessimists proved all too right. By 8 July Kluge's blow was shattered with heavy tank losses. Manstein made better progress, although also with heavy tank casualties, many due to mechanical breakdowns. By 9 July an encouraging penetration had been made in the South, but Manstein was still fifty-five miles distant from Kursk and ninety from Kluge's stalled spearheads.

Then on 10 July the Allied forces achieved strategic surprise with a powerful amphibious landing in Sicily. Three days later, bowing to the inevitable (despite Manstein's plea to continue Citadel in order to destroy the enemy's armoured reserves) Hitler ordered the withdrawal of forces to southern Europe, including the elite SS Panzer Corps, to help prop up the Italian and Balkan fronts and keep Italy in the war. Citadel was cancelled, though already on 12 July it was in jeopardy when mighty Russian forces launched the first of many blows aimed not only at defeating Citadel but as part of a general offensive intended to destroy the weakened Army Group South.

*   *   *

From this moment the war, from Germany's point of view, changed fundamentally. Henceforward, apart from one ill-judged major counter-offensive in the West in December 1944, the struggle deteriorated into one long withdrawal operation. Germany was squeezed from the East, the South and the West. Indeed, to all intents and purposes, a war on four fronts now engulfed Europe and hopelessly overstretched German resources. For not only was a desperate Zeitzler striving to hold together the Eastern Front, but also a strategically surprised Kesselring was shoring up the Southern Front, and Rundstedt (amazingly brought back by Hitler as Commander-in-Chief West in 1942) worrying about invasion of the Western one. Meanwhile Germany was being battered by the day and night bomber offensive the Allies had planned at the Casablanca Conference in January 1943, when also the decision to invade Sicily was taken. And, of immense help to Goebbels' propaganda stiffening German resolve, the policy of Unconditional Surrender was announced, without due consideration, by President Roosevelt.

Moreover there existed, also, a fifth front spanning the length and breadth of the Atlantic Ocean. After April, Admiral Dönitz (who had taken over as the Navy's Commander-in-Chief in January 1943 after Raeder fell out with Hitler) was compelled to admit defeat when U-boat losses soared to unsustainable quantities and he felt forced, by superior Allied tactics, techniques and technology, to withdraw the survivors from the vital hunting grounds. The Americans were thus able to reinforce Britain at will, assuring the moment when huge forces would invade the West.

Now, the tug-of-war between the theatres of war Commanders-in-Chief for adequate resources was stimulated. This posed awful dilemmas for those at OKW who struggled to advise a Führer whose judgement and intuitions became more impaired as signs of his failing health grew more apparent. The struggle was made no easier for Keitel and Jodl when Zeitzler seized the opportunity, offered by the invasion of Sicily, to attempt a reassertion of OKH influence over the Southern Front rather than leave it to OKW. Jealous as ever of OKW power, Jodl easily thwarted this ploy, but relations between the highest commanders and their staffs were not improved by it at a time of great tension when unity was essential.

Without abatement the squeezing of Germany continued throughout 1943. While Manstein and Kluge, with only occasional success in stopping the numerically superior Russians whenever they lacked logistic support, the Western Allies conquered Sicily in concert, on 25 July, with the removal of Mussolini from power. On both fronts the Germans and their now thoroughly unreliable Italian allies found themselves, as Manstein put it, 'waging a defensive struggle which could not be anything more than a system of improvisations and stop gaps'. It was a miracle, delivered by the skilful and staunch combat corps and divisions (despite the usual interventions by Hitler), that Army Group South remained in touch with Army Group Centre to retire reasonably intact behind the Dnieper and Desna at the end of September. The Russians then swiftly seized strategic bridgeheads on the west banks.

By then, however, the chances of reinforcement of Russia from Italy and the Balkans were remote in the extreme. For one thing German cities and factories were being laid waste by air attack, making the Luftwaffe divert immense resources to home defence. For another the Luftwaffe had played a disappointing and costly part in Citadel, though Jeschonnek had thrown everything possible into it. Things came to a head after Hamburg was devastated between 24 July and 2 August, the ball-bearing plant at Schweinfurt bombed in daylight on the 17th and the secret rocket research station at Peenemunde seriously damaged that night.

Much of the blame fell on Jeschonnek for his failure fully to appreciate the potential of Allied air power and to stand up to Hitler (before whom he used to stand like a cowed schoolboy) and Göring. And he knew it. Far too late now to cover his errors, he wrote a paper for Hitler, categorically laying the blame on Göring. But it was suppressed by Hitler's air adjutant, von Below. In consequence he telephoned Hitler and had a very stormy conversation in which the Führer stood by Göring and concluded with the words, 'You know what is left for you to do now!' The Chief of Air Staff obligingly shot himself, leaving behind a note saying, 'I can no longer work with the Reichsmarschall. Long live the Führer.' Thus, as Udet had committed suicide in 1941 to spare Göring, Jeschonnek spared Hitler, who was quite as much to blame.

But Hitler could not be blamed for the main disadvantages under which Germany and its Wehrmacht laboured, caused by the ready access of the British and Americans, via Ultra, to top-level, high-grade intelligence provided by decrypted radio communications. It was the Germans' misfortune that, although they sometimes questioned the immunity of the Enigma machines' codes, did envisage a Bombe type of code-breaking computer and did carry out investigations, they actually did nothing more than progressively make improvements to the machine. For they could neither find proof nor really accept that Enigma could be vulnerable. With supreme confidence in the technology at their disposal it seemed incomprehensible that anybody else could devise a method by which Enigma's enormous number of key-setting combinations could be broken quickly and in sufficient quantity to make the operation a threat to its security. Thus the Germans again fatally committed the military sin of despising their enemy.

One reason, of course, for this unwillingness of the Germans to face up to the danger was an arrogant confidence in the infallibility of their own superior genius compared with other peoples. They could not envisage the genius of the great British mathematician, Dr Alan Turing, who developed binary mathematics to improve beyond imagination the Polish Bombe computer, and helped build Colossus in 1944, the first electronic computer with a memory. Furthermore their complacency was compounded by the apparent technical superiority of their communication systems, as brilliantly employed for the Wehrmacht by Generals of Signals such as Erich Fellgiebel and Albert Praun. Another reason, however, may also have been a dread that, if Enigma had been compromised, the entire German radio network, through which so much traffic passed and upon which Wehrmacht operational command and control rested, would be rendered almost impotent, with appalling ramifications at a time when land lines were so often being cut by enemy action.

So the Germans complacently retained faith in Enigma, though prudently upgrading it as well as introducing still more sophisticated machines such as the Geheimschreiber (secret writer) teleprinter. They also took comfort in blaming their allies, especially the despised Italians, for breaches of secrecy and for betrayal.

This situation naturally placed generals, admirals and their subordinates at a dreadful, hidden disadvantage. Kesselring and OKW, for example, were not to know that many of their reports and plans for the defence of Sicily and Italy were being read by the enemy almost as soon as the addressees. Nor could they be aware that such information was of immense use to the Allies in checking the accuracy of the Germans' own knowledge of the enemy – and, maybe, how that information had been obtained. Thus it was all the easier for the Allies not only to deny German insight into their plans to strike at Sicily, but also confidently to devise deception measures which almost invariably completely fooled the Germans.

The dismal record of German forecasting of forthcoming Allied offensive operations from October 1942 onwards speaks for itself. OKW, OKH, OKM and OKL were fed so many false leads and so absolutely were denied sure and clear intelligence of enemy intentions, that they were reduced to guesswork about the destination and strength of operations in Russia and those directed against Tunisia, Sicily and Italy. Moreover, although radio intercept of a telephone conversation between Churchill and Roosevelt disclosed the coming defection of Italy, the Germans remained in ignorance of the negotiations leading up to Italy's exit from the Axis in September 1943.

This makes the frequently surprised Kesselring's clever defence of southern Europe all the more praiseworthy, especially since members of the High Command mistrusted and hampered him. Yet, at a time when Kesselring was being slandered by Göring (out of jealousy and for self-interest) with being the Luftwaffe's 'State Enemy Number 1'; when Milch was none too friendly; and Richthofen (commanding Second Air Fleet in Italy) was conspiring to undermine his plans, Hitler stayed ambivalent. At one moment he praised Kesselring and the next referred to him as a 'dupe' among 'those born traitors down there' (the Italians), and appointed Rommel (no friend of Kesselring's) as advisor on the Mediterranean theatre.

Nevertheless, when Richthofen and other generals anticipated an Allied landing in Sardinia, or even mainland Italy, Kesselring backed his appreciation that, because the Allies needed freedom of passage through the Mediterranean, the target would be Sicily. He heavily reinforced the island, and, after the Italian divisions defected, successfully defended it for more than a month. Meanwhile he made abundantly plain his unalterable strategic intention to defend the length of Italy and not, as Rommel and Jodl counselled, withdraw to the Alps.

Again, when Mussolini was deposed and Hitler, feeling sure the Italians would defect, planned, with encouragement by Jodl, to create a new Army Group B, commanded by Rommel, it was Kesselring who diplomatically kept the Italians in the Axis. It was he who skilfully thwarted Hitler's rash plan to seize Rome, the King and the Government while deftly making preparations to disarm the Italians (Operation Axis) should the need arise. It was also Kesselring who executed a masterly withdrawal from Sicily (which Rommel deemed impossible); and, when the Italians did defect on 8 September as the Allies invaded southern Italy and started to come ashore at Salerno, it also was he and his Chief of Staff, General Siegfried Westphal, who subtly managed to negotiate an almost bloodless Italian capitulation and disarmament at Rome (under threat of the Eternal City's bombardment). This was a lot more effective than Rommel's heavy-handedness in the North, which caused much more bloodshed along with a mass exodus of armed men who escaped transportation to form partisan bands in the hills.

At almost every stage of these hectic events, Kesselring was hampered by Hitler, Jodl, Keitel, Rommel and Richthofen. And indeed, those at OKW could claim the credit for out-guessing Kesselring in the belief that Salerno/Naples would be the Allied objective, and not Sardinia as Kesselring thought. It also damaged

Kesselring when he had to abandon Salerno on 16 September, having trumpeted that the Allies were on the eve of destruction. Yet Hitler, who had supported the withdrawal from Salerno after talking to Kesselring, made no move to sack him, though keeping an expectant Rommel in the north as a sort of Commander-in-Chief South West in waiting.

For Rommel, however, the call did not come. Instead Hitler had come to recognise that Kesselring had all the attributes of a 'great captain' who had proven himself master of not only all phases of the art of war (including conduct of withdrawal, the most difficult of all), of administration, but also, with distinction, of the rarest skill of co-operation with allies. He confirmed Kesselring in power in the south and, along with OKW staff, gradually warmed to his strategy of a slowly staged withdrawal, linked to a scorched earth policy, into a ninety-mile, main defensive, mountainous position, ten miles in depth, from the River Garigliano, in the west, to the Sangro in the east. Step by step as Kesselring withdrew, he craftily denigrated Rommel and convinced Hitler and Jodl of the practicality of his strategy which, he reckoned, would delay the enemy reaching the Apennines for from six to nine months longer than Rommel intended; and, moreover, would require eight fewer divisions.

Bit by bit Rommel's formations were detached to reinforce Kesselring. Time and again Kesselring defeated Rommel in debate and dialectics. Week after week Hitler procrastinated and played off one field marshal against the other. Almost out of the blue on 25 October he decided to retain Kesselring as Commander-in-Chief South West and also of a newly created Army Group C, with responsibilty for the whole of Italy. This would be separate from Field Marshal Weich's command as Commander-in-Chief South East, covering the Balkans, where guerrilla warfare was rife. In effect Kesselring was made administrator of most of Italy, a sort of Consul. Meanwhile, on 12 November, Rommel was sent away with his staff to inspect the Atlantic Wall defences.

Kesselring's success in winning (and thereafter retaining throughout difficult times) Hitler's confidence to an extent greater than any other of his commanders, with the possible exception of Admiral Dönitz, demands explanation. How was it that this intellectual Bavarian aristocrat and one-time soldier could woo and, to no mean extent, control the anti-general Hitler? Perhaps his wearing of a Luftwaffe uniform had something to do with it and no doubt his long-held anti-Communist views were influential. But although Kesselring was no Nazi, and frequently deplored the Party's and the SS's excesses and criminal activities, he must have seemed to Hitler as quite as much an ally as the favoured Keitel, Jodl, Rommel and Sepp Dietrich of the SS.

Unlike the members of that quartet, however, Kesselring was no lackey. He fought hard, shrewdly and effectively to win his own way and managed, on too many occasions to be gainsaid, to show how much more persuasive other intellectual and cultured generals might have been had they treated the Führer with reasonable respect instead of obsequiously or patronisingly. It is indeed remarkable how frequently he managed by clear, simply stated and well-aimed arguments to convince Hitler, often by flexibly sensing what the Führer wanted and meeting his whims if possible. At the same time it must not be overlooked that Kesselring, like Guderian, was adept and courageous in confronting Hitler and seeking ways to circumvent the more outrageous commands. But possibly it is Hitler himself, in the act of praising Kesselring at a later date, who provides the key: 'It is my opinion that military leadership without optimism is not possible.' Maybe, indeed, 'Smiling Albert' rather overdid the optimism as times grew worse. But like Manstein, Guderian and many another he too was striving to save his country from disaster, and his certainly was a better way than, for example, Keitel's and Jodl's.

It is therefore interesting to record that, towards the end of 1943 when Schmundt, probably in collaboration with Guderian and others, began trying to replace Keitel with an officer with experience of combat, his choice fell on Kesselring. Had he succeeded the course of events might have led to a startlingly different outcome. But in the event nothing came of it because, at that juncture, Kesselring could not be spared from Italy and, anyway, Hitler refused to do away with a field marshal who rushed ahead to open doors for him and was so obliging in every other way.

Kesselring was particularly fortunate in his brilliant Chief of Staff, Westphal, and the commander of Tenth Army in Italy, General Scheel Heinz von Vietinghoff, with both of whom he had an easy relationship. For although the brave Kesselring (who had been shot down five times) and Westphal issued comprehensive directives, which were not always received with approval, and frequently visited the front at critical moments to make decisions, he rarely interfered with their operations and supported them loyally even when Hitler interfered at the lower levels – which, significantly, he did less with Kesselring than others.

This team's conduct of the withdrawal to what became known as the Gustav Line, covering Rome, achieved almost everything promised by Kesselring, who had read the defensive nature of the terrain to perfection. The Allied armies, forced to assault a series of river lines, covering positions in often dreadful weather, made such slow progress that it was not until the end of October that the enemy had closed up to the Gustav Line where, exhausted and short of supplies, he was brought to a halt. Initial guerrilla warfare as yet was slight. But the loss of Sardinia and Corsica, which was inevitable in face of Allied naval and air supremacy, had exposed his right flank. His left, on the other hand, was secure since Allied landing in the Dodecanese islands had been efficiently checked by Weichs. He also had mopped up the Italians in Greece and Yugoslavia besides managing to retain adequate control over guerrilla forces who, often beneficially to the Germans, were engaged in bitter internecine warfare of racial and political natures.

Simultaneously, Manstein and Kluge, also harassed by partisans, had been fighting a very different, highly mobile campaign in Russia. Manstein especially had been under pressure as a result of repeated vetoing of his plans. Always at the back of his mind was resignation, as he indicated to Zeitzler in July: 'If the Führer thinks he can find any army group commander or headquarters staff with better nerves than we had during the past winter ... or with the ability to foresee the inevitable more clearly than we have done, I am fully prepared to hand over to them. As long as I remain at this post, however, I must have the chance to use my own head.'

Nothing changed, of course. Manstein, in spite of Hitler and those of his entourage like Göring, Himmler and Keitel, who wanted him replaced, went on fighting. But his resources were constantly reduced and his infantry units' parlous numbers of officers made them ever more prone to indiscipline and desertion – and ever more in need of spurious but uplifting Nazi indoctrination to keep them fighting.

Meanwhile, in the West, Rundstedt (who in Manstein's opinion was a 'tired, impotent man') was wrestling with defence of the Atlantic Wall. Not in the least fooled in the summer of 1943 by an elaborate Allied simulation of an impending invasion, he was, with

1,600 miles of coastline to defend and less than twenty divisions available (of which none were fully operational panzer divisions), in no condition to cope with the blow he knew must fall in 1944. This he stated in a report to Hitler on 28 October, in which he declared that although the Atlantic Wall was 'indispensable and valuable for battle as well as propaganda ... the outcome of the battle must depend on the use of a mobile and armoured reserve'.

Instantly Hitler responded with Directive No. 51 in which he admitted that a successful enemy landing in the West must have unpredictable consequences; and laid down that reinforcements must be made available for 'particularly those places from which the long-range bombardment [with V1 and V2 rocket weapons] will begin'. But, as Warlimont noted, all the Supreme Command could propose 'was little better than a series of expedients ... the defence against invasion would have to be undertaken primarily by the forces already available in the West' which had neither the necessary numbers nor capacity to do so.

Seeking a palliative, therefore, Hitler detailed Rommel and the staff of his Army Group B to make a report, prompting Rundstedt to ask Keitel if he was to be replaced by that field marshal. He was told that 'Rommel was suitable for "Seydlitz-like attacks as at Rossbach", but not for larger strategic operations. Only Field Marshal von Kluge could be considered a suitable replacement for me' – and Kluge was recovering from a serious motoring accident. Nevertheless, when Rommel reported on the state of the Atlantic Wall to Rundstedt on 19 December, he agreed that 'It all looks very black.'

Nevertheless, Rommel's appreciation of enemy intentions and potential tallied very closely with those of Rundstedt and with the need for much stronger armoured forces. Only later, after Hitler had ordered Rommel's Army Group B to command the forces in north-west Europe, under Commander-in-Chief West, would disagreements about their employment surface. In the meantime, however, on 20 December, Hitler had stated for the first time his realisation that 'if they attack in the West that attack will decide the war'. And thereupon he approved the creation of a new Panzer Group West, responsible to Rundstedt, while Rommel threw all his energy into strengthening the Atlantic Wall, upon which he believed the invasion would have to be broken if there was to be the slightest chance of repelling it.

Thus, to some considerable extent, the mere threat of invasion had gone some distance to hasten Germany's defeat. For Panzer Group West with its panzer divisons, plus many more infantry and lower grade fortification formations holding the Atlantic Wall, could only be found from the other fronts which were being remorselessly eroded by daily combat. Indeed, at the end of the year, although Kesselring had stabilised the front in Italy, in Russia the enemy pressed unrelentingly on all fronts but principally in the South. Kluge's Army Group Centre was thrown out of Smolensk on 23 September as the Red Army reached the Pripet Marshes. Kiev fell on 6 November and the Crimea was cut off when Hitler refused Manstein's plea that the peninsula should be evacuated, thus leaving Sevastopol under siege. Moreover the Russians did not stop there but, once the ground had frozen solid in December, pressed on into the Pripet Marshes and broke out of the Dnieper bridgeheads in an effort to complete the reconquest of Ukraine.

The New Year looked bleak indeed, regardless of promises of secret weapons which would turn the tide. By then, some thought, as Berlin crumbled under a sustained bomber offensive and the SS was forced to terrorise an apathetic populace to forestall collapse, there would be very little left to save.

Meanwhile conspirators, who were convinced that Germany's only hope rested on elimination of Hitler and his gang, were now, under the inspiration of Colonel Claus von Stauffenberg, ever more desperately plotting assassination and a putsch.

CHAPTER 17

Eclipse

The pressures piling upon the generals in 1944 were becoming unbearable and were producing stresses and strains which induced extremes of uncharacteristic behaviour. Few were affected more than Manstein as he struggled to cope, on the one hand, with the rolling Russian winter offensive in Ukraine and, on the other, with the infuriating incivility and tyranny of Hitler. Up to this moment he had endeavoured to accommodate the Führer's often irrational demands, while despising the man for his ignorance and vulgarity. Manstein was an excellent strategist, but could not match Kesselring for exceptional all-round statecraft, skill and steeliness in dealing with Hitler and his henchmen.

Matters began to come to a head on 27 January 1944 when Hitler called a conference of all Army Group and Army commanders to harangue them on the need for intensified Nazi indoctrination of the Army. In the process he deeply insulted the field marshals and generals twice, by innuendo, so angering Manstein that he interrupted the Führer to repudiate the aspersions. In response Hitler abandoned his speech, left the room in a rage and called in Manstein for a dressing down, which Manstein brushed aside with the proud remark 'I am a gentleman'. Manstein was neither prone to resignation nor, most emphatically, to plotting against Hitler because, as he boasted, 'Prussian Field Marshals do not mutiny.'

On 25 January the Russians had broken through on a wide front to the west of the Dnieper to encircle XXXXIV Panzer Corps and XI Corps in the Cherkassy salient. When Hitler insisted as usual on staying put and tampered with Manstein's orders to prepare a counterstroke to relieve the pocket prior to a break-out, yet another Stalingrad threatened in miniature. Snow and mud delayed the pincer-movement counter-attack. Yet when executed the results were like those of the old days with the capture of 700 enemy tanks and 750 guns, although only 2,000 prisoners. Nevertheless, with the relief force in sight of the pocket when bad weather and the state of the ground delayed the break-out, Hitler still forbade it. Manstein then did what Paulus should have done at Stalingrad. Regardless of Hitler's veto he ordered the break-out and managed to save 20,000 men out of 54,000 and much invaluable equipment, less the heavy artillery which was stuck in the mud.

Cavalier behaviour of this sort could not be permitted by Hitler. On 19 March he called another meeting of field marshals to enable them, with due ceremony, to present to him a declaration of loyalty, signed by them all. They wanted Rundstedt to act as their spokes-man and use the occasion to ask Hitler to give up his position as Army Commander-in-Chief, if only on the Eastern Front, and appoint one of them in his place. The weary Rundstedt refused because he thought that, as previously, he would be sent off 'with a flea in his ear'. In fact two of those present, Manstein and Kleist, were already booked for retirement as a result of lobbying by Göring, Himmler and Keitel. The two field marshals discovered this from Zeitzler when, without warning on 30 March, they were whisked off in Hitler's Condor airliner to Berchtesgaden. The Chief of Staff added that he had instantly tendered his resignation in protest only to be curtly refused.

The parting was conducted with dignity and the presentation of the Swords to their Knight's Crosses. The reason, according to Hitler, was the need for 'a new type of leadership ... under a new name and a new symbol'. Manstein was to be relieved by a Saxon, Field Marshal Walter Model, 'who would dash around the divisions and get the very utmost out of the troops'. A panzer general renowned for his ruthlessness and energy, his expertise in defensive warfare, extreme loyalty to Hitler and, yet, ability to stand up to the Führer and get away with it, Model was as good a choice as anybody in the circumstances. The same was true of Kleist's successor, Ferdinand Schörner, a Mountain general, holder of the Pour le Mérite and Hitler devotee, with a reputation for remorseless ferocity unlike any other Army general.

Not for nothing was Model known as 'The Führer's fireman'. He had saved Ninth Army at Rzhev in January 1942 and, recently, had taken command of Army Group North from General Georg Küchler after the Russians had completed the relief of Leningrad and thrown back the Germans in some disarray, which Küchler had earlier warned Hitler might happen. Küchler got the blame (though he had virtually saved his Army Group from envelopment before Model's arrival) and was retired.

Model, for his part, was lucky to be able, within four weeks, to bring the Russians to a halt on the Narva Line. He had the advantage, as Hitler's favourite, of being given two extra divisions, while the Russians struggled with difficult terrain, the spring thaw, and defective operational techniques. All of these combined to thwart the Russians' exploitation of initial success, for which good fortune Model was promoted field marshal. He was fortunate, too, in Ukraine, taking over from Manstein after the latter had all but checked the Russian winter offensive. Here, as in the North, he was helped by the thaw slowing down the Russian advance at a crucial moment.

Like Kesselring and Dönitz, Model had the knack of handling Hitler – in his case by introduction of a new formula he called 'Shield and Sword'. Similar to 'delaying defensive action', this catchword really was only a variation of existing doctrine, as practised by Manstein and Kesselring, whereby a withdrawal took place within the framework of a planned counter-offensive. But it sounded innovative, impressed Hitler and carried the advantage of a free hand for Model to withdraw as he chose in those circumstances.

*   *   *

As the Russians drew closer to Germany and invasion of France loomed larger, these threats had no decisive influence on the Italian Front because it had equal priority with the others. As Kesselring pointed out, this 'disclosed a strategic mistake by the Supreme German Command' regarding the main point of effort. He thought that to neglect the Italian front appeared justifiable, unless the potential importance of the Italian Theatre of War was considered from the viewpoint of air warfare and denial of air bases to the overwhelming enemy air forces.

The Allies, however, had the diversion of German forces from the other fronts more in mind. OKW's overall defensive strategy, which aimed to wear down the Allies to the point of exhaustion, certainly contributed to this. It was also debilitating in its own right since the Allies were by now so strong in men and materiel that attrition was hardly to Germany's benefit. Germany could hardly manage the replacements who, from 1944 onwards, arrived prematurely in the theatre and had to be trained in rear areas. Among them was an increasing number of Poles and Russians, whose fealty to Germany was anything but pronounced.

Kesselring's siting of layered lines of defence in depth as well as along the coasts was intended as much to fool the enemy and conceal his own strength as to mount genuine resistance. This deception, however, almost invariably failed due to excellent Allied intelligence. Their amphibious reconnaissance and raiding parties came and went without too much difficulty and their choice of Anzio as the site for a major, unopposed landing on 22 January 1944 was based on clear evidence of German weakness and bluff in that sector.

When the Allies came ashore, Kesselring's first reaction was anger at himself for being fooled; his second to order every available unit, less those in the Gustav Line, to the spot at once; and his third to gamble outrageously by forbidding Vietinghoff to abandon that Line even though it was in danger of being taken in rear. He coolly banked on the Allied Command failing to take advantage of apparent weaknesses and was fully repaid in his boldness when, having established a strong bridgehead, the enemy stood still throughout 22 and 23 January when, according to Westphal, almost any forward movement on the 23rd would have been irresistible.

So the Gustav Line held firm as Kesselring and General Georg von Mackensen sealed off the Anzio bridgehead and engaged in a grapple which did not end in stalemate until 29 February. In the meantime, the Allies launched costly, abortive frontal assaults on the Gustav Line with scant reward. It was a notable German defensive victory, yet robbed of its full value by Hitler's insistence not only on attempting the elimination of the bridgehead but also on dictating the tactics and a bad plan. Kesselring shared the blame for this and censured himself for not withstanding Hitler's intervention.

It was evidence of Kesselring's delusion, due to misleading information, that when the next Allied offensive hit the Gustav Line on 11 May, he had, only the day before, sent Vietinghoff on leave and a course on ideology. Caught off balance again, this time there was no respite. The Gustav Line was ruptured and the enemy poured through in a relentless thrust for Rome. Within four days withdrawal from the line was unavoidable and some German divisions were disintegrating. This time, so complete was defeat that it was impossible to effect much delay on the prepared lay-back positions. Had the American General Mark Clark, seeking glory from the capture of Rome, not diverged from the correct centre line, the

German right wing would have been overwhelmed. As it was Rome fell to Clark on 4 June and Tenth Army, covered by skilful rear-guards, withdrew in better order than it deserved.

Next stop was the Gothic Line, founded on the Apennines to guard Genoa, Bologna and the Po valley. It was not reached until mid-October due to a classic exhibition of delaying defensive action, straight out of the war-games manuals. But if Hitler had had his way by imposing halts at every juncture only remnants might have reached that position. As it was Kesselring was compelled to pay a flying visit to the Führer to put his case in person. It was a bad tempered meeting in which he lost patience when refuting the Führer's prevarications and made a 'short and heated reply'. Yet the upshot was a deal. In exchange for a free hand he would delay the enemy short of the Po into 1945. But that rather depended on events elsewhere which, in sheer magnitude if not necessarily strategic importance, dwarfed those in Italy and the Balkans.

*   *   *

At the beginning of 1944 overall Allied air superiority was becoming almost intolerable to the Germans. It was a miracle of determination, improvisation and organisation on Speer's part that industrial production continued to increase at a time when the defeat of the British night bomber offensive against German cities, due to appalling losses, was the Luftwaffe's last success. Come March, however, the American heavy day bombers were more than compensating for this Allied set-back; not only by hitting their targets more accurately but, by then escorted all the way by new, long-range fighter formations, also exterminating the German fighter force. In a single, so-called 'Big Week' in February, 692 German fighters were lost in the air and many more on the ground. Between March and May, shortly before the Allies launched their invasion of Normandy, no less than 2,442 fighters went down in combat in addition to some 1,500 lost from other causes. These losses were irreplaceable and presented the Allies with an air supremacy never to be lost.

Needless to say such catastrophic wastage had a profound effect on land operations. The Russians benefited and, at last after the disasters of June 1941, could provide more than adequate support for their advancing armies. Their latest machines and improved air crew training began to take a toll on an enemy who could no longer operate with impunity. On the Eastern Front, as almost everywhere, worthwhile German reconnaissance became extremely hazardous and at times impossible (even when later carried out by a few of the very fast jet aircraft as they entered service). Therefore the quality and quantity of intelligence fell calamitously.

In Italy and in the West the destruction wrought by air power corroded the German war effort. Soon after the Germans began constructing the sites from which jet-propelled V1 cruise missiles were to be launched, the RAF found and destroyed them. The planned long-range attack on England therefore had to be post-poned until more easily concealed launching ramps could be installed. Equally crippling was the systematic Allied pre-invasion attack on land communications which began in earnest on 6 March 1944. By day and night railway maintenance workshops and engine sheds, frequently co-located with marshalling yards and other route centres, were smashed. Progressively the entire railway system of France and Belgium was pulverised and paralysed to a planned pattern which suggested that the main landing would take place in the Pas de Calais. In May Rundstedt was told that only thirty-two trains per day were getting through instead of the necessary 100. Then, from 21 May, bridges across the River Seine were attacked, as well as locomotives. This further crippled the railways, making it all the more difficult to transfer troops to and from the Pas de Calais and Normandy – with telling strategic as well as logistic effect.

Meanwhile airfields were under intensive attack. This severely hampered Luftwaffe operations in any role and made virtually impossible reconnaissance not only of the harbours, whence the Allied invasion would be launched, but also adequate defence against enemy bombers, which attacked with impunity.

*   *   *

The air threat induced the controversy which most bedevilled German defensive strategy in France and Belgium. Rundstedt clung to the orthodox doctrine that, since an enemy lodgement was unstoppable by the coastal defences, the correct response was the classic one of massed counter-attack by mobile armoured forces from depth at the earliest moment. But Rommel, whose Army Group B was subordinated to Rundstedt and responsible for both countries, thought otherwise. Based on his experience of Allied air attacks in North Africa, and now underlined in devastation by the awe-inspiring demonstration before his very eyes, he considered

that, in the face of such firepower, it would be impossible to
assemble an effective armoured concentration from depth. Moreover, in 1943 he had written a paper declaring that numerous relatively cheap anti-tank guns sited in depth were a better anti-armour
weapon system than far more expensive tanks. He concluded
therefore that the invasion must be destroyed within 'the first 24
hours' amid the coastal fortifications; backed by panzer divisions
located within a few miles of the beaches tasked to intervene without
delay.

The panzer debate raged while Rommel strove to strengthen the
coastal defences in order to fight an old-fashioned infantry and
artillery contest among them. Guderian, who visited France in
April, sided with Rundstedt, as did the commander of Panzer Group
West, General Geyr von Schweppenburg. After the war Guderian
admitted that he and Geyr had made a mistake, probably because
they had no personal experience of the devastating effect of Anglo-
American air power. In the event, however, the matter was referred
to Hitler who resolved it with a politician's compromise. Six panzer
divisions would be spread out within immediate striking distance of
the coast, while four would be held back in depth (three of them
straddling the Seine to the north-west of Paris). But only six of these
divisions were fully operational on 6 June because OKH had been
dilatory in moving remnants from the East. Meanwhile, come that
date, only eighteen per cent of the planned defences in Seventh
Army's sector (including Normandy) were complete.

There was no disagreement among generals, however, regarding
their appreciation of where the main Allied blow would fall.
Applying straight military logic they decided it had to be the Pas de
Calais, a conclusion put beyond doubt by confirmatory intelligence
reports from air reconnaissance, radio intercepts and agents. What
the Germans were unaware of, however, was that they were the
victims of one of the most elaborate spoofs of all time. Such
reconnaissance aircraft as did penetrate British air space brought
back little of value due to excellent enemy camouflage of what
mattered and subtle disclosure of decoys. Enemy radio traffic was
also very secure yet arranged to mislead. As D Day for Operation
Overlord drew near, Britain was sealed off from neutral countries,
such as Eire and Spain, to prevent leakage of information through
them. Furthermore, every German agent had been captured and
'turned' to transmit false information.

Naturally receptive to confirmation of their own convictions, Rundstedt, Rommel and everybody else, with the notable exception of Hitler, were induced to believe what they wanted to believe – that the Pas de Calais was the principal target, although they also assumed there would be diversionary landings for which forces would have to be provided. Towards the end of April, however, the Führer, who already had contributed two or three wild intuitions about the likely target, hit the jackpot. Noting that air reconnaissance seemed to disclose larger concentrations of enemy shipping west of the Isle of Wight than elsewhere, he chose Normandy which, like the Pas de Calais, was within fighter aircraft range. This notion Rundstedt could not ignore. But although he made reluctant adjustments, which alarmed the enemy when they detected them, he remained, on naval advice, steadfast in his belief in the Pas de Calais solution, and wrote off the shipping concentrations as part of a deception ploy.

Rommel, on the other hand, lent credence to the Normandy threat. But when the enemy's D Day dawned he was visiting his wife at Ulm on her birthday, absent from his headquarters like several of his generals. General Edgar Feuchtinger, commanding 21st Panzer Division near Caen in Normandy, was in close attendance to his mistress in Paris.

As so often on crucial occasions, the Germans were completely surprised – this time not only because of Allied deception measures and security, but chiefly due to the not unreasonable conclusion that, owing to bad weather (which did indeed delay D Day by twenty-four hours), an amphibious operation was impossible. It was simply the Germans' misfortune that the Allies, with better basic meteorological information at their disposal, were aware of an interval of calm in the weather pattern which had eluded the German meteorologists.

But much more than the surprise of timing upset the Germans on 6 June. To begin with they were shattered by unexpected Allied tactics and technology when the assault echelons, led by specialised armoured vehicles behind an unprecedentedly heavy air, artillery and rocket bombardment, came in two hours prior to high water. To some extent this neutralised the beach obstacles and they also overran the front line defences (in most places) at high speed and with light casualties. Rommel and his staff had no more imagined the breaching of minefields and other obstacles, along with the overwhelming of strongpoints, within only a few hours, than they had anticipated the rapid exploitation inland by armoured forces which nearly took Caen at nightfall. Nor could they deal effectively with those forces when 21st Panzer Division was delayed by indecision in launching its planned counter-attack. The defeat was exacerbated by Rommel's absence, Rundstedt's reluctance to commit his reserved panzer divisions until the position was clarified, and Jodl's unwillingness to awake Hitler to obtain permission for their release – which was not granted until 1600 hours.

By then, of course, Rommel's plan to defeat the enemy within forty-eight hours was in ruins. Henceforward the Germans were condemned to roping off the gradually expanding Allied bridgehead under a storm of gunfire and air attack which made tactical movement during daytime extremely difficult and only possible at night with long intervals between vehicles. The only two concentrated counterstrokes collapsed. Inevitably, also, the semi-isolation of the armies by air power so delayed the arrival of logistic resources as well as reinforcements that on 1 July Rundstedt warned Keitel by telephone that 'the writing was on the wall'. This, coming on top of the collapse of Army Group Centre at the hands of the Russians, seems badly to have shaken Keitel who cried, 'What shall we do? What shall we do?' At which Rundstedt had barked: 'Make peace you fools, what else can you do?' His outburst led to his immediate retirement and replacement by Kluge.

To make matters worse for the defenders of Normandy, however, Kluge continued to deny them adequate reinforcements from Fifteenth Army in the Pas de Calais. Completely deceived until mid-July that Normandy was only a feint and that far more Allied divisions than they thought were still waiting in England, he too clung to Rundstedt's original opinion with fatal results. Naturally, too, the Germans wanted to secure the V1 launching sites, although in fact this was not of major military consequence once the weapon's inaccuracy and enemy countermeasures took their toll.

When Kluge first took over on 4 July he at first gave the impression (probably for Hitler's benefit) that all would be well. Yet in his heart he realised that Germany was in desperate straits and that the conspirators with whom he was involved to remove Hitler were on the eve of striking. Like Guderian and Geyr von Schweppenburg, he at first underestimated the effect of Allied firepower and sedulously sought to obey the Führer's order to hold fast to

Normandy. He may or may not have been upset on 17 July when Rommel was seriously wounded by an air attack, but he was buoyed up next day when a big, anticipated British attack at Caen was checked with heavy losses. But on 20 July he, like many another general, was on the horns of a dilemma when word was received that Hitler had been killed by a bomb planted in the conference room at Rastenburg.

*   *   *

At the beginning of July General Beck, Dr Karl Goerdeler (a former Burgomeister of Leipzig) and Colonel von Stauffenberg had decided that they must assassinate Hitler, before the front in Normandy collapsed and the Russians reached Poland, and then seize control of the government. On three occasions between 6 and 15 July, Stauffenberg was called to a conference with the Führer and took the bomb with him in his brief case. But since on neither occasion were Hitler, Göring and Himmler all present, he took the bomb away with him. On 20 July, however, he decided to explode the device regardless of those present. In the event neither Göring nor Himmler were there, though, among others, Keitel, Jodl, Warlimont and Schmundt were.

Stauffenberg primed the bomb, joined the conference after it had started, placed the briefcase close to Hitler and then made an excuse to leave the room. As he was walking away there was a heavy explosion, so he kept going and caught his aeroplane to Berlin, without checking the results. Meanwhile General Fellgiebel, also without checking, had phoned the success signal to the conspirators in Berlin and then sabotaged the Rastenburg telephone exchange.

Sure of Hitler's death, the conspirators set in motion the planned putsch, only to discover, when it was too late, that Hitler had survived; that Fellgiebel had failed to put the communication system out of action; and therefore that General Fritz Fromm, the Commander-in-Chief Home Army, would not authorise sending of the code-word for action to quell internal disorder, which included arrest of SS officers by the Army. Three hours were then wasted by Beck in indecision until Stauffenberg arrived to confirm Hitler's death. Fromm then was arrested and the codeword issued, but confusion then reigned supreme after Keitel spoke by telephone to Goebbels and word of the Führer's survival was spread.

It was the conspirators' intention, once Hitler was dead, to have

Kluge and Rommel (mainly as a popular figurehead) make instant contact with the Allies in France to arrange an Armistice. But, with Rommel in hospital (and never, in fact, a fully committed plotter), only Kluge could take action. And he, like Beck, vacillated long enough for Warlimont to get in touch by phone to convince him that Hitler was indeed alive. Meanwhile Goebbels had taken charge in Berlin and had alerted an SS battalion which released Fromm from arrest. Fromm, anxious to clear himself from blame, had Stauffenberg and his immediate accomplices shot and also had persuaded Beck to commit suicide. Before midnight Hitler had spoken on the radio and the incompetently planned and thoroughly bungled putsch had collapsed. The thoroughly honourable General Staff officers, several of them still conscience-smitten at the thought of breaking the Oath to Hitler, were not the right players for that kind of subversive game.

In his book *The Struggle for Europe*, Chester Wilmot wrote: 'Hitler's speech was the start of a blood-bath far exceeding that of the Röhm purge in 1934'. Not only would many field marshals (including Kluge, Rommel and Erwin von Witzleben), generals and other less senior officers pay with their lives by suicide and execution, but so too would civilians such as Goerdeler. Even more crushing was the unleashing by Hitler, Keitel and Jodl of a policy to humiliate the Army generals and initiate moves aimed at the total elimination of the General Staff.

*   *   *

In the meantime the war continued with ever increasing intensity. The withdrawal in Italy went on; the front in Normandy was on the verge of breaking; and the Eastern Front was already asunder. For on 22 June 1944, the anniversary of Germany's attack on Russia, the Red Army with some 2.5 million men, 5,200 tanks and 5,300 aircraft, struck on a 35-mile front in the direction of Minsk at the start of an expanding offensive into Belorussia. Its intention was to wipe out Army Group Centre, commanded by Field Marshal Ernst Busch.

Busch, by no means the brightest of the field marshals, was an enthusiastic Nazi Party supporter from the early days whose obedience to Hitler remained absolute. He had taken over Army Group Centre from Kluge in October 1943 and now had at his disposal a mere 700,000 men in thirty-eight under-strength infantry divisions and only two panzer divisions. His force was without sufficient reserves, attenuated in part by the demands of the other theatres of war and by Hitler's conviction that Army Groups North and South Ukraine were the principal enemy objectives. But at least Busch was not taken by surprise. Considerable evidence of the enemy build-up on his front had been acquired. Furthermore, Model shared his opinion that his own Army Group North Ukraine would not be attacked.

Busch's rigid plan of defence was based on Hitler's insistence upon holding the route centres of Vitebsk, Orsha, Mogilev and Bobruisk with six infantry divisions tasked to 'fight to the last man'. Such meagre reserves as were at his disposal in Third Panzer Army (under General Georg-Hans Reinhardt) were to counter-attack as required. But, despite his acute anxiety about the apparent magnitude of the enemy build-up, OKH made light of the threat and forbade the construction of a lay-back position along the Berezina river.

Preceded by intensive guerrilla activity against the German communications, which pinned down reserves and disrupted rail movement, the Russians broke through everywhere behind a vast artillery barrage, supplemented by air attacks the Luftwaffe could not counter. Within thirty-six hours five divisions in LI Corps were threatened with encirclement at Vitebsk and Reinhardt was calling on Busch to authorise withdrawal. This Busch, ever true to his revered Führer, rejected – a refusal endorsed the following afternoon (24 June 1944) by Zeitzler after he had consulted Hitler. Two hours later Vitebsk was cut off at about the same time as Hitler ordered a break-out, though with the proviso that one division stay behind to fight to the death. By 27 June, however, all was over. LI Corps had been overrun with the loss of some 35,000 men, along with all their equipment, as the prelude to Army Group Centre's disintegration.

Next day Hitler sacked the faithful Busch and, automatically, sent for Model, the miracle worker, to save something from yet another wreck of his own making. But all Model could do, with diminishing resources, was bend to the Russian storm – and, in due course, extract formations from Army Group North Ukraine (which he continued to command wth enormous energy) to provide forces for a counterstroke. Invoking his agreement with Hitler and using his Shield and Sword doctrine, Model withdrew in haste as best he could. Bobruisk was taken on 27 June, Minsk on 3 July and the

Polish frontier crossed on the 10th. Huge, encircled pockets were left for the Russians to swallow in the same manner as the Germans had swallowed Russians on the same ground in 1941.

Also reminiscent of 1941, the German army groups on the flanks of the virtually extinct Army Group Centre were under heavy pressure and retreating fast as Marshal Zhukov progressively widened the frontage of the Red Army's offensives to engulf the entire Eastern Front. His main thrust line continued to point at Warsaw, en route to Berlin. But starting on 10 July 1944 in the North, strong thrusts also penetrated Finland and the Baltic States and neared the East Prussian frontier. In the South, a concerted advance into Ukraine and southern Poland proved well-nigh irresistible until signs began to develop of inevitable Russian logistic deficiencies.

These hopeful signs of relief were not, however, evident on 19 July after the exhausted and, by now, thoroughly exasperated Zeitzler had resigned as Chief of Staff. He was disgraced, and forbidden to wear uniform, by a vindictive Hitler who then decided to replace him by General Walther Buhle. But Buhle was injured by Stauffenberg's bomb. As a temporary measure, Guderian was made acting Chief of Staff, though continuing to be Inspector of Panzer Forces.

Since becoming Inspector in February 1943, Guderian had assumed an ambivalent role in his dealings with Hitler. Well aware of Germany's parlous state and, like Manstein and many another general, bent on trying to save Germany by a peace forged of some miraculous stalemate, he deluded himself into imagining that he possessed Hitler's close confidence – as if anybody, let alone a general, would have enjoyed that privilege. Also, like Manstein, he would have nothing to do with the conspirators, one of whom, in the aftermath of Rommel's wounding, asked Guderian to become the titular head of a new government. Unhesitatingly, he had unequivocally refused on the grounds of the Oath, his duty as an officer and the fact that Beck and Kluge (both of whom he considered too indecisive) were involved. At the same time, however, he kept secret the information that an assassination was imminent and, on 20 July, took good care to be well out of contact while walking round the estate Hitler had given him for services rendered.

Facing up now to what his wife called '... this dreaded development and the task that would be set you', which they often had discussed, he felt bound in honour to tackle only one of the problems

Zeitzler attempted on his appointment. That was to be 'permitted to give instructions to all General Staff Officers of the Army on such subjects as concerned the General Staff as a whole' and to consolidate his relationship with Hitler by demanding that 'Each General Staff officer must be a National Socialist officer'; by attempting to thwart Himmler's insistent ambition to supplant the Army with the SS and Keitel's and Jodl's intention to abolish the General Staff; and to shore up the Eastern Front long enough for a stalemate to make feasible a peace by diplomatic means.

In none of the above aims would he succeed, although, in collaboration with Model, he did manage to impose a temporary halt on the enemy advance to the Vistula. With Russian collusion when Stalin, for devious political motives, unnecessarily stopped before Warsaw, he also put down the Polish Home Army's uprising in Warsaw. But there was nothing he could do to prevent the defection of Bulgaria on 8 September 1944, the conquest of Romania that same month and the consequent collapse of the German right flank. These catastrophes made inevitable a withdrawal from Greece and southern Yugoslavia in October, with its attendant threat to the flank and rear of the Italian Front, as Anglo-American forces, after their overwhelming victory in Normandy in August, reached the Siegfried Line.

In Normandy, of course, Kluge had not only been frustrated by Hitler's persistent unwillingness to give ground and insistence upon a suicidal order to counter-attack the initial American breakout at St Lo, but also had been distracted by his personal involvement with the conspiracy and aware that this must soon be disclosed to the Führer with fatal consequences. In the tactical sense, too, he had been forced into error due to the need to hold the line with panzer divisions instead of the infantry divisions, whose role that was. Unfortunately, however, those less mobile formations not only were below strength but also contained significant numbers of Russians and Poles who only waited for an opportunity to change sides.

These mistakes he now compounded when, against his better judgement but in a despairing attempt to redeem himself in Hitler's eyes, he ordered a piecemeal death ride of the attenuated panzer divisions towards Avranches to sever the Allied thrusts into Brittany and towards Paris. Needless to say, against an enemy with vastly superior land forces and absolute air supremacy, there was no chance of success for a blow lacking in surprise. Inevitably it was stopped dead by the Americans at Mortain as the prelude to the encirclement and destruction of those battered panzer divisions, and much else besides, in the Falaise pocket in mid-August. The disaster was exacerbated on 15 August when the Allies landed against scant opposition in southern France, compelling General Friedrich Wiese's Nineteenth Army to beat a hasty and nearly disastrous retreat northwards to merge with Kluge's remnants fleeing for the Siegfried Line.

It was incidental in the current state of play that Kluge, who had been told to report to Berlin for investigation, committed suicide on 18 August. But it was a sign of the seriousness of the situation, in Hitler's opinion, when he replaced Kluge with Model. All that Model could do, as elsewhere whenever playing his familiar 'fireman's' role, was fall back to the next line of prepared positions and hope for the enemy to grind to a halt due to logistic shortages. In this case, that meant manning the Siegfried Line guarding Germany's western frontier and extending that line of defence along the Maas and the Scheldt in order to hold Holland as a launching base for naval operations and the long-range V2 rockets against England.

Model's Army Group B, indeed, was in worse shape at that moment than the commands of Kesselring in Italy, Weichs in Yugoslavia and Guderian on the Eastern Front. All three were clinging by the fingernails to what few holds remained along Germany's perimeter, each without the slightest hope of standing fast for long wherever the enemy chose to exert his overwhelming strength.

Kesselring's and Vietinghoff's masterly retirement into the Gothic Line delayed the rearguard's arrival in the main position until the end of September. On ground mostly ideal for defence they had, with forces little better than at fifty per cent strength, held up an opponent who also suffered from logistic troubles on land, but whose air power was overwhelming. Contrary to OKW's belief (as postulated by Warlimont) that the retreat to the Gothic Line should be rapid, Kesselring pulled back no faster than he deemed necessary. His skilful and parsimonious handling of reserves, along with complete and (at times for theatrical effect) vitriolic personal grip on his subordinates, was exercised with an energy every bit as dynamic as Model's. Making the best of a combination of route demolitions and delaying actions on river lines, bad weather and an exhaustion which brought the enemy to a virtual standstill by the end of October, he saw his Army Group through to the Apennines. This was despite guerrilla sabotage and air attacks which cut railways and forced much traffic onto minor roads, mainly by night.

Ironically, at the end of July during the post-Bomb Plot turmoil, Hitler had been under some pressure to bring Kesselring back to Germany for the task of restoring the Luftwaffe. His refusal to do so must have been difficult at a time when so few of the very experienced air commanders were left or acceptable and when scapegoats were more than ever in demand to prop up the Führer's dwindling image of infallibility. For not only Army officers were on the shortlist for disgrace since even Göring was discredited in Hitler's and OKW eyes. The inability of German fighters and anti-aircraft guns to prevent devastating attacks on Germany's cities, oil supplies and lines of communication at last were laid at Göring's door. However, in June, Milch, who knew fighters were vital to defence, had been already sacked as State Secretary because the new jet fighter aircraft had not been developed as bombers as Hitler desired. And a disillusioned Sperrle, commander of Third Air Fleet in Northern France, was about to be retired, blamed for his inability, due to acute fighter and fuel shortages, as well as rampaging enemy fighters, to protect the Navy and the routed Army as they fled for a dubious safety at home.

It was Guderian who initiated the proposal to have Kesselring work under Hitler to revitalise the Luftwaffe and eliminate Göring's right of interference. But General von Greim got the unenviable job since Kesselring was considered indispensable where '... the entire front, long subject to inhuman demands, depended upon his contagiously inspiring temperament'.

Kesselring's days in Italy were numbered, however. Like Guderian he had been aware of the Bomb Plot and had adopted a wait-and-see attitude, especially since he was of the opinion that open resistance by the General Staff 'would have been doomed to failure in view of the structure of the Wehrmacht itself [including the SS] and the attitude of the German people'. Surviving the plot's aftermath without official reproach, he was on 23 October on the eve of success as, in accordance with his shrewd anticipation, the Allied offensive slowed to the point of stalling. But that day, during a visit to the front, he was badly injured in a motor car accident and put out of action for three months, leaving Vietinghoff in command to secure the Gothic Line into 1945.

Meanwhile, in the Balkans, Field Marshal von Weichs also had kept his nerve in September 1944 when faced with the arrival of Russian forces on the Yugoslavian frontier. Overcoming Hitler's initial insistence on the defence of Greece, and, thereafter, resisting an OKW suggestion for precipitate withdrawal, he allayed panic by means of a cool, slow and systematic thinning out of his nearly 1 million strong Army Groups E and F, with minimum loss of stores and equipment. Pulling out of the Greek islands in mid-September and harried by air attacks and enemy amphibious raids, he only accelerated through Greece in October when the Red Army and Yugoslav partisans drew close to Belgrade. It was a remarkable and often overlooked feat that, despite local reverses against the Russians, Weichs managed to keep his command intact and deftly brush aside the partisans attacking his lines of communication. In November he stabilised the front, with a foothold in Bosnia and Croatia, without serious losses, thus temporarily securing Vietinghoff's front in Italy.

Likewise Model and the compliant and weary Rundstedt (whom Hitler had restored as Commander-in-Chief West in September) won a brief respite when the Allies, due to logistic deficiencies, also stalled along the Siegfried Line and the Maas by mid-November. On the Eastern Front, Guderian fought a losing battle both against the Russians, vanishing allies, the Führer and OKW.

The collapse of Romania and the desertions of Bulgaria and Hungary from Germany's side stretched the Southern Front to breaking point as the Red Army headed for Belgrade and Budapest. Simultaneously, in the North on 5 October, a renewed enemy offensive surged into the Balkan states to seize Memel and thus isolate Field Marshal Schörner's Army Group North in the Kurland peninsula. Henceforward, at the very moment when the Russians also entered East Prussia and the guns could be heard by Hitler in Rastenburg, these valuable troops would have to be supplied by sea and, more critical yet, were denied a part in the last ditch defence of the Reich.

Needless to say, it was Hitler who, despite Guderian's and Schörner's protests, had delayed a withdrawal from Kurland far too long. On 15 August, Guderian already had engaged in the first of many rows to come with Hitler as he realised there was no special understanding between them. Nevertheless he tended to blame Keitel most of all for OKW's shortcomings at the same time as he endeavoured to thwart Himmler being given an Army command.

Yet a change in manners compared with that of previous Chiefs of Staff did exist for better or worse. Warlimont wrote of Guderian's 'use of strong language even at the briefing conferences'; commenting, however, that this frankness 'was unlikely to bring any change in the unhappy relationship between the top levels of the Wehrmacht'. Thus animosities flourished with Guderian's many subsequent attempts to evacuate or break out from Kurland. One of the most virulent of them arose as he haggled in competition with Rundstedt and Kesselring for reinforcements to check the Russian armies which stood within striking distance of Budapest, Silesia and Berlin.

Nor were the animosities entirely of Guderian's making. He had no part in Hitler's decision at the beginning of August to make Himmler responsible for combing out industrial manpower in order to form a new People's Army of 25 Volksgrenadier divisions, imbued with National Socialist ideals – thus accelerating the fall in industrial production already in decline from the enemy bomber offensive. Nor was he party to Hitler's decision on 19 August, as the Falaise pocket snapped shut, when Jodl recorded the Führer saying: 'Prepare to take the offensive in November when the enemy air forces can't operate. Main point: some 25 divisions must be moved to the West in the next one or two months.' His intuition was said to be based on a concept of Clausewitz (even if Hitler was unaware of it) that: 'When the disproportion of Power is so great that no limitation of our own object can ensure us safety from catastrophe ... forces will, or should, be concentrated in one desperate blow.'

Suicidal as that might be, it was a Hitlerian intuition of desperation which gave birth to what would become known as the Ardennes offensive. It also resulted, with more immediate impact on Guderian, in Jodl's frequent diversion to the West of formations Guderian managed to scrape together for defence of the East. Similarly stocks of captured enemy weapons (the existence of which Keitel and Jodl denied until convinced otherwise) which Guderian had requested for his own use in the East were transferred to the West.

CHAPTER 18

Obliteration

Paradoxically, and yet in complete accord with his increasing tendency to grasp at straws, Hitler very nearly agreed with Guderian's policy of continuing defence in the East when, on 31 August 1944, he remarked, 'The moment will arrive when disagreements between the Allies have become so great that a break will come ... I intend to carry on the fight until there is a prospect of peace that is reasonable, of a peace tolerable for Germany which will safeguard its existence for this and future generations.'

Yet although he still had in mind an attempt to provoke those disagreements it was not until 16 September that the inspiration came, when Jodl was reporting minor successes against the Americans in the Ardennes. Suddenly he announced: 'I have just made a momentous decision. I shall go over to the counter-attack. Here, out of the Ardennes with Antwerp as the objective.'

Everybody present stood aghast. But Keitel and Jodl knew well that to oppose him in that mood was a waste of nervous energy and time. Expending no effort in repeating the exhaustive war-gaming which had preceded the *Sichelschnitt* operation of 1940, they spent the next four weeks producing five separate options. Hitler rejected them all, combining the first two to match his original, high-risk concept. Obediently OKW passed what now was code-named Operation *Wacht am Rhein* to Model and Rundstedt (who yet again had been recalled as Commander-in-Chief West having almost completed the odious task of helping to liquidate the Army plotters), each of whom also was horrified.

As Rundstedt saw it, the twenty-eight divisions of variable quality allotted to him, backed up by a mere 1,000 out-classed aircraft, had no chance of success against a victorious enemy who had sound morale, superior numbers and air supremacy. In December, when the counterstroke was to be launched, his three armies (Sixth SS Panzer, Fifth Panzer and Seventh) would be lacking 3,500 officers and 115,000 men. Artillery tactics would be seriously impaired by the technical disparity of too many diverse pieces (many of them foreign), along with ammunition shortage. Armoured formations, though containing many AFVs superior to those of the enemy, were fifteen per cent below establishment, under-trained and short of fuel.

Indeed it was logistic shortages which worried Rundstedt the most. His staff had calculated that only thirty per cent of the fuel needed to reach Antwerp was available – regardless of Jodl's bland assurance that ample supplies would be available when required. Moreover transport problems caused by air attacks on lines of communication were crippling. Worst of all, however, there was no way of forecasting what the weather might do. This made nonsense of Hitler's dependence on a protracted period of poor visibilty to ground enemy aircraft.

Planning and preparations proceeded in an atmosphere of fantasy and mistrust. Rundstedt and Model tried hard to water down what they called the Large Solution (a two-army thrust between Monschau and Echternacht to Antwerp) by substitution of the Small Solution – a pincer movement, closing at Liège on the River Meuse, designed to envelop a single American Army. Hitler would have none of that, yet the two field marshals persisted in working stealthily towards that end. Nevertheless, on 12 December, after Hitler inflicted on his generals the usual two-hour pre-battle harangue, Rundstedt said: 'We are staking our last card. We cannot fail.' This was after a humiliating reception when, as General Fritz Bayerlein described it, 'We were all stripped of our weapons and brief-cases . . . and led between a double row of SS troops into a deep bunker.'

This tight security, of course, was a direct consequence of the failed Bomb Plot which put nearly all German generals beyond the Nazi pale. Nevertheless it was much to the credit of their military security, spiced by more than a little luck that, for once, the Germans achieved complete surprise when, after three postponements, they attacked in dense mist on 16 December. It was the thwarting of Ultra, caused by OKW's total ban on radio communications, as well as by good physical concealment, which assisted most of all. Yet the Allies actually were in possession from various other sources of sufficient evidence for their most senior Intelligence Officer (with a reputation for pessimism) to give an accurate warning of what threatened. His advice was brushed aside by senior American generals who, not unreasonably, simply could not imagine such a ludicrous venture being attempted.

German intelligence about their enemy on this occasion was good, however. They were aware of and encouraged by the meagre forces opposed to them in the Ardennes. Furthermore, in Rundstedt's judgement, the morale of his own troops, bolstered by intensive Nazi indoctrination, was remarkably high. Yet *Wacht am Rhein*, renamed *Herbstnebel* (Autumn Mist), failed to benefit from these important advantages, even though it overran some American formations and caused a few days' panic in certain high as well as lowly places.

At the end of the first day on the northern flank, the elite and better equipped Sixth SS Panzer Army (commanded by Oberstgruppenführer Sepp Dietrich) already had fallen behind schedule due to a combination of American resistance, the notoriously intricate Ardennes countryside and the icy roads, which increased fuel consumption. General Hasso von Manteuffel's Fifth Panzer Army on the left, on the other hand, made better progress and continued to do so throughout the operation. This then was the proper moment to reinforce Manteuffel's success. But Hitler refused to favour an Army formation to the detriment of his SS favourites. When at last he did relent, three days later, Manteuffel was in serious logistic difficulties. He had failed to do two vitally necessary things: to capture enemy fuel stocks and to seize the strategic route centre of Bastogne, which the Americans continued to hold unyieldingly.

With Sixth SS Panzer Army stalled and Fifth Panzer Army overstretched, Rundstedt asked Hitler on 22 December to call off Autumn Mist. This sensible proposal coincided with a break in the weather and the commencement of unrelenting attacks from the full might of enemy airpower. Needless to say Hitler refused. So Manteuffel, under mounting pressure from counter-attacks against the flanks of his narrowing salient by an opponent now exactly informed by Ultra of German objectives and deployment, continued to struggle as best he could towards the Meuse. He was stopped on 23 December, out of fuel, three miles short of Dinant.

That day, too, Guderian, increasingly worried by accumulating evidence of an imminent major Russian offensive in the East, decided that the complete victory which 'For the sake of my country I had hoped for' was no longer attainable. On 26 December he asked

Hitler to cancel Autumn Mist and transfer Sixth SS Panzer Army to the East, but was fobbed off with platitudes and a mere dribble of reinforcements because Hitler, supported by Jodl, determined to persist with offensive action of a sort in the Ardennes. This meant abandoning manoeuvre for attritional warfare under intense and continuous bombardment in an ever shrinking salient: something Germany could never afford, especially at this moment of severe deprivation in manpower, equipment and fuel.

Now Hitler began comparing his desperate situation with that of Frederick the Great in the fifth year of the Seven Years' War, when the monarch, poised for defeat, decided to continue the eventually victorious struggle despite his once superb Army then being, in his opinion, 'a muck-heap' which lacked leaders and had incompetent generals, poor commanding officers and was replete with wretched troops. In that mood it was therefore unlikely that when, on 9 January 1945, Guderian tried once more to make Hitler change tack, he would get far – especially since, in the course of this meeting, he lost his temper when the Führer denounced General Reinhard Gehlen, OKH's chief intelligence officer, as a lunatic who must be sacked. Guderian had then snapped back to insist Gehlen was '… one of my very best General Staff officers' whom he refused to dismiss. He added, when Hitler tried to calm him with flattery, 'The Eastern Front is like a house of cards. If the front is broken through at one point the rest will collapse.'

Precisely this happened on 12 January (the exact date predicted by Gehlen) when the Russians, with a ten to one superiority, thrust forward along twenty-four axes across the length of the Eastern Front. Within three days the German line was shattered. Steadily the Russians advanced far beyond the Prussian border and the Vistula on their way to the Oder Neisse river line, raping those German women who stayed behind and pillaging East Prussia, Upper Silesia and Hungary as they progressed. In those horrendous circumstances, as evidence of the German extermination and concentrations began to appear irrefutably, and when the Russians wrought vengeance for the abominations inflicted on their own nation, many distraught German soldiers saw no alternative but to fight fanatically to the death. Yet not even Field Marshal Schörner's merciless hangings, without trial, of laggards and deserters could stem the rout of his Army Group A. Meanwhile, on 21 January as the situation raced out of control, Hitler decided, to the despair of Guderian, to appoint the military ignoramus Himmler as commander of what was left of Army Group Vistula.

Only here and there, at cities such as Königsberg, Danzig, Poznan and the ancient brick-built stronghold of the Teutonic Knights at Malbork, did islands of resistance coalesce – Malbork suffering fifty per cent damage during a two-month siege before it fell. The Kurland peninsula was left far to the rear with Hitler resolutely defying Guderian's vehement calls for its evacuation by sea. Meanwhile, as the Allies returned to the offensive in the West, Hitler had been forced to abandon Autumn Mist and, far too late, transfer mobile troops to Guderian. But their piecemeal arrival was badly delayed by transport difficulties on railways suffering from devastating air attacks and mechanical breakdowns of worn-out rolling stock. And their commital to protect the Lake Balaton oilfields in Hungary was, to say the least, a controversial decision (brought about by Hitler's latest brainstorm that Berlin was of less importance than Vienna or his native Austria) at the moment when Berlin was threatened. For on 3 February, when little stood in their way, the Russians began appearing in strength on the Oder between Kustrin and the Czech border.

Yet amazingly (and extremely fortuitously for the Germans) there the Russians temporarily halted instead of driving, as they could have done, to Berlin and Central Germany. They did so partly for logistic reasons (exacerbated by the German route denial programme) and partly for Stalin's political purposes during the crucial Yalta Conference (4 to 9 February) with President Roosevelt and Prime Minister Churchill. But the turmoil was aggravated in OKW and OKH where Guderian engaged in a sequence of rows with the obdurate (and seriously ailing) Hitler and with Jodl, who lived their weird, day by day existence in a world of total unreality, behaving as if something might yet be saved from the wreck. Normally a general in Guderian's position might have resigned. But Guderian clung to power, not because, as Milch said, with a degree of exaggeration at Nürnberg, 'For us there was only one kind of resignation – death', but due to his deep feeling (shared with other generals) that there was an almost sacred mission to complete, if possible, regardless of the consequences.

The first major altercation occurred on or about 5 February when Guderian, fired up by a few drinks with the Japanese Ambassador, outfaced Hitler over the Kurland issue – 'With eyes flashing and the hairs of his moustache literally standing on end', as Speer recorded it – but to no avail. There would be several more rows in which Guderian put his life at risk by contradicting Hitler to his face while, behind his back, managing to manoeuvre the incompetent Himmler out of his Army Group Vistula command; and successfully persuading the badly frightened SS leader to attempt secret, though ineffectual, armistice approaches to the enemy through neutral countries.

Likewise Guderian's efforts to persuade Foreign Minister Ribbentrop to initiate serious peace moves got nowhere – until, that is, his clandestine activities came to the ears of Hitler, Keitel and Jodl, who determined to rid themselves of an Army Chief of Staff who was engaged, at great personal risk, in manipulating the government in the old-fashioned General Staff way. Indeed, this could not go on. On 21 March Hitler demonstrated his respect for Guderian by quietly asking him to take leave. But Guderian, to whom sick leave was no more acceptable than resignation, doggedly kept on trying to achieve some sort of peace settlement, clinging to his post on the pretext of the need to find suitable replacements (of whom there was a dire shortage) for senior staff officers who had been wounded in the heavy bombing of his HQ at Zossen on 15 March.

Germany by now was as defenceless in the air as on the ground. The Luftwaffe, crippled by losses from bombing or enemy occupation of most of its factories, training bases and operational airfields, was reduced to a heterogeneous collection of 2,000 mainly obsolete machines. OKL, evacuated from Berlin and dispersed all over the place (including a lunatic asylum in Wasserburg as first stop prior to moving into a vaguely projected Redoubt in the Bavarian and Austrian Alps) had no coherent control over it. The new jet aircraft, though much faster than more reliable Allied machines, were too few in number to turn the tide. Enemy bombers flew as they chose from all directions, including Italy, where Vietinghoff's front had been left in a state of relative calm while the exhausted but more reliable Allies, deprived since Christmas of strength for offensive action, stood awaiting reinforcements. Aerial mining of the Danube crippled movement of supplies along that vital waterway. An apathetic populace, terrified by the oppression of the SS and Gestapo, cringed as their country was pulverised by air and land action. In the concentration camps, Himmler's minions commenced the liquidation of individuals such as survivors of the Bomb Plot whose testimony in peacetime would be damning.

In February, as the Russians dug in along the Oder and invaded Hungary, most attention switched to the West where the Allies launched three successive major offensives to clear the west bank of the Rhine. From the central headquarters that he never left to visit the front, Rundstedt presided over loss of home ground from attacks which started at Nijmegen on his right and spread systematically southwards to consume his left. This worn out, disreputable doyen of the General Staff no longer possessed hope or ideas. He simply sat in a state of detachment in his headquarters monitoring, in as much as decaying communications allowed, the inevitable forfeiture of the Rhineland and the piecemeal destruction of its defenders.

Remorselessly pushed back by overwhelming forces, Rundstedt's men nevertheless fought quite well in the circumstances (even though, to Guderian's intense indignation, Hitler accused them of cowardice). All the bridges except one were blown in succession as the fatally debilitated armies reeled back. But that one exception, at Remagen, which fell almost intact into American hands on 7 March from a highly enterprising American coup de main (to present them with a welcome foothold on the east bank), was to shake Hitler and his generals to the roots, and actuate yet another dramatic change of Commander-in-Chief West.

Once more, and for the last time, Hitler removed Rundstedt and called on another favoured 'fireman' as replacement: none other than the redoubtable Kesselring who, barely recovered from a fractured skull, had resumed command in Italy in February. There was no handover from one field marshal to another, though each was called to Berlin for an interview with Hitler. Rundstedt, who symbolised the empty shell of a General Staff reduced to impotence, was to say farewell for the last time and receive the highest honour – the Knight's Cross. Kesselring was to be given a cynically misleading briefing from his Führer, Keitel and Jodl prior to assuming his last appointment.

Kesselring must surely have been aware of the hopeless task thrust upon him. His initial greeting of his old friend, General Westphal, who once more was his Chief of Staff, with the ironic remark, 'I am the new V3' gives the lie to Westphal's and Model's subsequent suggestions that he actually had been taken in by the over-optimistic and thoroughly unrealistic pep talks and briefings spouted by Hitler,

Keitel and Jodl.

Ever a trier, Kesselring on this occasion admitted, 'I felt utterly at sea ... Even if my ways were different I could still understand von Rundstedt's, though I could not persuade myself to adopt them ... The laxity of discipline everywhere required personal contact with commanders and troops ... One had to have a glimpse into men's hearts'.

He immediately achieved this when Westphal, registering Kesselring's seeming disbelief of his own extremely gloomy assessment of the situation, asked to be dismissed, only to be assured of the new Commander-in-Chief's complete confidence. Kesselring repeated this placatory performance when, with even greater asperity, Model exploded in bitterness, regardless of who might overhear, at the very mention of Hitler's, Keitel's and Jodl's views: 'From them I want to hear nothing. All our troubles come from them.'

In practice, due to the perils of flying in the face of enemy fighter swarms and motoring along damaged roads under constant threat of air attack, Kesselring hardly ever managed to visit commanders and troops in order to scan their hearts. Like Rundstedt, he mostly was penned in his headquarters, listening to staff officers reporting the rapid collapse of the Western Front. He learnt from OKH, by telephone and enemy-monitored radio messages, of the failure, due to lack of fuel and to tough enemy resistance, of Sixth SS Panzer Army's counter-attack in Hungary.

Meanwhile Guderian crossed swords with Hitler again and again as he struggled to eliminate enemy bridgeheads over the Oder at Kustrin and have the Navy rescue forces cut off in coastal fortresses. Likewise Kesselring, with what miserable reserves he could scrape together, did all he could to rope off the inexorably expanding American bridgehead at Remagen. But there nothing of lasting value could be achieved either. On 23 March at Oppenheim, American troops, at meagre cost, bounced a second crossing over the Rhine. Next day the British and Americans, launching massive amphibious and airborne forces, seized additional lodgements in depth over that river on a wide frontage in the vicinity of Wesel. The point of dissolution had been reached, at which effective counteraction was no longer possible anywhere, since, apart from a few scattered armoured detachments, mobile combat forces no longer existed. Realising this, Model retired with the 325,000 men of his Army Group B amid the ruins of the Ruhr industrial complex, which

American pincers completely encircled on 28 March prior to its gradual elimination by siege warfare.

That same day Guderian attended his last conference with Hitler in the Reich Chancellery bunker. He did so in the knowledge that the Rhine no longer posed a barrier to enemy progress in the West; that Frankfurt-am-Main had fallen; the Ruhr soon must be encircled; northern Germany was defenceless; Hungary and Silesia overrun; and that the counter-attack at Kustrin had failed with catastrophic losses. As before Hitler urged another attempt at Kustrin and laid charges of dereliction of duty by General Busse, the commander at that front. Once more Guderian vehemently interrupted the Führer to repudiate such scurrilous accusations.

Hitler adjourned the conference and, in the presence of Keitel alone, ordered Guderian to take six weeks' leave, replacing the last (though still only acting) Army Chief of Staff with General Hans Krebs. This appointment lacked substance, since, to all intents and purposes in the final month of the war, Jodl was in charge and busily engaged with Keitel in formalising his long-cherished ambition – the abolition of the General Staff.

Already, of course, due to the rapid shrinkage of the Third Reich in its closing period, the once all-powerful General Staff had no role to play. Only a few surviving proud members would play parts in a tragedy of disintegration on the eve of obliteration. They registered the advance of Yugoslavian partisans making previously unthinkable progress towards Trieste, thus threatening Vietinghoff's rear in Italy as an overture to the British smashing his left at Lake Comacchio on 9 April. This was a prelude to crushing defeat when the Americans chimed in on 14 April, breaking into the Po valley defences, seizing Bologna on 21 April and scooping up the majority of Tenth Army's equipment as it exploited to and then across the river. Virtually unopposed, the Allies fanned out through northern Italy towards Lake Como, to enter Genoa on 28 April (the day when, almost incidentally, Mussolini was executed by anti-Fascist partisans); and to take Milan, Turin and Venice prior to crossing the Piave on the 29th. Vietinghoff, without authority from a dissolving High Command, asked the enemy for an armistice.

Meanwhile, the German Navy (with Hitler's grudging approval) had scored Germany's final triumph when it managed, in a brilliant use of seapower, to evacuate an estimated 1.5 million soldiers and civilians from the Kurland peninsula, supplemented by survivors from the beleaguered coastal garrisons of Danzig, Gdynia, Königsberg, Pillau and Kolberg. However, it dropped many of them into the lap of the Russians as they opened their final drive on Berlin on 16 April, three days after Hitler's precious Vienna had fallen during bitter fighting.

By then, indeed, a rare mood touching realism had seized Hitler and OKW as the map symbols displayed the nation's dissolution. What Warlimont termed 'precautionary orders' had been issued on 11 April for 'the formation of dispersed headquarters (one in the north and one in the south) because of the increasing difficulty of centralised direction'. As a reward for his loyalty and the Navy's enhanced reputation for its Dunkirk-type operations in the Baltic, Grand Admiral Dönitz (with his headquarters at Plon) was appointed commander of the northern sector, with responsibility for Norway, Denmark and what remained of the Western and Eastern fronts. Kesselring was allocated the southern sector of Germany, Austria and northern Italy.

On 21 April resistance ended in the Ruhr where Model, con- science-stricken by his involvement with the ruination of his country by a dishonourable clique, and finally disillusioned by Hitler's manic call for a scorched earth policy, found a way round the strictures of the Oath. On his own authority he released the survivors of Army Group B from their obligations and, in the certain knowledge that he would stand trial for the death of 577,000 Latvians in con- centration camps, blew out his brains.

Meanwhile Hitler had celebrated his fifty-sixth birthday on 20 April by summoning to Berlin the still supposedly loyal Party members and military commanders to present their good wishes; presumably without saying 'Many Happy Returns of the Day'. For those who had to make the return journey from outside a city with the Russians already at its outskirts, this was indeed an extremely perilous as well as futile business. Yet, one by one, Göring, Dönitz, Kesselring, Keitel and Jodl were solemnly called to the presence and given a pep talk before departing to carry on the fight.

On 22 April, faithful to the suicide syndrome he had preached to others, Hitler made the irrevocable decision to take his own life in the Reich Chancellery bunker. Having announced that resolve, he ordered Keitel and Jodl to transfer themselves with OKW to the West. Keitel and Jodl, with the title OKW North, was sent to join

Dönitz; General August Winter to join Kesselring in the South.

Simultaneously in its closing hours of existence, what was left of OKH evacuated from Zossen, leaving Krebs, the new 'official' Chief of Staff, to find death in action in Berlin. This was a worthy fate for the last Chief of Staff, bearing in mind that, on 25 April (the day the Russians completed the encirclement of Berlin), Jodl had proudly recorded in his diary, 'The Führer signs the order for the command organisation and the centralisation of the staffs'. This document was, as Warlimont put it, 'a personal, though belated, triumph for which he had striven for almost ten years'. It abolished OKH and placed the Führer over OKW, the Commander-in-Chief Navy and the Commander-in-Chief Air. Its legal validity lasted barely a month.

Those weeks, nevertheless, were punctuated by the most bizarre fantasies as senior members of the German military, clinging to the binding Oath of Loyalty to a sickly, demented Führer, assiduously salved their consciences by obeying his worthless and corrupt orders almost to the letter. Moved by a genuine, if blatantly impractical, desire to save as many men as possible from the Russian clutches, these misguided hangers-on prolonged a struggle beyond all sense and reason.

The traumas afflicting Kesselring may have been more complex than those imposed on Dönitz, but they were none the less daunting in their Byzantine confusion. Faced with Hitler's orders to inflict fundamental damage on the German economy and its people's well-being by carrying out a scorched earth policy, Kesselring procrastinated when Speer (who on one occasion flourished a pistol saying, a trifle late in the day, that assassination of the Führer was the only way to end the tragedy) in desperation pleaded with him to spare public utilities and bridges from destruction. Informed by Göring on 22 April that he intended to assume the Führer's powers, since the latter was isolated in Berlin, he was told next day that Göring had been placed under arrest by an infuriated Hitler, and might soon be shot. Distressed, therefore, on 29 April by news that Vietinghoff had applied for an armistice with the enemy, this also prompted Kesselring to cover his own back by instantly dismissing the Commander-in-Chief South for exceeding his authority.

To the last moment Hitler tried to impose his authority. A mere eighteen hours before taking his life, he was radioing crazy questions to Jodl about the movements of Army formations which really existed only on paper. At last, on 30 April as ferocious fighting within Berlin drew to a climax, the generals were let off the hook, by a message saying Hitler was dead, having committed suicide in the bunker along with the mistress he had married at the last moment. He had nominated Dönitz his successor as President and Supreme Commander of the Wehrmacht.

Released from the oath but hampered by corrupt signal communications across a divided country, Dönitz and Kesselring at once expressed 'a determination to obtain peace as speedily as possible – without letting our soldiers on the Eastern Front fall into the hands of the Russians'.

Dönitz, to save face, naively proclaimed: 'I assume command of all Services of the armed forces with the firm intention of continuing the fight against the Bolsheviks until our troops and the hundreds of thousands of German families in our eastern provinces have been saved from slavery or destruction. Against the English and the Americans I must continue to fight for as long as they persist in hindering the accomplishment of my primary mission.'

Yet his naivety can be seen as a justifiable last effort to save his people, if it is taken into account that the Americans, advancing at a rate of twelve miles per day against evaporating resistance from enemy troops only too anxious to become prisoners in the West, had reached the Elbe, a mere sixty miles from Berlin, on 11 April (five days before the Russian advance had begun). Thus it was possible for the Allies to reach the capital city long before the Russians. Dönitz was clinging, quite unavailingly, to the dutiful hope that the standstill order imposed by General Eisenhower for political reasons might yet be reversed.

In the real world, however, he and Kesselring realised that such a change of Allied heart in the context of Unconditional Surrender and enemy solidarity was a fantasy. They were far more pragmatic when negotiating immediately for the truce which was announced, after delays due to communication difficulties, on the afternoon of 2 May for implementation early on the 3rd. The Russians were left to occupy those parts of the Third Reich set aside for them by agreements between the Allies.

Thus the last rites of the Third Reich, which had collapsed into chaos, were in the hands of the military, as they had been in 1918. However, this time there would be no mercy, no attempt to retain German unity and no mention of stabs in the back by people at

home. When, as General Alfred Jodl and Admiral Hans von Friedeburg – the plenipotentiaries of President Grand Admiral Karl
Dönitz – signed an instrument of Unconditional Surrender with the
Americans at Rheims on 7 May, and Field Marshal Wilhelm Keitel,
Friedeburg and Luftwaffe General Hans Jurgen Stumpff repeated
the ceremony before the Russians at Berlin next day, they made an
all-military group. This time there were no German civilian signa-
tories upon whom to foist the blame in the years to come, and only
one surviving signatory (Stumpff) had a clean record. For Friedeburg would commit suicide two weeks later and Keitel and Jodl
would pay with their lives for war crimes.

Within a matter of days, indeed, there was no longer a Wehrmacht
or a German government, as Keitel and Kesselring were made
prisoners of war on 13 and 15 May respectively, prior to the arrest of
the entire government, including Dönitz and Jodl, on the 23rd.

CHAPTER 19

A Fractured Destiny

When the generals were herded into prison camps to await investigation by the Allies for trial for war crimes and for denazification procedures, they had ample time to talk among themselves. They were able to reflect upon the reasons for their failure – as individuals and as a nation – in the pursuit of conquest and glory. Indeed many, at the subsequent urging of their captors, compiled between them millions of words of immense value for political and historical analysis – not a few of which have been quoted in this book.

No doubt the interrogators were conscious of the aftermath of World War I when the German generals spread the stab-in-the-back myth. Therefore they were prepared for the emergence of a central theme of exculpation concerning the reasons for Germany's terrible misfortunes in successive wars, above all in World War II. Almost to a man the generals and admirals laid the blame on Adolf Hitler, thus making he who constantly sought scapegoats the greatest scapegoat of all.

Furthermore, rare indeed was the general who acknowledged that the national disasters of the twentieth century were the by-products of the previous century's political unifications. These, after all, had been more at the dictates of generals through the Great General Staff junta than the elected, civilian representatives they despised. But the trail of misadventure and miscalculation stretched much further back even than that.

It could be traced, at least, to the fifteenth century when the Knights of the Teutonic Order overstretched themselves and met disaster at the Battle of Grunwald in 1410. For even at that early date the Germanic tribes were exhibiting those same aggressive characteristics that would lie at the root of their triumphs and disasters in the centuries to come. These were the traits of arrogance and excess which so often blinded them to reality and drove them either to despise other peoples or attempt 'to make possible the impossible', as Guderian once said when up against such a challenge.

Again and again this deadly syndrome was to be repeated. We have seen how it reappeared virulently with the emergence of Prussia as a power to be reckoned with early in the eighteenth century. This tribal revitalisation culminated in the wars of Frederick the Great, who, due to the opportune death of the hostile Elizabeth of Russia and succession as Tsar of the sympathetic Peter III in 1762, most luckily escaped total disaster brought on by overstretching his forces. Again a pronounced and fatal over-confidence can be detected when the Prussian generals, faced by the threat of Napoleon's victorious armies, rejected an urgently needed modernisation of the out-dated Army Frederick had bequeathed them.

One has to admire the remarkable recovery of Prussia after the disaster at Jena in 1806, and her contribution to the final defeat of France in 1815. But, in the light of what was to follow a century later in 1914, there have to be reservations about the progressive strengthening of the State and its armed forces by the General Staff. The great victories of the 1860s and 1870s made feasible German unification under the politico-military hegemony of this body. With hindsight, we can see that these events stimulated an age-old arrogance and over-confidence which falsely convinced war-mongering generals and admirals that the subjugation of Europe was within their grasp.

However, from the outset in 1914, the generals failed in their aim due to incompetence and internal divisions, and in the war's aftermath the Germans did not fully learn the lessons thrust upon them by complete defeat. It is not so strange that the proud generals yearned for the day when a Saviour would appear and they could restore the General Staff denied them by the Treaty of Versailles. They would then be able to set a course to retrieve Germany's old power and influence – by arms if necessary. For the generals remained incorrigible war-mongers and the advent of the war-loving Adolf Hitler as Chancellor was a godsend to many among them, as well as to many of the people.

It was natural, therefore, that in 1945 the generals sought new scapegoats, of whom Hitler was the favourite for denigration. It was easy to blame him, and tacitly set aside their euphoria in 1940, when, regardless of the fact that their political influence had already vanished, their country was benefiting enormously from military successes. It was easier still to forget their acute disappointments as the tragedy (as many of them saw it) worsened when their ill-gotten gains were snatched away.

But it was the people's tragedy, as well as the generals', that they had been, in many cases, contentedly seduced by Hitler. Once legally elected, this despot had elevated himself immediately to a position of absolute power wielded with almost unrivalled criminality and barbarism. He did so, moreover, with such consummate ease – in admittedly special circumstances – that he fooled, almost all of the time, all of the people of an erstwhile democratic nation (albeit saddled with a flawed constitution) as to his real intention to go to war.

In other words, it was the German people's tragedy that to their own cost they voted into power a blatantly corrupt and violent political party in 1933, and then stood complacently, for the most part, on the sidelines. They allowed a demagogic war-lover to neutralise the General Staff, which was the only checking power capable of protecting a gullible nation from the abuses and outrages of a visibly corrupt politician and his gang. This calamity was made all the worse in that it coincided with the inspired creation, by that same General Staff, of a military machine governed by doctrines which, initially, seemed to hold the key to the conquest of those out-moded opponents who had imposed upon them the strictures of the hated Versailles Treaty.

There was a grim irony in the situation in which a war-mongering General Staff, ostensibly steeped in codes of honour related to ostensibly high standards of civilisation and decent behaviour, found itself snared by traditional grasping ambition. It was eager to restore, by hook or by crook, Germany's former military and political prestige and power through the application of an advanced military education, allied to technological progress. At the same time it was contentedly being driven to raise and train highly efficient defence forces possessing immense offensive potential. This Wehrmacht was capable of doing far more than simply neutralise the looming threat of the militaristic Russian Communist regime, which was loathed almost as much as the upholders of the reviled Versailles Treaty – France and Britain.

It was one of many paradoxes that the generals' tragedy was induced by the same much vaunted standards of conduct, within the General Staff's arrogant closed society, that had become so out-dated in the aftermath of World War I as to be incapable of coping with modern gangsterism and a corrupt propaganda system beyond its comprehension. Germany and her Army General Staff were duped and undermined from within, as have been so many militaristic states and organisations throughout history, and were left vulnerable during World War II to destruction by external forces. Yet they became their own eventual executioners by creating military forces that overwhelmed many (though fortunately not all) of the nations that they eventually contemptuously provoked or drove into effective opposition.

It was quite as much a paradox, however, that Hitler was incapable of making rational or full use of one of the most competent military organisations ever assembled and trained in peacetime. Between 1939 and 1942 Germany's forces defeated all comers in battle, making Germany master of Western Europe (with the notable exception of Britain) and creating an opportunity, in alliance with her satellite Axis partners, to dominate the world – if only her leaders possessed the wisdom to do so.

How was it then that things went so badly awry for the Germans?

To begin with, it was a disaster for Germany that Hitler's fear of antagonising the populace induced a sense of political insecurity that deterred him from gearing the nation to wage Total War in the manner of General Ludendorff in 1916. For how else can one explain his tardiness in fully pushing German production to maximum capacity until 1943? Or his unwillingness, to the bitter end, to direct women to work outside the home, in the same manner as did Britain, for example, instead of employing as he did inefficient slave labour with the many security and sabotage risks involved?

It may be argued that the nation was as blameworthy in permitting war as its war-mongering generals, and the members of a General Staff who, in collaboration with the governments of the day, deliberately failed to assuage the people's sense of guilt for provoking the previous World War. This created, however hesitantly, an atmosphere which enabled a triumphant Hitler to commence hostilities without arousing any sort of effective opposition. Say what they might, before and after September 1939 the people got what they deserved. Having acquiesced to what Hitler and his generals desired, no compromise was possible. There could only be total victory or utter defeat for a General Staff that was trapped within a rigid system of its own making and under a sacred oath to Head of State and Supreme Commander Hitler.

Ironically, therefore, an inherent reason for things ultimately going wrong was the creation by the generals of systems and methods to make total victory against all comers seem easily within Germany's grasp. Those brilliant 'Blitzkrieg' victories of 1939 and 1940 were so complete as to instil a familiar, dangerous over-confidence within a vain and proud sect. Somewhat to their surprise, as well as satisfaction, the generals convincingly demonstrated that (in present day parlance) the 'manoeuvre warfare' doctrine created by the Truppenamt and the restored General Staff, and further developed by Hitler's initially well-informed intuition, was irresistible. Suddenly, to their own amazed delight, they seemed to have hit on a doctrine similar to one the British Army Staff College and the United States Marine Corps would adopt in 1995: '... a warfighting philosophy which seeks to defeat the enemy by shattering his morale and physical cohesion – his ability to fight as an effective, co-ordinated whole – rather than to destroy him physically through incremental attrition'.

But just as no battle plan long survives the onset of combat, so Hitler's politically centred Grand Strategy and the generals' military strategy soon ran into difficulties. This was despite retaining the steadily improving, extremely competent tactical and technical systems devised and practised by commanders in the field with supremely trained and well-led formations and units. The leaders of these organisations, having won the first evocative victories, con-tributed to an ill-considered lust for even more ambitious conquests – as had been the effect in wars gone by.

This led to misdirected campaigns conducted with such arrogance and lack of moral principle as not only to induce attritional struggles with powerful yet despised opponents, but also to antagonise their own equally despised allies. It is indeed remarkable that, repeatedly, Germany's rulers have grossly underestimated the French, the Slavic peoples (including the Russians, of course), the Italians and the Americans. They have tackled their enemies with such racially inspired savagery as to outrage all and sundry into becoming implacably dedicated to overcoming Germany and more and more impervious to the morale-destroying aspect of 'manoeuvre warfare'. And they have so upset Germany's friends as to make them only too ready to change sides.

Germany's potency was eroded all the more, by no means incidentally, by numerous failures of German Intelligence and Security. A glance through this book reveals but a few of the vast catalogue of Intelligence failures subsequent to the overrunning of France in June 1940. They start with the incorrect evaluation of Britain's emaciated military strength in the immediate aftermath of Dunkirk; proceed along the downhill pathway of events leading to a faulty Mediterranean and Baltic strategy; and continue to the bitter end through the fatal underestimation of Soviet Union powers of resistance, allied to contempt for British and American determination and strength.

Time and again, at all levels, Hitler and his generals were let down by seriously flawed Intelligence services. This deficiency was compounded by the fundamental breach of their high-grade radio signal codes and cyphers which placed them at a disastrous military disadvantage from mid-1940 onwards. An avoidable error, this was arguably a consequence of that same arrogance and over-confidence that allowed them to dismiss the possibility of Enigma being vulnerable to breaking. They simply could not imagine anybody else matching their own technical prowess of invention and efficiency. Thus they laid themselves wide open to self-, as well as enemy, deceptions on a massive scale.

How apt it was that a thoroughly undermined society and organisation should be served so assiduously and harmfully by brilliantly conceived and yet corrupted communications. For at the war's outbreak Germany's electronic systems, especially their civil and military radio networks, were not only among the best in the world, but also the most single-mindedly organised and directed for the waging of manoeuvre warfare in all its psychological aspects as a vital adjunct to land, air and naval operations. Moreover, it was ironic that the self-same superior radio communications, which lay at the heart of Blitzkrieg, presented Germany's enemies with unprecedented insight into the minds of Hitler and his generals. The Allies were thus able to forestall a majority of Axis plans with a confidence and dexterity that contributed significantly to Germany's defeat.

Not to be overlooked, of course, is the triumph of propaganda campaigns. These were hydras which deluded the German people and generals as to Hitler's true intentions in much the same way as they at first so thoroughly bamboozled Germany's enemies, whose morale and political cohesion they destroyed as a result. Until 1 September 1939, the propaganda successes matched the standard set by the military philosopher of the fifth century BC, Sun Tzu: 'To defeat the armies of your enemies without ever having to fight them'. As time went by and incremental attrition at the hands of an unforgiving enemy began to take its toll, the brainwashing of the Germans was extremely effective in maintaining morale and the determination of the people and the military to fight on – despite the mounting evidence of impending doom due to heavy defeats and awful destruction by aerial bombing. This was a pernicious obstinacy linked to Goebbels's successful endeavours to sustain a false belief in Hitler's infallible genius as well as the virtues of National Socialism.

*   *   *

Today, after more than fifty years since the events producing the last of Germany's successive triumphs and disasters, and at a moment when many armies, including those of the USA and Britain, focus their studies of future war on the German systems of the 1930s and 1940s, it is perhaps worth while reflecting that this is not the first period in which Prussian methods have, with unfortunate results, been embraced as models. Prior to the rise of French techniques and the genius of Napoleon, the methods formulated and practised by Frederick the Great were emulated by many another nation in arms, revolutionary America not least among them in the eighteenth century. Likewise, the elder Moltke's teachings and his routing of the Austrians in 1866 and of the French in 1870 again inspired emulation of Prussian methods. And even after the Germans were defeated in World War I, there were nations, such as China and Argentina, which chose to learn from German instructors.

The many admirable attributes, talents and skills of the individuals who made Germany's military methods so widely respected were overshadowed by arrogance, excess, rigidity of mind, bullying and a blindness to the lessons of history. These flaws in part stemmed from the problem of defending a land with few natural barriers. Not only the Prussians but also the entire Germanic people, historically and right up to and including World War II, feared the prospect of violation by peoples they saw as barbarians who, over the centuries, had invaded or threatened from the East. The habit of pre-emptive attack as the best form of defence fostered the ambition, over-confidence and inflexibility that in many cases made Germany her own worst enemy.

Without much doubt the same zealous motivations which, long ago, set the Teutonic Knights against the early Prussian tribes, the Poles, Lithuanians and others, existed with some strength in the first part of the twentieth century. However, Germany has established safeguards against the possible active resurgence of these factors. Since 1945, it has acquired a constitution and democratic system which seem reasonable proof against the emergence of another dictator or governing General Staff. Today it benefits from an electorate that consistently sets its face against periodic outbreaks of racial hatred, violence and offensive action. It maintains sceptical surveillance of a by no means ill-equipped or ineffective Bundeswehr, which is subject to strict State political control – and, in the midst of prosperity, finds it none too easy to recruit sufficient personnel for those armed forces.

Bibliography

Unpublished Sources

US Army Historical Division European Command

ETHINT 2. Interview with General Walter Warlimont on Norway, North Africa, French Resistance, German American Relations, Dieppe, Sitzkrieg

ETHINT 38. Panzer Tactics in Normandy by General Heinz Guderian

ETHINT 39. Employment of Panzer Forces on the Western Front by General Heinz Guderian

MS B-270. Concerning the general strategy of the Italian campaign by Field Marshal Albert Kesselring and General Siegfried Westphal

MS C-059a. Seelöwe by Ministerialrat Dr Helmuth Greiner

MS C-075. Final Commentaries on the Campaign in North Africa 1941–1943 by Field Marshal Albert Kesselring

MS P-041g. Army High Command. Duties of Army Training Branch by General Edgar Röhricht

MS P-031a. Training and Development of German General Staff Officers
Vol X by Generaloberst Franz Halder
Vol XVII by Field Marshal Albert Kesselring
Vol XVIII by Generaloberst Heinz Guderian

MS P-041k. The Signal Services in the Service of OKH by General der Nachrichtentruppe Albert Praun

MS P-151. Operational Basis for the First Phase of the French Campaign in 1940 by Generaloberst Franz Halder

MS T-28. Battle of Moscow 1941–1942 by General Hans von Greiffenberg and General Günther Blumentritt

Published Sources

Anon, *Führer Conferences on Naval Affairs 1939–1945* (London, 1990)

Anon, *The Rise and Fall of the German Air Force* (Old Greenwich, 1969)

Ansel, W., *Hitler Confronts England* (Durham, NC, 1960)

Barnett, C. (ed.), *Hitler's Generals* (London, 1989)

Bartov, O., *The Eastern Front, 1941–45: German Troops and the Barbarisation of Warfare* (London, 1985)

Bekker, C., *The Luftwaffe War Diaries* (New York, 1969)

Clausewitz, K. von, *The Campaign of 1812 in Russia* (1843, and London, 1992)

Cruttwell, C.R.M., *History of the Great War 1914–1918* (Oxford, 1934)

Deichmann, P., *German Air Force Operations in Support of the Army* (Arno, 1962); published in a revised edition as *Spearhead for Blitzkrieg* ed. Dr Alfred Price (London, 1996)

Farrar-Hockley, A., *Student* (New York, 1973)

Gill, J., *With Eagles to Glory: Napoleon and his German Allies in the 1809 Campaign* (London, 1992)

Glantz, D.M., *The Initial Period of War on the Eastern Front* (London, 1993)

Görlitz, W., *History of the German General Staff* (New York, 1955)

Gröner, W., *Feldherr wider Willen* (Berlin, 1931)

Guderian, H., *Achtung! Panzer!* (London, 1994)

Guderian, H., *Panzer Leader* (London, 1953)

Halder, F., *Hitler als Feldherr* (Munich, 1949)

Halder, F., *War Diary 1939–1942* (Novato, 1988)

Hinsley, J., et al, *British Intelligence in the Second World War*, five volumes (London, 1979)

Hitler, A., *Mein Kampf*

Howard, M., *The Franco-Prussian War* (London, 1961)

Horne, A., *To Lose a Battle: France 1940* (London, 1969)

Lehmann, R., *The Leibstandarte* (Winnipeg, 1987)

Ludendorff, E., *My War Memoirs* (London, 1919)

Ludendorff, E., *The General Staff and its Problems* (London, 1920)

Kesselring, A., *Memoirs* (London, 1989)

Macksey, K., *Tank Warfare* (London, 1971)

Macksey, K., *Guderian: Panzer General* (London, 1975, 1992)

Macksey, K., *The Partisans of Europe* (London, 1975)

Macksey, K., *Kesselring: The Making of the Luftwaffe* (London, 1978); republished as *Kesselring: German Master Strategist of the Second World War* (London, 1996)

Macksey, K., *Rommel: Battles and Campaigns* (London, 1979)

Macksey, K., *For Want of a Nail* (London, 1989)

Manstein, E. von, *Lost Victories* (London, 1987)

Messenger, C., *The Last Prussian – von Rundstedt* (London, 1991)

Messenger, C., *Hitler's Gladiator – Dietrich* (London, 1988)

Moltke, H. von, *Memoirs* (Berlin, 1922)

Petre, F., *Napoleon's Conquest of Prussia 1806* (London, 1907, 1993)

Pitt, B. (ed.), *Purnell's History of World War 1* (London, 1969)

Pitt, B. (ed.), *Purnell's History of World War 2* (London, 1966)

Rabenau, F. von, *Seeckt* (Leipzig, 1940)

Seaton, A., *The Russo-German War 1941–45* (London, 1971)

Seeckt, H. von, *Thoughts of a Soldier* (London, 1930)

Stahlberg, A., *Bounden Duty* (London, 1990)

Suchenwirth, R., *Command and Leadership of the German Air Force* (Arno, 1969)

Suchenwirth, R., *The Development of the German Air Force 1919–1939* (Arno, 1968)

Tirpitz, A. von, *My Memoirs* (London, 1919)

Warlimont, W., *Inside Hitler's Headquarters* (London, 1989)

Westphal, S., *Erinnerungen* (Mainz, 1975)

Wheeler-Bennett, J., *Hindenburg: The Wooden Titan* (London, 1936)

Wheeler-Bennett, J., *The Nemesis of Power* (London, 1953)

Wilmot, C., *The Struggle for Europe* (London, 1952)

Index